KT-433-180

EVERY BOY'S NEW Handbook

HAMLYN

First published 1985
Fifth impression 1990
Published by The Octopus Publishing Group Limited
Michelin House, 81 Fulham Road, London SW3 6RB, England

ISBN 0 600 38982 0

Printed in Yugoslavia

Some of the illustrations in this book have previously appeared in other books published by The Octopus Publishing Group Limited. Additional illustrations especially for this book are by Bob Mathias.

CONTENTS

CONTENTS

CONTENTS

CONTENTS

INTRODUCTION

The main purpose of sport is enjoyment. It brings a sense of achievement as skill and performance improve. But it also brings other things. If we train and play hard, we become fitter. Our bodies become suppler and stronger.

There is a Latin phrase, '*mens sana in corpore sano*' (a sound mind in a sound body), which expresses the fact that if your body is fit then your mind will be too.

Try to take part in some active sport at least once a week, and you will feel a much healthier and happier person.

You do not need to be good at sports to enjoy them – according to the Olympic ideal it is the taking part, not the winning, which is important, though nowadays this is sometimes forgotten.

Whatever type of person you are, there is a sport which will suit you, and there are many different ones to choose from.

If you like team games, try rowing, football, rugby, cricket or hockey. You may play these at school. Games for you to play with a friend include badminton, squash and tennis; and if you enjoy competing as an individual, try swimming, jogging, golf or athletics.

Different sports may be suitable for different times of the year – cricket and swimming in summer; skiing and tobogganing in winter; though many sports do not depend on the weather since they are played indoors. For water sports, such as sailing or windsurfing, a wet suit can be worn in winter to enable you to continue enjoying them.

Many unusual sports are becoming popular nowadays – hang-gliding, parachuting, karate, kendo, motorcycle trial racing; but the traditional sports are still just as much fun.

Go to your local sports centre and see what facilities are available; or a teacher at school may be able to help you find local facilities if there is a sport you are particularly keen to try. You could always go on a sporting holiday, such as a sailing or riding holiday.

The sections that follow will not teach you to be a top sportsman – only hard work and skill will make you that – but they will act as an introduction to various different kinds of sports, showing you what is involved in each one.

The lists of records and winners will prove interesting reading – and you never know, maybe if you train hard, one day *your* name will be added to a list of record-breaking sportsmen!

ARCHERY

Archery is an Olympic sport, having been restored to the Olympic Games in 1972. There are also world archery championships and the governing body is the Fédération Internationale de Tir à l'Arc (International Archery Federation).

The main form of the sport is target archery. Field archery, where targets are set out over two courses, and crossbow archery, which is similar to target archery but archers use a crossbow instead of a long bow, are also practised.

In target archery, competitors shoot a certain number of rounds. In each round, archers shoot arrows from different distances. Men shoot at 90 m, 70 m, 50 m and 30 m. Each

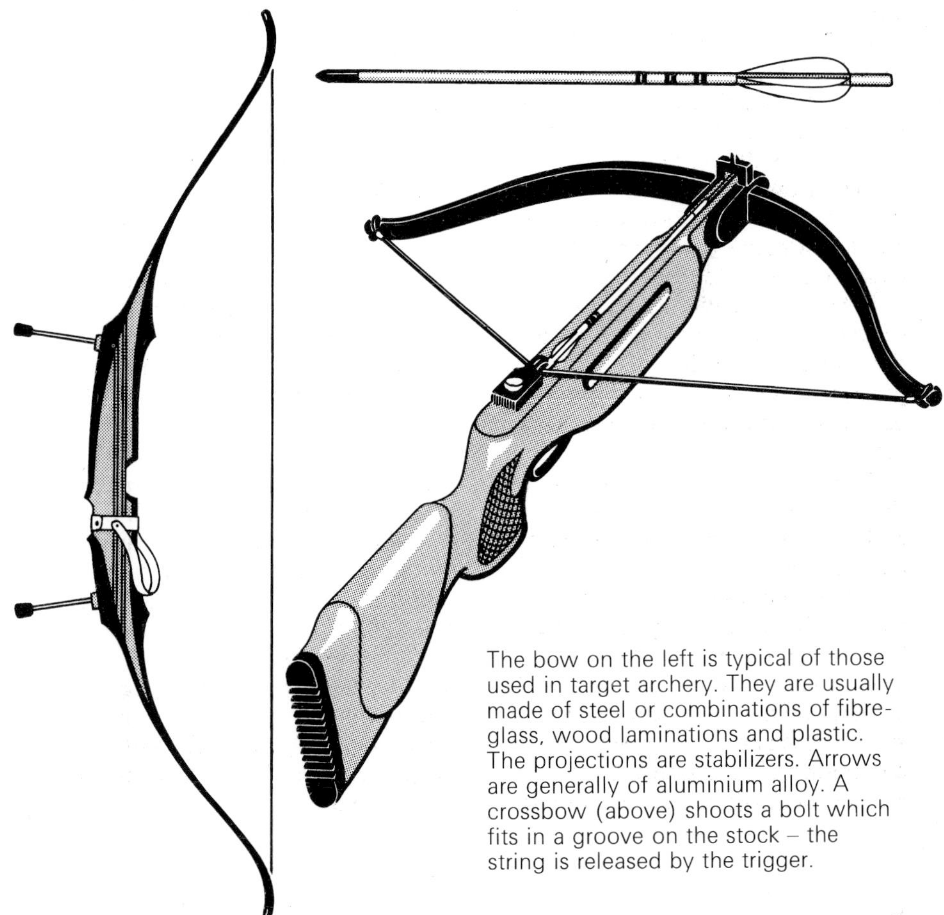

The bow on the left is typical of those used in target archery. They are usually made of steel or combinations of fibre-glass, wood laminations and plastic. The projections are stabilizers. Arrows are generally of aluminium alloy. A crossbow (above) shoots a bolt which fits in a groove on the stock – the string is released by the trigger.

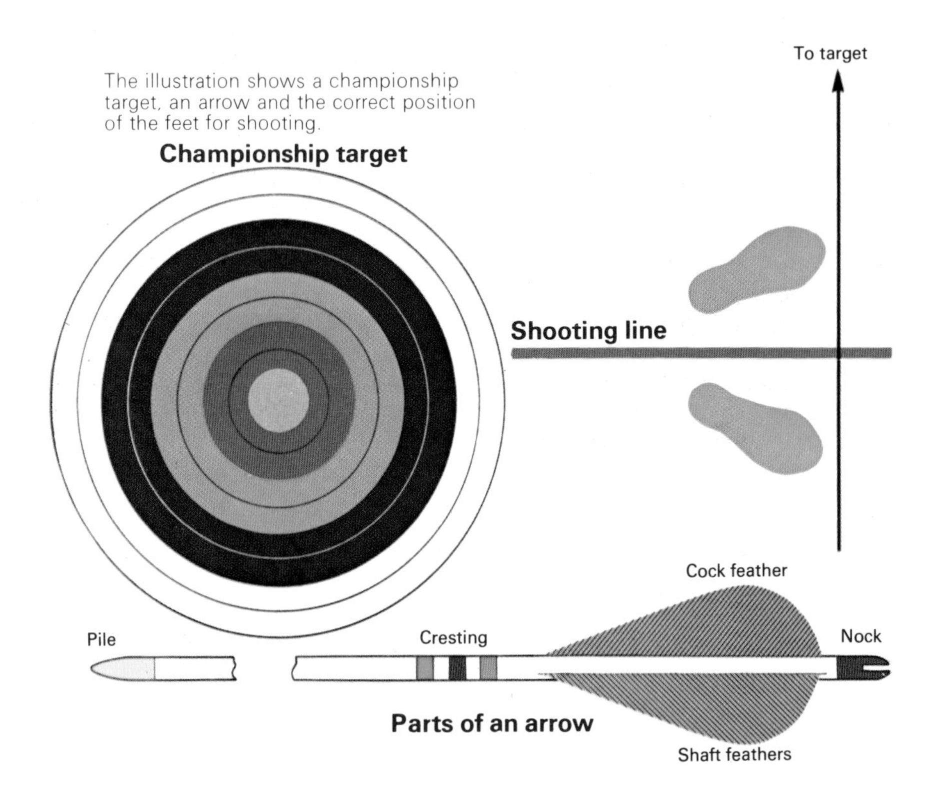

The illustration shows a championship target, an arrow and the correct position of the feet for shooting.

arrow that hits the target scores and is added to the archer's total.

The standard international target is based on the British five-zone target in which the five zones (concentric bands) score as follows: white 1; black 3; blue 5; red 7; yellow 9. In the international target each zone is divided into two, the two white zones scoring 1 and 2, the two black zones 3 and 4, the two blue zones 5 and 6, the two red zones 7 and 8, and the central yellow zones 9 and 10. Archery has the attraction that it can be enjoyed by people of all ages. Many young people make bows from yew branches and shoot sticks as arrows, but if you do this, remember that a stick can put out an eye, and never shoot if somebody is in front of you, within your range.

Archery has its own terminology and the parts of a bow and arrow have their special names. Bows may be fitted with sights or marks and the archer wears a quiver to hold the arrows. Some parts of an arrow are illustrated here. The positions of the hands, and the techniques of sighting and drawing the bow, are best learned by instruction from an expert, so if archery interests you, join a club where you will be welcomed and taught to become an archer.

ASSOCIATION FOOTBALL

Association football is played with a round ball on a rectangular pitch by two sides of 11 people. The object is to score goals, i.e. force the ball into the opponents' goal, which is formed by two upright posts upon which is mounted a crossbar. One of the players is a goalkeeper, who is allowed to use his hands within the goal area. Other players can play the ball with any part of the body except the hands. The modern game of football began in Britain in the 19th century. It is now the most widespread ball game, with about 150 countries affiliated to the Fédération Internationale de Football Associations (FIFA), the governing body.

The main international

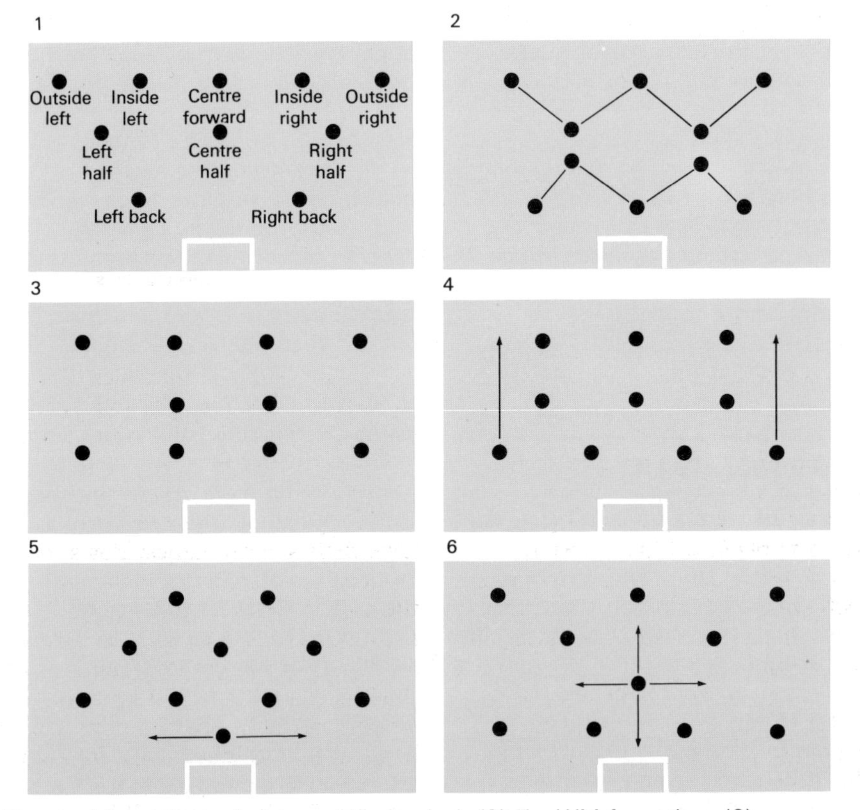

Standard formations of players: (1) classical; (2) the WM formation; (3) the 4-2-4 formation; (4) the 4-3-3 formation; (5) the *catenaccio* system with a sweeper; (6) the mid-field sweeper.

competition, the World Cup, is held every four years, and has been won by Brazil (3 times), Italy (3), West Germany (2), Uruguay (2), Argentina (2) and England. These countries have the strongest 'soccer' traditions, with Scotland, Hungary, Holland, Austria and Czechoslovakia among the other strong nations.

In Britain the most important tournaments, the Football Association Challenge Cup (first played in 1872) and the Football League (formed 1888), with their Scottish counterparts, are the oldest competitions in the world. Since 1956 competitions have been organized between European clubs, principally the European Champions' Cup. The main winners have been Real Madrid (6), Liverpool (3), Bayern Munich (3), Ajax Amsterdam (3), Inter Milan (2), AC Milan (2), Benfica (2), and Nottingham Forest (2).

Outside Europe, South America contains the strongest teams.

FOOTBALL TACTICS

The art of team play is to bring out the collective best in the eleven people in the side. The system of play should be tailored to the needs of the players, rather than the other way around.

Defensively there are two main styles of play. The most usual system in England is to play with two full-backs, a centre-half who attacks the ball and a covering central defender. This orthodox back four adopts 'zonal marking', whereby each defender has responsibility for areas of the field, rather than following specific opponents throughout the match. For example, the right-back is responsible for the opposing left-winger while he is on that side of the field, but if he switches to the other flank, the left-back takes care of him.

The alternative is the system of 'man-for-man marking', which is the one played in many European countries, notably Italy and West Germany. Here, each defender dogs the footsteps of one particular opponent wherever he runs on the field. The only player who does not do this is one defender, the sweeper (or *libero*), who is free to take over if an attacker beats the defender marking him near the goal.

As you progress as a player, specific coaches will teach you the positional demands of a particular team. The most important thing to learn is that whatever position you play, your work off the ball is just as vital as what you do when you are in possession of the ball.

Once you are in a regular position in a school or a club team, aim to learn as much as you can about your role. Defenders must defend primarily, but full-backs can add important width to attacks and central defenders are able to use their abilities in the air to go forward for corners and free-kicks. Midfield players have responsibilities all over the field, while forwards must watch for opposing defenders turning offensive as well as hunting for goals.

FOOTBALL FACTS AND FIGURES

Goalscoring: The biggest score recorded in British soccer is Arbroath 36, Bon Accord 0 in the Scottish Cup on 5 September 1885. On the same day Dundee Harp beat Aberdeen Rovers 35-0.

The highest individual score in British soccer is 13 goals scored by John Petrie for Arbroath in the above match. In English league soccer the record is held by Joe Payne, who scored 10 for Luton Town against Bristol Rovers in the Third Division (South) on 13 April 1936.

The most goals scored in a career is 1329 by Arthur Friedenreich in Brazilian soccer between 1910 and 1930. In British soccer Arthur Rowley scored 434 league goals for West Bromwich Albion, Leicester City and Shrewsbury Town between 1946 and 1965. Jimmy McGrory, for Celtic and Clydebank, scored 410 in 408 Scottish league matches between 1922 and 1938.

World Cup Records: The only player to play in five World Cup final tournaments is Antonio Carbajal of Mexico, who kept goal on eleven occasions in the finals of 1950, 1954, 1958, 1962 and 1966. The most appearances in World Cup finals were made by Uwe Seeler, of West Germany, who played 21 times in 1958, 1962, 1966 and 1970. Pelé of Brazil played 14 times in the same four final tournaments, and on three occasions was in the World Cup winning squad, although he did not play in the Final itself in 1962 because of injury.

Gerd Muller of West Germany has scored the most goals in World Cup final tournaments, his 14 came as ten in 1970 and four in 1974. Just Fontaine of France is the highest scorer for a single World Cup final tournament, with 13 goals in 1958. In 1970, Jairzinho of Brazil became the only player to score in every match of the World Cup final tournament, including the Final.

WORLD CUP WINNERS

1930 Uruguay
1934 Italy
1938 Italy
1950 Uruguay
1954 West Germany
1958 Brazil
1962 Brazil
1966 England
1970 Brazil
1974 West Germany
1978 Argentina
1982 Italy
1986 Argentina

FA CUP WINNERS

1880–1	Old Carthusians
1881–2	Old Etonians
1882–3	Blackburn Olympic
1883–4	Blackburn Rovers
1884–5	Blackburn Rovers
1885–6	Blackburn Rovers
1886–7	Aston Villa
1887–8	West Bromwich Albion
1888–9	Preston N.E.
1889–90	Blackburn Rovers
1890–1	Blackburn Rovers
1891–2	West Bromwich Albion

1892–3	Wolverhampton Wanderers
1893–4	Notts County
1894–5	Aston Villa
1895–6	Sheffield Wednesday
1896–7	Aston Villa
1897–8	Nottingham Forest
1898–9	Sheffield United
1899–1900	Bury
1900–1	Tottenham Hotspur
1901–2	Sheffield United
1902–3	Bury
1903–4	Manchester City
1904–5	Aston Villa
1905–6	Everton
1906–7	Sheffield Wednesday
1907–8	Wolverhampton Wanderers
1908–9	Manchester United
1909–10	Newcastle United
1910–11	Bradford City
1911–12	Barnsley
1912–13	Aston Villa
1913–14	Burnley
1914–15	Sheffield United
1915–19	*No competition*
1919–20	Aston Villa
1920–1	Tottenham Hotspur
1921–2	Huddersfield Town
1922–3	Bolton Wanderers
1923–4	Newcastle United
1924–5	Sheffield United
1925–6	Bolton Wanderers
1926–7	Cardiff City
1927–8	Blackburn Rovers
1928–9	Bolton Wanderers
1929–30	Arsenal
1930–1	West Bromwich Albion
1931–2	Newcastle United
1932–3	Everton
1933–4	Manchester City
1934–5	Sheffield Wednesday
1935–6	Arsenal
1936–7	Sunderland
1937–8	Preston N.E.
1938–9	Portsmouth
1939–45	*No competition*
1945–6	Derby County
1946–7	Charlton Athletic
1947–8	Manchester United
1948–9	Wolverhampton Wanderers
1949–50	Arsenal
1950–1	Newcastle United
1951–2	Newcastle United
1952–3	Blackpool
1953–4	West Bromwich Albion
1954–5	Newcastle United
1955–6	Manchester City
1956–7	Aston Villa
1957–8	Bolton Wanderers
1958–9	Nottingham Forest
1959–60	Wolverhampton Wanderers
1960–1	Tottenham Hotspur
1961–2	Tottenham Hotspur
1962–3	Manchester United
1963–4	West Ham United
1964–5	Liverpool
1965–6	Everton
1966–7	Tottenham Hotspur
1967–8	West Bromwich Albion
1968–9	Manchester City
1969–70	Chelsea
1970–1	Arsenal
1971–2	Leeds United
1972–3	Sunderland
1973–4	Liverpool
1974–5	West Ham United
1975–6	Southampton
1976–7	Manchester United
1977–8	Ipswich
1978–9	Arsenal
1979–80	West Ham United
1980–1	Tottenham Hotspur
1981–2	Tottenham Hotspur
1982–3	Manchester United
1983–4	Everton
1984–5	Manchester United
1985–6	Liverpool
1986–7	Coventry City
1987–8	Wimbledon

FOOTBALL LEAGUE CHAMPIONS

1890–1	Everton
1891–2	Sunderland
1892–3	Sunderland
1893–4	Aston Villa
1894–5	Sunderland
1895–6	Aston Villa
1896–7	Aston Villa
1897–8	Sheffield United
1898–9	Aston Villa
1899–1900	Aston Villa
1900–1	Liverpool
1901–2	Sunderland
1902–3	Sheffield Wednesday
1903–4	Sheffield Wednesday
1904–5	Newcastle United
1905–6	Liverpool
1906–7	Newcastle United
1907–8	Manchester United
1908–9	Newcastle United
1909–10	Aston Villa
1910–11	Manchester United
1911–12	Blackburn Rovers
1912–13	Sunderland
1913–14	Blackburn Rovers
1914–15	Everton
1915–19	*No competition*
1919–20	West Bromwich Albion
1920–1	Burnley
1921–2	Liverpool
1922–3	Liverpool
1923–4	Huddersfield Town
1924–5	Huddersfield Town
1925–6	Huddersfield Town
1926–7	Newcastle United
1927–8	Everton
1928–9	Sheffield Wednesday
1929–30	Sheffield Wednesday
1930–1	Arsenal
1931–2	Everton
1932–3	Arsenal
1933–4	Arsenal
1934–5	Arsenal
1935–6	Sunderland
1936–7	Manchester City
1937–8	Arsenal
1938–9	Everton
1939–46	*No competition*
1946–7	Liverpool
1947–8	Arsenal
1948–9	Portsmouth
1949–50	Portsmouth
1950–1	Tottenham Hotspur
1951–2	Manchester United
1952–3	Arsenal
1953–4	Wolverhampton Wanderers
1954–5	Chelsea
1955–6	Manchester United
1956–7	Manchester United
1957–8	Wolverhampton Wanderers
1958–9	Wolverhampton Wanderers
1959–60	Burnley
1960–1	Tottenham Hotspur
1961–2	Ipswich
1962–3	Everton
1963–4	Liverpool
1964–5	Manchester United
1965–6	Liverpool
1966–7	Manchester United
1967–8	Manchester City
1968–9	Leeds
1969–70	Everton
1970–1	Arsenal
1971–2	Derby County
1972–3	Liverpool
1973–4	Leeds United
1974–5	Derby County
1975–6	Liverpool
1976–7	Liverpool
1977–8	Nottingham Forest
1978–9	Liverpool
1979–80	Liverpool
1980–1	Aston Villa
1981–2	Liverpool
1982–3	Liverpool
1983–4	Liverpool

1984–5	Everton
1985–6	Liverpool
1986–7	Everton
1987–8	Liverpool

FOOTBALL LEAGUE CUP WINNERS (1983–1986 Milk Cup)

1960–1	Aston Villa
1961–2	Norwich City
1962–3	Birmingham City
1963–4	Leicester City
1964–5	Chelsea
1965–6	West Bromwich Albion
1966–7	Queen's Park Rangers
1967–8	Leeds United
1968–9	Swindon Town
1969–70	Manchester City
1970–1	Tottenham Hotspur
1971–2	Stoke City
1972–3	Tottenham Hotspur
1973–4	Wolverhampton Wanderers
1974–5	Aston Villa
1975–6	Manchester City
1976–7	Aston Villa
1977–8	Nottingham Forest
1978–9	Nottingham Forest
1979–80	Wolverhampton Wanderers
1980–1	Liverpool
1981–2	Liverpool
1982–3	Liverpool
1983–4	Liverpool
1984–5	Norwich City
1985–6	Oxford United
1986–7	Arsenal
1987–8	Luton Town

SCOTTISH CUP WINNERS

1890–1	Hearts
1891–2	Celtic
1892–3	Queen's Park
1893–4	Rangers
1894–5	St. Bernard's
1895–6	Hearts
1896–7	Rangers
1897–8	Rangers
1898–9	Celtic
1899–1900	Celtic
1900–1	Hearts
1901–2	Hibernian
1902–3	Rangers
1903–4	Celtic
1904–5	Third Lanark
1905–6	Hearts
1906–7	Celtic
1907–8	Celtic
1908–9	*Cup withheld (riot)*
1909–10	Dundee
1910–11	Celtic
1911–12	Celtic
1912–13	Falkirk
1913–14	Celtic
1914–19	*No competition*
1919–20	Kilmarnock
1920–1	Partick Thistle
1921–2	Morton
1922–3	Celtic
1923–4	Airdrieonians
1924–5	Celtic
1925–6	St Mirren
1926–7	Celtic
1927–8	Rangers
1928–9	Kilmarnock
1929–30	Rangers
1930–1	Celtic
1931–2	Rangers
1932–3	Celtic
1933–4	Rangers
1934–5	Rangers
1935–6	Rangers
1936–7	Celtic
1937–8	East Fife
1938–9	Clyde
1939–46	*No competition*
1946–7	Aberdeen
1947–8	Rangers
1948–9	Rangers
1949–50	Rangers

1950–1	Celtic
1951–2	Motherwell
1952–3	Rangers
1953–4	Celtic
1954–5	Clyde
1955–6	Hearts
1956–7	Falkirk
1957–8	Clyde
1958–9	St Mirren
1959–60	Rangers
1960–1	Dunfermline
1961–2	Rangers
1962–3	Rangers
1963–4	Rangers
1964–5	Celtic
1965–6	Rangers
1966–7	Celtic
1967–8	Dunfermline
1968–9	Celtic
1969–70	Aberdeen
1970–1	Celtic
1971–2	Celtic
1972–3	Rangers
1973–4	Celtic
1974–5	Celtic
1975–6	Rangers
1976–7	Celtic
1977–8	Rangers
1978–9	Rangers
1979–80	Celtic
1980–1	Rangers
1981–2	Aberdeen
1982–3	Aberdeen
1983–4	Aberdeen
1984–5	Celtic
1985–6	Aberdeen
1986–7	St Mirren
1987–8	Celtic

SCOTTISH LEAGUE CHAMPIONS

1891–2	Dumbarton
1892–3	Celtic
1893–4	Celtic
1894–5	Hearts
1895–6	Celtic
1896–7	Hearts
1897–8	Celtic
1898–9	Rangers
1899–1900	Rangers
1900–1	Rangers
1901–2	Rangers
1902–3	Hibernian
1903–4	Third Lanark
1904–5	Celtic
1905–6	Celtic
1906–7	Celtic
1907–8	Celtic
1908–9	Celtic
1909–10	Celtic
1910–11	Rangers
1911–12	Rangers
1912–13	Rangers
1913–14	Celtic
1914–15	Celtic
1915–16	Celtic
1916–17	Celtic
1917–18	Rangers
1918–19	Celtic
1919–20	Rangers
1920–1	Rangers
1921–2	Celtic
1922–3	Rangers
1923–4	Rangers
1924–5	Rangers
1925–6	Celtic
1926–7	Rangers
1927–8	Rangers
1928–9	Rangers
1929–30	Rangers
1930–1	Rangers
1931–2	Motherwell
1932–3	Rangers
1933–4	Rangers
1934–5	Rangers
1935–6	Celtic
1936–7	Rangers
1937–8	Celtic
1938–9	Rangers
1939–46	*No competition*
1946–7	Rangers

1947–8	Hibernian
1948–9	Rangers
1949–50	Rangers
1950–1	Hibernian
1951–2	Hibernian
1952–3	Rangers
1953–4	Celtic
1954–5	Aberdeen
1955–6	Rangers
1956–7	Rangers
1957–8	Hearts
1958–9	Rangers
1959–60	Hearts
1960–1	Rangers
1961–2	Dundee
1962–3	Rangers
1963–4	Rangers
1964–5	Kilmarnock
1965–6	Celtic
1966–7	Celtic
1967–8	Celtic
1968–9	Celtic
1969–70	Celtic
1970–1	Celtic
1971–2	Celtic
1972–3	Celtic
1973–4	Celtic
1974–5	Rangers
1975–6	Rangers
1976–7	Celtic
1977–8	Rangers
1978–9	Celtic
1979–80	Aberdeen
1980–1	Celtic
1981–2	Celtic
1982–3	Dundee United
1983–4	Aberdeen
1984–5	Aberdeen
1985–6	Celtic
1986–7	Rangers
1987–8	Celtic

HOME INTERNATIONAL CHAMPIONSHIP (since 1946)

1946–7	England
1947–8	England
1948–9	Scotland
1949–50	England
1950–1	Scotland
1951–2	Wales and England
1952–3	England and Scotland
1953–4	England
1954–5	England
1955–6	England, Scotland, Wales and Ireland
1956–7	England
1957–8	England and Ireland
1958–9	England and Ireland
1959–60	England, Wales and Scotland
1960–1	England
1961–2	Scotland
1962–3	Scotland
1963–4	England, Scotland and Ireland
1964–5	England
1965–6	England
1966–7	Scotland
1967–8	England
1968–9	England
1969–70	England, Scotland and Wales
1970–1	England
1971–2	England and Scotland
1972–3	England
1973–4	England and Scotland
1974–5	England
1975–6	Scotland
1976–7	Scotland
1977–8	England
1978–9	England
1979–80	Ireland
1980–1	*Not completed*
1981–2	England
1982–3	England
1983–4	Northern Ireland

Note: The Championship ended in 1983–4

EUROPEAN CUP WINNERS

1956 Real Madrid
1957 Real Madrid

1958 Real Madrid
1959 Real Madrid
1960 Real Madrid
1961 Benfica
1962 Benfica
1963 AC Milan
1964 Inter-Milan
1965 Inter-Milan
1966 Real Madrid
1967 Celtic
1968 Manchester United
1969 AC Milan
1970 Feyenoord
1971 Ajax Amsterdam
1972 Ajax Amsterdam
1973 Ajax Amsterdam
1974 Bayern Munich
1975 Bayern Munich
1976 Bayern Munich
1977 Liverpool
1978 Liverpool
1979 Nottingham Forest
1980 Nottingham Forest
1981 Liverpool
1982 Aston Villa
1983 SV Hamburg
1984 Liverpool
1985 Juventus
1986 Steaua Bucharest
1987 FC Porto
1988 PSV Eindhoven

EUROPEAN CUP-WINNERS CUP WINNERS

1961 AC Fiorentina
1962 Atletico Madrid
1963 Tottenham Hotspur
1964 Sporting Club Lisbon
1965 West Ham United
1966 Borussia Dortmund
1967 Bayern Munich
1968 AC Milan
1969 Slovan Bratislava
1970 Manchester City
1971 Chelsea
1972 Rangers
1973 AC Milan
1974 FC Magdeburg
1975 Dynamo Kiev
1976 Anderlecht
1977 SV Hamburg
1978 Anderlecht
1979 Barcelona
1980 Valencia
1981 Dynamo Tbilisi
1982 Barcelona
1983 Aberdeen
1984 Juventus
1985 Everton
1986 Dynamo Kiev
1987 Ajax Amsterdam
1988 Mechelen

UEFA CUP WINNERS (until 1971, European Fairs Cup)

1958 Barcelona
1960 Barcelona
1961 AS Roma
1962 Valencia
1963 Valencia
1964 Real Zaragoza
1965 Ferencvaros
1966 Barcelona
1967 Dynamo Zagreb
1968 Leeds United
1969 Newcastle United
1970 Arsenal
1971 Leeds United
1972 Tottenham Hotspur
1973 Liverpool
1974 Feyenoord
1975 Borussia Moenchengladbach
1976 Liverpool
1977 Juventus
1978 PSV Eindhoven
1979 Borussia Moenchengladbach
1980 Eintracht Frankfurt
1981 Ipswich Town
1982 IFK Gothenburg
1983 Anderlecht
1984 Tottenham Hotspur
1985 Real Madrid
1986 Real Madrid
1987 IFK Gothenburg
1988 Bayer Leverkusen

ATHLETICS

Athletics is the simplest and oldest of sports, being the basis of the ancient Olympic Games. It nowadays embraces running, walking, jumping and throwing contests, those involving running on a track known as track events and the others as field events. The following men's events are currently in the Olympic Games. Running: 100 m, 200 m, 400 m, 800 m, 1500 m, 5000 m, 10000 m, marathon (42195 m, 110-m hurdles, 400-m hurdles, 3000-m steeplechase, 4 × 100-m relay, 4 × 400-m relay; walking: 20 km and 50 km; jumping: high jump, long jump, triple jump, pole vault; throwing: shot, discus, hammer, javelin. There are separate events for men and women, although women run 3000 metres instead of 5000 and do not compete in a steeplechase, walking races, triple jump, hammer, and pole vault. There are also combined competitions, a decathlon (10 events) for men, and a heptathlon (seven events) for women.

Until recently, those countries which used imperial measurements ran races at distances of 100 yards, mile, 3 miles, etc, but nowadays, only the mile remains as a common event.

Athletics is administered internationally by the International Amateur Athletic Federation, although it is possible now for top athletes to earn huge incomes, as professionals. Many Olympic champions have turned professional, but professional athletics has so far failed to capture public enthusiasm.

Apart from the Olympic Games, the principal athletic competitions are the Commonwealth Games, the European Championships and the Pan-American Games.

Athletics can be the loneliest of sports. Although competitors may be numerous at meetings, the training is often performed alone, and can be a test of the athlete's willpower.

An international athlete is likely to have his own coach to map out his training schedules for him. The novice athlete can help himself by improving his general fitness and by using a training routine suited to his particular event.

Whatever his event, qualities which will help the athlete are: strength, skill, stamina, speed and flexibility (or suppleness). Various exercises have been devised for each, and the serious athlete can obtain a manual which details exercises for specific athletic events.

ATHLETICS CLUBS

If you are prepared to devote the time and effort necessary to achieve a high standard, join an athletics club, where you will find others of a similar mind, facilities for training and experienced athletes and coaches to help you.

WORLD RECORDS

Event	*Record*	*Holder*	*Nation*	*Year*
100 m	9.83 sec	Ben Johnson	Canada	1987
200 m	19.72 sec	Pietro Mennea	Italy	1979
400 m	43.29 sec	Butch Reynolds	USA	1988
800 m	1 min 41.73 sec	Sebastian Coe	GB	1981
1500 m	3 min 29.46 sec	Said Aouita	Morocco	1985
Mile	3 min 46.32 sec	Steve Cram	GB	1985
5000 m	12 min 58.39 sec	Said Aouita	Morocco	1987
10000 m	27 min 13.81 sec	Fernando Mamede	Portugal	1984
Marathon	2 hr 06 min 50 sec	Belayneh Densimo	Ethiopia	1988
110-m hurdles	12.93 sec	Renaldo Nehemiah	USA	1981
400-m hurdles	47.02 sec	Edwin Moses	USA	1983
3000-m steeplechase	8 min 05.40 sec	Henry Rono	Kenya	1978
High jump	2.43 m	Javier Sotomayor	Cuba	1988
Pole vault	6.01 m	Sergey Bubka	USSR	1986
Long jump	8.90 m	Bob Beamon	USA	1968
Triple jump	17.97 m	Willie Banks	USA	1985
Shot put	23.06 m	Ulf Timmermann	GDR	1988
Discus	74.08 m	Jurgen Schult	GDR	1986
Hammer	86.74 m	Yuriy Sedykh	USSR	1986
Javelin	87.66 m	Jan Zelezny	Czechoslovakia	1987
Decathlon	8,847 points	Daley Thompson	GB	1984
4 × 100 m relay	37.83 sec	National team	USA	1984
4 × 400 m relay	2 min 56.16 sec	National team	USA	1968 and 1988

Event	*Record*	*Holder*	*Nation*	*Year*
Decathlon (new tables)	8847 pts	Daley Thompson	GB	1985
Relays:				
4 × 100 m	37.83 sec		USA	1984
4 × 200 m	1 min 20.26 sec	University of Southern California	USA	1978
4 × 400 m	2 min 56.16 sec		USA	1977
4 × 800 m	7 min 03.89 sec		GB	1982
4 × 1500 m	14 min 38.8 sec		FRG	1977

WORLD MILE RECORD

Year	*Athlete*	*Nation*	*Time*
1913	John Paul Jones	USA	4 min 14.4 sec
1915	Norman Taber	USA	4 min 12.6 sec
1923	Paavo Nurmi	Finland	4 min 10.4 sec
1931	Jules Ladoumègue	France	4 min 9.2 sec
1933	Jack Lovelock	New Zealand	4 min 7.6 sec
1934	Glenn Cunningham	USA	4 min 6.8 sec
1937	Sydney Wooderson	GB	4 min 6.4 sec
1942	Gunder Haegg	Sweden	4 min 6.2 sec
1942	Arne Andersson	Sweden	4 min 6.2 sec
1942	Gunder Haegg	Sweden	4 min 4.6 sec
1943	Arne Andersson	Sweden	4 min 2.6 sec
1944	Arne Andersson	Sweden	4 min 1.6 sec
1945	Gunder Haegg	Sweden	4 min 1.4 sec
1954	Roger Bannister	GB	3 min 59.4 sec
1954	John Landy	Australia	3 min 58.0 sec
1957	Derek Ibbotson	GB	3 min 57.2 sec
1958	Herb Elliott	Australia	3 min 54.5 sec
1962	Peter Snell	New Zealand	3 min 54.4 sec
1964	Peter Snell	New Zealand	3 min 54.1 sec
1965	Michel Jazy	France	3 min 53.6 sec
1966	Jim Ryun	USA	3 min 51.3 sec
1967	Jim Ryun	USA	3 min 51.1 sec
1975	Filbert Bayi	Tanzania	3 min 51.0 sec
1975	John Walker	New Zealand	3 min 49.4 sec
1979	Sebastian Coe	GB	3 min 49.0 sec
1980	Steve Ovett	GB	3 min 48.8 sec
1981	Sebastian Coe	GB	3 min 48.53 sec
1981	Steve Ovett	GB	3 min 48.4 sec
1981	Sebastian Coe	GB	3 min 47.33 sec
1985	Steve Cram	GB	3 min 46.32 sec

OLYMPIC CHAMPIONS (1988)

Event	*Winner*	*Nation*	*Time/distance*
100 m*	C Lewis	USA	9.92 sec
200 m	J DeLoach	USA	19.75 sec
400 m	S Lewis	USA	43.87 sec
800 m	P Ereng	Kenya	1 min 43.45 sec
1500 m	P Rono	Kenya	3 min 35.96 sec
3000 m steeplechase	J Kariuki	Kenya	8 min 05.51 sec
5000 m	J Ngugi	Kenya	13 min 11.70 sec
10000 m	B Boubayeb	Morocco	27 min 21.46 sec
Marathon	G Bordin	Italy	2 hr 10 min 32 sec
110 m hurdles	R Kingdom	USA	12.98 sec
400 m hurdles	A Phillips	USA	47.19 sec
20 km walk	J Pribilinec	Czechoslovakia	1 hr 19 min 57 sec
50 km walk	V Ivanenko	USSR	3 hr 38 min 29 sec
High jump	G Avdeyanko	USSR	2.38 m
Pole vault	S Bubka	USSR	5.90 m
Long jump	C Lewis	USA	8.72 m
Triple jump	C Markov	Bulgaria	17.61 m
Shot put	U Timmermann	GDR	22.47 m
Discus	J Schult	GDR	68.82 m
Hammer	S Litvinov	USSR	84.80 m
Javelin	T Korjus	Finland	84.28 m
Decathlon	C Schenk	GDR	8488 points
4 × 100 m relay		USSR	38.19 sec
4 × 400 m relay		USA	2 min 56.16 sec

* Ben Johnson finished first, but was later disqualified for having taken a banned substance

BADMINTON

Badminton is played on an indoor court by two sides of one or two players. It is played with rackets and a shuttle made of feathers fixed in a cork base, although nylon or plastic may be used. The object is to hit the shuttle over a 1.55 m-(5 ft 1 in) high net to the floor on the opponents' side, which wins the rally. Only the serving side scores a point for winning a rally. Service changes when the server loses a rally. In doubles, both partners serve before the serve passes to the other side, so the non-servers must win two rallies to obtain the service. Men's games are to 15 points, women's to 11, a match being the best of three games. However, especially in round-robin tournaments, a match might consist of one game of 21 points.

The game started about 1870 at the Duke of Beaufort's seat at Badminton, from which it took its name. The principal event for individuals was for many years the All-England Championships, but recently World Championships have been introduced. The Men's International Championship for the Thomas Cup has been won most times by Indonesia. The Ladies' Championship is for the Uber Cup with the USA and Japan being the most successful teams. England, Denmark, and Malaysia have also been strong countries. The governing body is the International Badminton Federation.

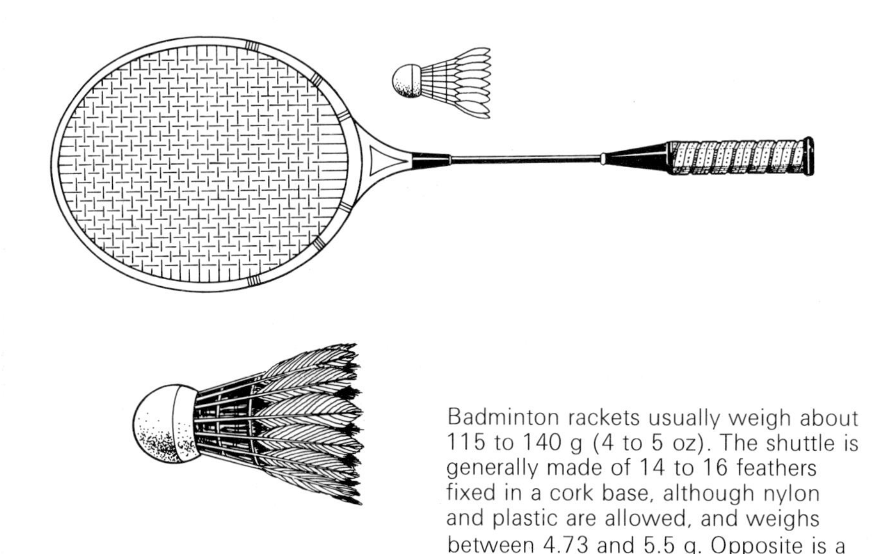

Badminton rackets usually weigh about 115 to 140 g (4 to 5 oz). The shuttle is generally made of 14 to 16 feathers fixed in a cork base, although nylon and plastic are allowed, and weighs between 4.73 and 5.5 g. Opposite is a standard court with dimensions.

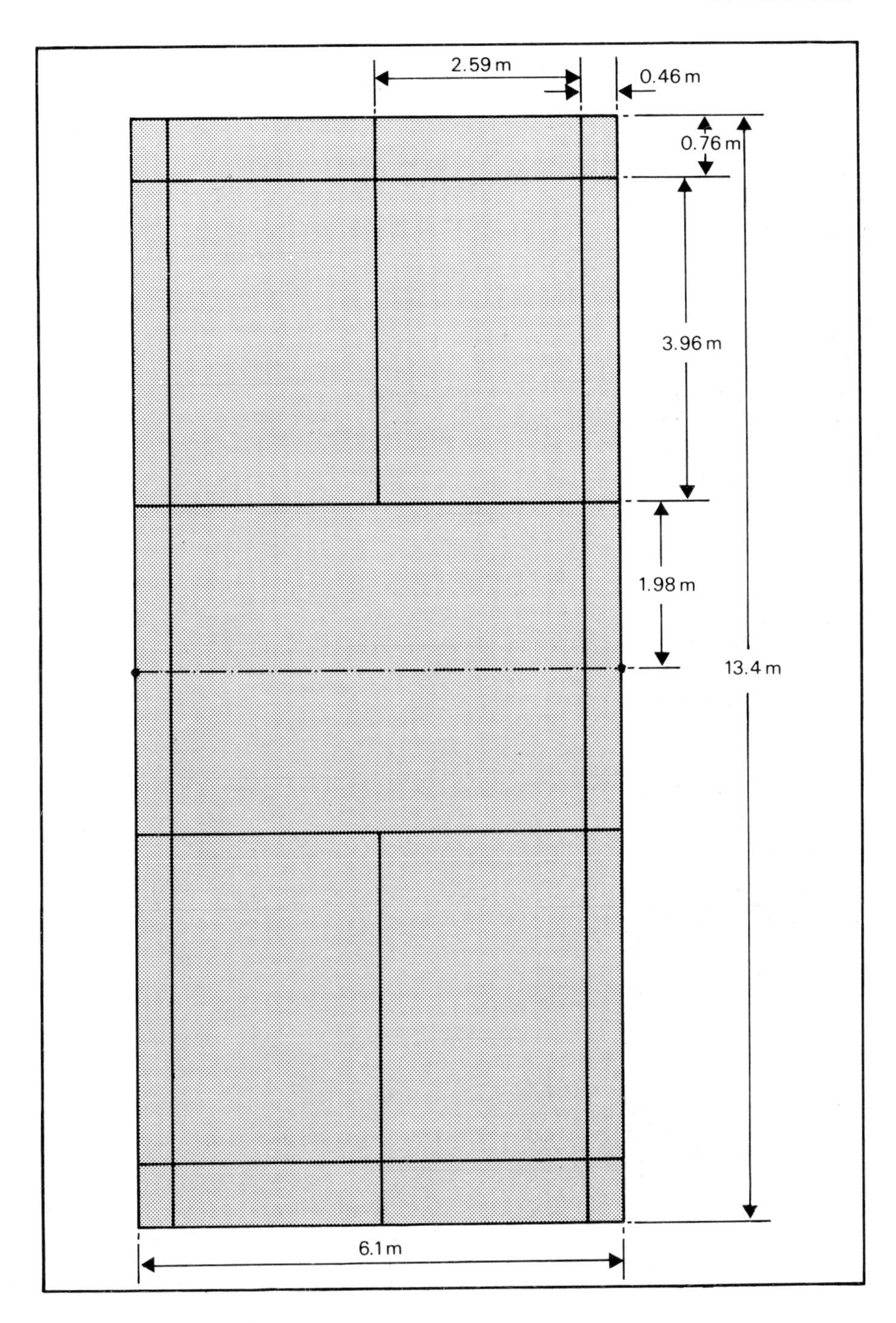
2.59 m
0.46 m
0.76 m
3.96 m
1.98 m
13.4 m
6.1 m

CRICKET

Cricket is a bat and ball game played between two teams of 11. Each side bats in turn and attempts to make more runs than their opponents, who attempt to dismiss them. It is played on a grass arena, usually oval in shape. In the centre of the arena is the pitch, with a wicket at each end consisting of three vertical stumps with two horizontal bails on the top.

The fielding side has all 11 players on the field together. One is a wicket-keeper who is positioned behind the wicket. Two of the batting side take up position, one at each wicket, and when either is dismissed, they are replaced by another member of the team. So, two batsmen are always playing. When ten batsmen have been dismissed, there is no one left to come in, and the team is therefore all out.

A member of the fielding side bowls from one end of the pitch to the batsman at the opposite wicket. When six balls have been bowled, it is the end of an over and another bowler bowls from the other end at the batsman who is positioned at the opposite wicket.

A run is scored when, after a batsman hits the ball, or the ball is in play, both batsmen run to their opposite wicket. If the ball is hit over the boundary the batsman scores six runs and does not run between the wickets. If the ball touches the ground before going over the boundary, the batsman

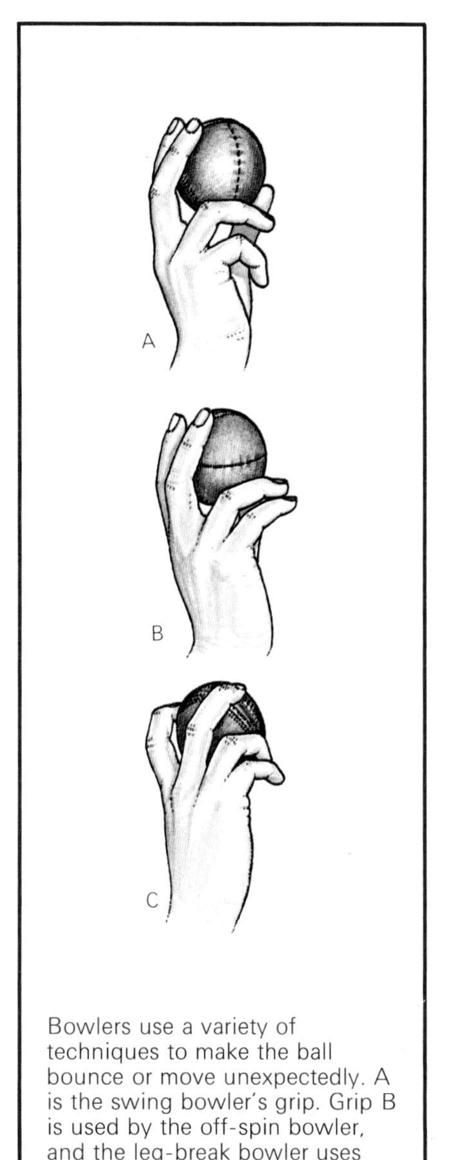

Bowlers use a variety of techniques to make the ball bounce or move unexpectedly. A is the swing bowler's grip. Grip B is used by the off-spin bowler, and the leg-break bowler uses grip C.

These are some of the commonest fielding positions for a right-handed batsman:
1 wicket-keeper, 2 first slip, 3 second slip, 4 third slip, 5 fourth slip, 6 gully, 7 third man, 8 silly point, 9 point, 10 cover point, 11 extra cover, 12 deep extra cover, 13 silly mid-off, 14 mid-off, 15 long off, 16 fine leg, 17 short leg, 18 short square leg, 19 silly mid-on, 20 square leg, 21 deep square leg, 22 deep fine leg, 23 mid-wicket, 24 mid-on, 25 long on.

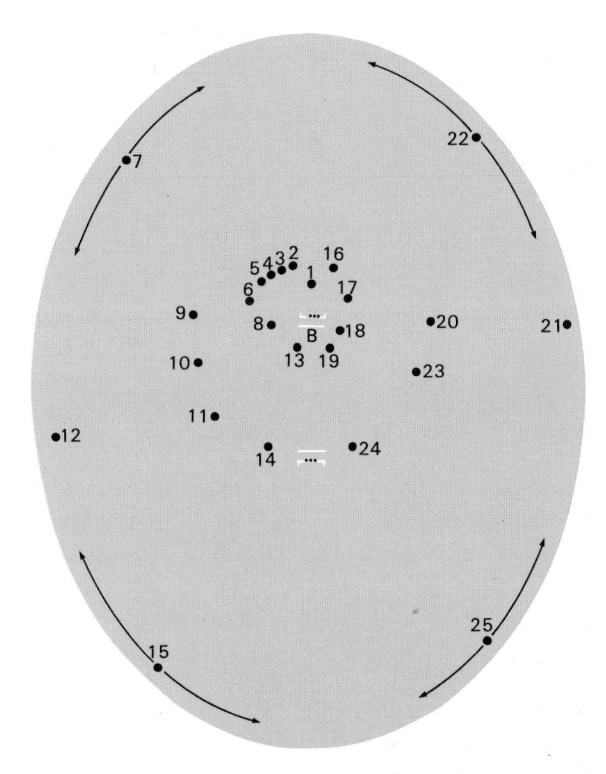

scores four runs.

A batsman can be dismissed in several ways. Bowled: when the ball delivered by the bowler hits the wicket so that a bail is dislodged. Leg before wicket (lbw): when any part of the body except the hand prevents the ball hitting the wicket, and the ball has not touched the bat or hand first and did not pitch outside leg stump. Caught: when a fielder catches the ball before it touches the ground after leaving the bat or batsman's gloves. Hit wicket: when the batsman breaks the wicket with bat or body while playing a shot or starting a run. Run out: when the fielding side breaks the wicket with the ball when the batsman is out of his ground while the ball is in play. Stumped: when the batsman moves out of his ground when receiving the ball and the wicket-keeper breaks the wicket with the ball.

Each team plays one or two innings in a match. Matches can be a certain amount of time, or a specified number of overs. Play can finish before time if a result has been obtained.

The first discovered reference to cricket dates from the year 1550, and the game was well-established in England in the 18th century. Lord's in London is the home of the Marylebone Cricket Club, for many years the game's governing body. This is now the International Cricket Conference.

CRICKET RECORDS

Highest score in first-class cricket – 499 not out (Hanif Mohammed, in Pakistan, 1959)
Highest score in Test cricket – 365 not out (G. Sobers, West Indies, against Pakistan, in Kingston, 1958)
Highest known score in School cricket – 628 not out (A. E. Collins, in a match at Clifton College, Bristol, 1899)
Greatest number of runs in first class cricket – 61 237 between 1905 and 1934 (Sir J. B. Hobbs)
Greatest number of runs in Test cricket – 10122 (S. M. Gavaskar of India between 1970 and 1987)
Most runs scored off a six-ball over – 36 (G. Sobers of Nottinghamshire, off M. Nash of Glamorgan, at Swansea, 1968 and Ravi Shastri of Bombay off Tilak Raj of Baroda, at Bombay, 1985)
Highest batting partnership – 641 (T. Patton and N. Rippon in Australia, 1913–14)
Highest score in a season – 3816 (D. C. S. Compton, in 1947, with an average of 90.85)
Greatest number of wickets by a bowler in one match – 19 (J. C. Laker, for England against Australia, at Old Trafford, 1956, for 90 runs)
Greatest number of wickets in first-class cricket – 4187 between 1898 and 1930 (W. R. Rhodes)
Greatest number of wickets in Test cricket – 396 (R. J. Hadlee of New Zealand between 1972 and 1988)
Greatest total – 1107 (by Victoria against New South Wales, 1926)

TEST MATCH RESULTS

1. *England v Australia (The Ashes)*

1876/7	Aus 1	Eng 1
1878/9	Aus 1	Eng 0
1880	Eng 1	Aus 0
1881/2	Aus 2	Eng 0 dr 2
1882	Aus 1	Eng 0
1882/3	Aus 2	Eng 2
1884	Eng 1	Aus 0 dr 2
1884/5	Eng 3	Aus 2
1886	Eng 3	Aus 0
1886/7	Eng 2	Aus 0
1887/8	Eng 1	Aus 0
1888	Eng 2	Aus 1
1890	Eng 2	Aus 0
1891/2	Aus 2	Eng 1
1893	Eng 1	Aus 0 dr 2
1894/5	Eng 3	Aus 2
1896	Eng 2	Aus 1
1897/8	Aus 4	Eng 1
1899	Aus 1	Eng 0 dr 4
1901/2	Aus 4	Eng 1
1902	Aus 2	Eng 1 dr 2
1903/4	Eng 3	Aus 2
1905	Eng 2	Aus 0 dr 3
1907/8	Aus 4	Eng 1
1909	Aus 2	Eng 1 dr 2
1911/12	Eng 4	Aus 1
1912	Eng 1	Aus 0 dr 2
1920/1	Aus 5	Eng 0
1921	Aus 3	Eng 0 dr 2
1924/5	Aus 4	Eng 1
1926	Eng 1	Aus 0 dr 4
1928/9	Eng 4	Aus 1
1930	Aus 2	Eng 1 dr 2
1932/3	Eng 4	Aus 1
1934	Aus 2	Eng 1 dr 2
1936/7	Aus 3	Eng 2
1938	Aus 1	Eng 1 dr 2
1946/7	Aus 3	Eng 0 dr 2
1948	Aus 4	Eng 0 dr 1

1950/1 Aus 4 Eng 1
1953 Eng 1 Aus 0 dr 4
1954/5 Eng 3 Aus 1 dr 1
1956 Eng 2 Aus 1 dr 1
1958/9 Aus 4 Eng 0 dr 1
1961 Aus 2 Eng 1 dr 2
1962/3 Eng 1 Aus 1 dr 3
1964 Aus 1 Eng 0 dr 4
1965/6 Eng 1 Aus 1 dr 3
1968 Aus 1 Eng 1 dr 3
1970/1 Eng 2 Aus 0 dr 4
1972 Eng 2 Aus 2 dr 1
1974/5 Aus 4 Eng 1 dr 1
1975 Aus 1 Eng 0 dr 3
1976/7 Aus 1 Eng 0
1977 Eng 3 Aus 0 dr 2
1978/9 Eng 5 Aus 1
1979/80 Aus 3 Eng 0
1980 dr 1
1981 Eng 3 Aus 1 dr 2
1982/3 Aus 2 Eng 1 dr 1
1985 Eng 3 Aus 1 dr 2
1986/7 Eng 2 Aus 1 dr 2
1987/8 dr 1

2. *England v South Africa*

1888/9 Eng 2 SA 0
1891/2 Eng 1 SA 0
1895/6 Eng 3 SA 0
1898/9 Eng 2 SA 0
1905/6 SA 4 Eng 1
1907 Eng 1 SA 0 dr 2
1909/10 SA 3 Eng 2
1912 Eng 3 SA 0
1913/14 Eng 4 SA 0 dr 1
1922/3 Eng 2 SA 1 dr 2
1924 Eng 3 SA 2
1927/8 Eng 2 SA 2 dr 1
1929 Eng 2 SA 0 dr 3
1930/1 SA 1 Eng 0 dr 4
1935 SA 1 Eng 0 dr 4
1938/9 Eng 1 SA 0 dr 4
1947 Eng 3 SA 0 dr 2
1948/9 Eng 2 SA 0 dr 3
1951 Eng 3 SA 1 dr 1
1955 Eng 3 SA 2
1956/7 Eng 2 SA 2 dr 1
1960 Eng 3 SA 0 dr 2
1964/5 Eng 1 SA 0 dr 4
1965 SA 1 Eng 0 dr 4

3. *England v West Indies*

1928 Eng 3 WI 0
1929/30 Eng 1 WI 1 dr 2
1933 Eng 2 WI 0 dr 1
1934/5 WI 2 Eng 1 dr 1
1939 Eng 1 WI 0 dr 2
1947/8 WI 2 Eng 0 dr 2
1950 WI 3 Eng 1
1953/4 WI 2 Eng 2 dr 1
1957 Eng 3 WI 0 dr 2
1959/60 Eng 1 WI 0 dr 4
1963 WI 3 Eng 1 dr 1
1966 WI 3 Eng 1 dr 1
1967/8 Eng 1 WI 0 dr 4
1969 Eng 2 WI 2 dr 1
1973 WI 2 Eng 0 dr 1
1973/4 WI 1 Eng 1 dr 3
1976 WI 3 Eng 0 dr 2
1980 WI 1 Eng 0 dr 3
1980/1 WI 2 Eng 0 dr 2
1984 WI 5 Eng 0
1985/6 WI 5 Eng 0
1988 WI 4 Eng 0 dr 1

4. *England v New Zealand*

1929/30 Eng 1 NZ 0 dr 3
1931 Eng 1 NZ 0 dr 2
1932/3 dr 2
1937 Eng 1 NZ 0 dr 2
1946/7 dr 1
1949 dr 4
1950/1 Eng 1 NZ 0 dr 1
1954/5 Eng 2 NZ 0
1958 Eng 4 NZ 0 dr 1
1958/9 Eng 1 NZ 0
1965 Eng 3 NZ 0
1965/6 dr 3
1969 Eng 2 NZ 0 dr 1
1970/1 Eng 1 NZ 0 dr 1
1973 Eng 2 NZ 0 dr 1
1974/5 Eng 1 NZ 0 dr 1
1977/8 Eng 1 NZ 1 dr 1
1978 Eng 3 NZ 0
1983 Eng 3 NZ 1

1983/4 NZ 1 Eng 0 dr 2
1986 NZ 1 Eng 0 dr 2
1987/8 dr 3

5. England v India

1932 Eng 1 Ind 0
1933/4 Eng 2 Ind 0 dr 1
1936 Eng 2 Ind 0 dr 1
1946 Eng 1 Ind 0 dr 2
1951/2 Eng 1 Ind 1 dr 3
1952 Eng 3 Ind 0 dr 1
1959 Eng 5 Ind 0
1961/2 Ind 2 Eng 0 dr 3
1963/4 dr 5
1967 Eng 3 Ind 0
1971 Ind 1 Eng 0 dr 2
1972/3 Ind 2 Eng 1 dr 2
1974 Eng 3 Ind 0
1976/7 Eng 3 Ind 1 dr 1
1979 Eng 1 Ind 0 dr 3
1979/80 Eng 1 Ind 0
1981/2 Ind 1 Eng 0
1982 Eng 1 Ind 0 dr 2
1984/5 Eng 2 Ind 1 dr 2
1986 Ind 2 Eng 0 dr 1

6. England v Pakistan

1954 Eng 1 Pak 1 dr 2
1961/2 Eng 1 Pak 0 dr 2
1962 Eng 4 Pak 0 dr 1
1967 Eng 2 Pak 0 dr 1
1968/9 dr 3
1971 Eng 1 Pak 0 dr 2
1972/3 dr 3
1974 dr 3
1977/8 dr 3
1978 Eng 2 Pak 0 dr 1
1982 Eng 2 Pak 1
1983/4 Pak 1 Eng 0 dr 2
1987 Pak 1 Eng 0 dr 4
1987/8 Pak 1 Eng 0 dr 2

7. England v Sri Lanka

1981/2 Eng 1 Sri Lanka 0
1984 dr 1
1988 Eng 1 Sri Lanka 0

8. Australia v South Africa

1902/3 Aus 2 SA 0 dr 1
1910/11 Aus 4 SA 1
1912 Aus 2 SA 0 dr 1
1921/2 Aus 1 SA 0 dr 2
1931/2 Aus 5 SA 0
1935/6 Aus 4 SA 0 dr 1
1949/50 Aus 4 SA 0 dr 1
1952/3 Aus 2 SA 2 dr 1
1957/8 Aus 3 SA 0 dr 2
1963/4 Aus 1 SA 1 dr 3
1966/7 SA 3 Aus 1 dr 1
1969/70 SA 5 Aus 0

9. Australia v West Indies

1930/1 Aus 4 WI 1
1951/2 Aus 4 WI 1
1954/5 Aus 3 WI 0 dr 2
1960/1 Aus 2 WI 1 tie 1 dr 1
1964/5 WI 2 Aus 1 dr 2
1968/9 Aus 3 WI 1 dr 1
1972/3 Aus 2 WI 0 dr 3
1975/6 Aus 5 WI 1
1977/8 WI 3 Aus 1 dr 1
1978/9 WI 2 Aus 0 dr 1
1981/2 Aus 1 WI 1 dr 1
1983/4 WI 3 Aus 0 dr 2
1984/5 WI 3 Aus 1 dr 1

10. Australia v New Zealand

1945/6 Aus 1 NZ 0
1973/4 Aus 2 NZ 0 dr 1
1973/4 Aus 1 NZ 1 dr 1
1976/7 Aus 1 NZ 0 dr 1
1980/1 Aus 2 NZ 0 dr 1
1981/2 Aus 1 NZ 1 dr 1
1985/6 NZ 2 Aus 1
1985/6 NZ 1 Aus 0 dr 2
1987/8 Aus 1 NZ 0 dr 2

11. Australia v India

1947/8 Aus 4 Ind 0 dr 1
1956/7 Aus 2 Ind 0 dr 1
1959/60 Aus 2 Ind 1 dr 2
1964/5 Aus 1 Ind 1 dr 1
1967/8 Aus 4 Ind 0
1969/70 Aus 3 Ind 1 dr 1
1977/8 Aus 3 Ind 2
1979/80 Ind 2 Aus 0 dr 4
1980/1 Aus 1 Ind 1 dr 1
1985 Aus 0 Ind 0 dr 3
1985/6 dr 3

12. Australia v Pakistan

1956/7 Pak 1 Aus 0

1959/60 Aus 2 Pak 0 dr 1
1964/5 dr 1
1964/5 dr 1
1972/3 Aus 3 Pak 0
1976/7 Pak 1 Aus 1 dr 1
1978/9 Pak 1 Aus 1
1979/80 Pak 1 Aus 0 dr 2
1981/2 Aus 2 Pak 1
1982/3 Pak 3 Aus 0
1983/4 Aus 2 Pak 0 dr 3

13. *Australia v Sri Lanka*
1982/3 Aus 1 SL 0
1987/8 Aus 1 SL 0

14. *South Africa v New Zealand*
1931/2 SA 2 NZ 0
1952/3 SA 1 NZ 0 dr 1
1953/4 SA 4 NZ 0 dr 1
1961/2 SA 2 NZ 2 dr 1
1963/4 dr 3

15. *West Indies v New Zealand*
1951/2 WI 1 NZ 0 dr 1
1955/6 WI 3 NZ 1
1968/9 WI 1 NZ 1 dr 1
1971/2 dr 5
1979/80 NZ 1 WI 0 dr 4
1984/5 WI 2 NZ 0 dr 2

16. *West Indies v India*
1948/9 WI 1 Ind 0 dr 4
1952/3 WI 1 Ind 0 dr 4
1958/9 WI 3 Ind 0 dr 2
1961/2 WI 5 Ind 0
1966/7 WI 2 Ind 0 dr 1
1970/1 Ind 1 WI 0 dr 4
1974/5 WI 3 Ind 2
1975/6 WI 2 Ind 1 dr 1
1978/9 Ind 1 WI 0 dr 5
1982/3 WI 2 Ind 0 dr 3
1983/4 WI 3 Ind 0 dr 3
1987/8 Ind 1 WI 1 dr 2

17. *West Indies v Pakistan*
1957/8 WI 3 Pak 1 dr 1
1958/9 Pak 2 WI 1
1974/5 dr 2
1976/7 WI 2 Pak 1 dr 2
1980/1 WI 1 Pak 0 dr 3
1987/8 WI 1 Pak 1 dr 1

18. *New Zealand v India*
1955/6 Ind 2 NZ 0 dr 3
1964/5 Ind 1 NZ 0 dr 3
1967/8 Ind 3 NZ 1
1969/70 Ind 1 NZ 1 dr 1
1975/6 Ind 1 NZ 1 dr 1
1976/7 Ind 2 NZ 0 dr 1
1980/1 NZ 1 Ind 0 dr 2

19. *New Zealand v Pakistan*
1955/6 Pak 2 NZ 0 dr 1
1964/5 dr 3
1964/5 Pak 2 NZ 0 dr 1
1969/70 NZ 1 Pak 0 dr 2
1972/3 Pak 1 NZ 0 dr 2
1976/7 Pak 2 NZ 0 dr 1
1978/9 Pak 1 NZ 0 dr 2
1984/5 Pak 2 NZ 0 dr 1
1984/5 NZ 2 Pak 0 dr 1

20. *New Zealand v Sri Lanka*
1982/3 NZ 2 SL 0
1983/4 NZ 2 SL 0 dr 1

21. *India v Pakistan*
1952/3 Ind 2 Pak 1 dr 2
1954/5 dr 5
1960/1 dr 5
1978/9 Pak 2 Ind 0 dr 1
1979/80 Ind 2 Pak 0 dr 4
1982/3 Pak 3 Ind 0 dr 2
1983/4 dr 3
1984/5 dr 2

22. *India v Sri Lanka*
1982/3 dr 1
1985 SL 1 Ind 0 dr 2

23. *Pakistan v Sri Lanka*
1981/2 Pak 2 SL 0 dr 1
1985/6 Pak 2 SL 0 dr 1
1985/6 SL 1 Pak 1 dr 1

WORLD CUP

1975 West Indies
1979 West Indies
1983 India
1987 Australia

ENGLISH COUNTY CHAMPIONSHIP

1873	Gloucestershire and Nottinghamshire
1874	Derbyshire
1875	Nottinghamshire, Lancashire and Sussex
1876	Gloucestershire
1877	Gloucestershire
1878	Middlesex
1879	Notts and Lancs
1880	Nottinghamshire
1881	Lancashire
1882	Notts and Lancs
1883	Nottinghamshire
1884	Nottinghamshire
1885	Nottinghamshire
1886	Nottinghamshire
1887	Surrey
1888	Surrey
1889	Surrey, Lancashire and Nottinghamshire
1890	Surrey
1891	Surrey
1892	Surrey
1893	Yorkshire
1894	Surrey
1895	Surrey
1896	Yorkshire
1897	Lancashire
1898	Yorkshire
1899	Surrey
1900	Yorkshire
1901	Yorkshire
1902	Yorkshire
1903	Middlesex
1904	Lancashire
1905	Yorkshire
1906	Kent
1907	Nottinghamshire
1908	Yorkshire
1909	Kent
1910	Kent
1911	Warwickshire
1912	Yorkshire
1913	Kent
1914	Surrey
1915–18	*No competition*
1919	Yorkshire
1920	Middlesex
1921	Middlesex
1922	Yorkshire
1923	Yorkshire
1924	Yorkshire
1925	Yorkshire
1926	Lancashire
1927	Lancashire
1928	Lancashire
1929	Nottinghamshire
1930	Lancashire
1931	Yorkshire
1932	Yorkshire
1933	Yorkshire
1935	Yorkshire
1936	Derbyshire
1937	Yorkshire
1938	Yorkshire
1939	Yorkshire
1940–5	*No competition*
1946	Yorkshire
1947	Middlesex
1948	Glamorgan
1949	Middlesex and Yorkshire
1950	Lancashire and Surrey
1951	Warwickshire
1952	Surrey
1953	Surrey
1954	Surrey
1955	Surrey
1956	Surrey
1957	Surrey
1958	Surrey
1959	Yorkshire
1960	Yorkshire
1961	Hampshire

1962	Yorkshire	1976	Middlesex
1963	Yorkshire	1977	Middlesex and Kent
1964	Worcestershire	1978	Kent
1965	Worcestershire	1979	Essex
1966	Yorkshire	1980	Middlesex
1967	Yorkshire	1981	Nottinghamshire
1968	Yorkshire	1982	Middlesex
1969	Glamorgan	1983	Essex
1970	Kent	1984	Essex
1971	Surrey	1985	Middlesex
1972	Warwickshire	1986	Essex
1973	Hampshire	1987	Nottinghamshire
1974	Worcestershire	1988	Worcestershire
1975	Leicestershire		

GILLETTE CUP/NATWEST TROPHY

1963	Sussex	1972	Lancashire	1981	Derbyshire
1964	Sussex	1973	Gloucestershire	1982	Surrey
1965	Yorkshire	1974	Kent	1983	Somerset
1966	Warwickshire	1975	Lancashire	1984	Middlesex
1967	Kent	1976	Northamptonshire	1985	Essex
1968	Warwickshire	1977	Middlesex	1986	Sussex
1969	Yorkshire	1978	Sussex	1987	Nottinghamshire
1970	Lancashire	1979	Somerset	1988	Middlesex
1971	Lancashire	1980	Middlesex		

JOHN PLAYER REFUGE ASSURANCE LEAGUE CHAMPIONS

1969	Lancashire	1976	Kent	1983	Yorkshire
1970	Lancashire	1977	Leicestershire	1984	Essex
1971	Worcestershire	1978	Hampshire	1985	Essex
1972	Kent	1979	Somerset	1986	Hampshire
1973	Kent	1980	Warwickshire	1987	Worcestershire
1974	Leicestershire	1981	Essex	1988	Worcestershire
1975	Hampshire	1982	Sussex	(Cup: Lancashire)	

BENSON AND HEDGES CUP

1972	Leicestershire	1978	Kent	1984	Lancashire
1973	Kent	1979	Essex	1985	Leicestershire
1974	Surrey	1980	Northants	1986	Middlesex
1975	Leicestershire	1981	Somerset	1987	Yorkshire
1976	Kent	1982	Somerset	1988	Hampshire
1977	Gloucestershire	1983	Middlesex		

GOLF

Golf is a game played with clubs and a small ball, the object being to play the ball from a starting point (a tee) into a small hole in as few strokes as possible. A golf course usually has 18 such holes. The hole is usually on a relatively flat green of very short grass, with a fairway of well-mown grass between tee and green. On either side of the fairway is longer grass (the rough) and other common hazards are occasional trees and bushes and bunkers of sand.

There are two main forms of competition. Stroke-play (or medal play) is used for almost all major championships, in which golfers count their total strokes for the round or rounds, the one with the lowest total winning. Match-play is when two sides play on a hole-by-hole basis, the winner being the side that wins most holes. Most major professional championships consist of four rounds of stroke-play.

The game is played throughout the world, and a universal handicapping system allows players of unequal skill to compete satisfactorily. The origins of the game are obscure, but Scottish claims to its invention are as strong as any.

Various countries and continents have 'circuits' consisting of a number of tournaments, the American circuit being one of the richest in terms of prize money.

Since the 1960s, open championships of countries such as Britain and America have become tremendously popular with spectators, and are highly-prized titles.

Two major competitions are contested between Britain and America every two years – the Ryder Cup and the Walker Cup – with America having won well over 80 per cent of the matches since their inauguration in the 1920s.

Golf is taught at some schools. A young player may face difficulties in learning the game because of the expense of the equipment and the shortage of public courses. However, you can practise putting on a putting green, and longer shots in a field, with no more than a club and ball.

Golf is best learned from a good coach. If you want to play seriously, seek advice about where you can learn, or write to the secretaries of local golf clubs, and ask for advice about facilities for learning the game.

GOLF CLUBS

Players may use a maximum of 14 clubs. They may replace damaged clubs during a round, or add extra clubs if they started with fewer than 14, provided they do not exceed the total. The 14-club rule also applies to partners sharing a set of clubs.

There are three types of clubs:

* a wood has a head that is quite broad from front to back, and is usually made of wood, plastic or light metal. Woods are numbered

from 1 to 7 according to shape, and are used for long shots.
* an iron has a head that is quite narrow from front to back, and is usually made of steel. Irons are numbered from 1 to 10 and are used for shorter shots.
* a putter is a light metal club for playing the ball on the putting green.

View of a typical hole with tee, green and bunkers. Inset is a range of clubs, from woods (left) through irons to the putter (right).

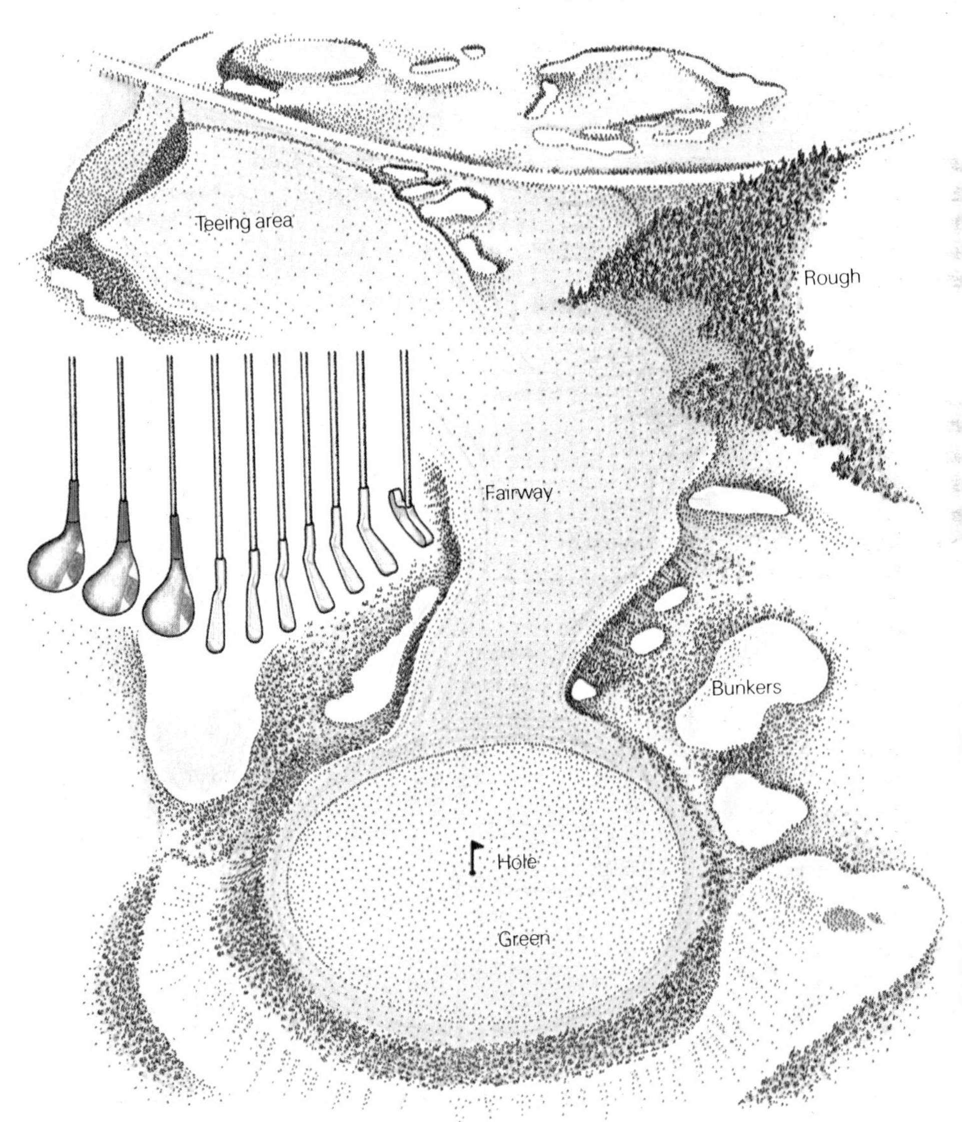

OPEN CHAMPIONSHIP WINNERS (since 1948)

1948 T.H. Cotton (Great Britain)
1949 A.D. Locke (South Africa)
1950 A.D. Locke
1951 M. Faulkner (Great Britain)
1952 A.D. Locke
1953 B. Hogan (USA)
1954 P.W. Thomson (Australia)
1955 P.W. Thomson
1956 P.W. Thomson
1957 A.D. Locke
1958 P.W. Thomson
1959 G.J. Player (South Africa)
1960 K. Nagle (Australia)
1961 A. Palmer (USA)
1962 A. Palmer
1963 R.J. Charles (New Zealand)
1964 A. Lema (USA)
1965 P.W. Thomson
1966 J.W. Nicklaus (USA)
1967 R. de Vicenzo (Argentina)
1968 G.J. Player
1969 A. Jacklin (Great Britain)
1970 J. Nicklaus
1971 L. Trevino (Mexico)
1972 L. Trevino
1973 T. Weiskopf (USA)
1974 G.J. Player
1975 T. Watson (USA)
1976 J. Miller (USA)
1977 T. Watson
1978 J. Nicklaus
1979 S. Ballesteros (Spain)
1980 T. Watson
1981 B. Rogers (USA)
1982 T. Watson
1983 T. Watson
1984 S. Ballesteros
1985 S. Lyle (Great Britain)
1986 G. Norman (Australia)
1987 N. Faldo (Great Britain)
1988 S. Ballesteros

RYDER CUP (since 1947)*

1947	USA	1961	USA	1975	USA
1949	USA	1963	USA	1977	USA
1951	USA	1965	USA	1979	USA
1953	USA	1967	USA	1981	USA
1955	USA	1969	Tie	1983	USA
1957	GB	1971	USA	1985	Europe
1959	USA	1973	USA	1987	Europe

* until 1979 between USA and Great Britain and Northern Ireland; since 1979 between USA and Europe

WALKER CUP (for Amateurs) (since 1947)

1947	USA	1961	USA	1975	USA
1949	USA	1963	USA	1977	USA
1951	USA	1965	Tie	1979	USA
1953	USA	1967	USA	1981	USA
1955	USA	1969	USA	1983	USA
1957	USA	1971	GB	1985	USA
1959	USA	1973	USA	1987	USA

ICE HOCKEY

Ice hockey is played on an ice rink between two teams of six men wearing ice skates and protective clothing, using sticks to play a circular rubber disc called a puck into the opponents' goal. Up to eleven substitutes are allowed. The game originated in Canada about 1860. Canada remains a strong nation, but has been overtaken in the amateur game by the USSR. Sweden, Czechoslovakia, USA and Finland are also strong. There are strong professional leagues in the USA and Canada, where the Stanley Cup is the chief prize.

ICE SKATING

Skating consists of three main sports, apart from ice hockey.

SPEED SKATING

This takes place on outside circuits. Both men and women compete in the Winter Olympic Games, at distances from 500 m to 10 000 m. Europeans have usually dominated, but the American Eric Heiden gained five golds in 1980, and Canadian Gaetan Boucher won two in 1984.

FIGURE SKATING

This is the longest established Winter Olympic sport and there are world championships. Events are for men, women and man/woman pairs. In senior solo competitions there are three elements: compulsory figures, a short prescribed free-skating phase, and a free-style phase. Pairs only perform the last two phases. Performances are assessed by a panel of judges. Among the best known figure skaters are Richard Button (USA), John Curry and Robin Cousins (Great Britain), Sonja Henie (Norway) and the Protopopovs (USSR).

ICE DANCING

This is derived from figure skating, and competitions are organized in a similar way. The main differences are that certain movements used in figure skating are not valued, and competitors (man/woman pairs) are confined to recognized groups of dances.

At the 1984 Winter Olympics in Sarajevo, Yugoslavia, Britain's Jayne Torvill and Christopher Dean won the gold medal, proving themselves to be among the greatest ice dancers ever.

ROWING

Rowing competitions take place mainly on inland waterways. In competition rowing, each person has a single oar – competitions in which each has a pair of oars are known as sculling. There are two main types of competition: regattas, in which competitors row in heats on a knock-out basis, which culminate in a final; and head of the river races in which competitors start at regular intervals, the winners being decided by time taken to complete the course. A crew for a rowing race almost always consists of two, four or eight people with oars; a sculling race has one, two or four. Eights are always steered by a coxswain, who sits at the stern; pairs and fours might also be coxed.

Distances for international regattas are 2000 m for men, 1000 m for women and 1500 m for men under 18. The construction and design of boats is unrestricted, though typical lengths are as follows: single sculls, 8.2 m (27 ft); double sculls, 10.4 m (34 ft); coxless pair 10.7 m (35 ft); coxless four, 13.4 m (44 ft); coxed four, 13.7 m (45 ft); eight, 18.9 m (62 ft).

The modern sport was developed in England, the oldest sculling race in the world, for Doggett's Coat and Badge, being instituted in 1715. Henley Regatta began in the early 19th century, and competition was soon established in the USA, Australia, Europe and Russia.

The sport is now almost entirely amateur, a professional phase having declined. A number of events are held in the Olympic Games and in the 1960s world championships replaced the European championships in four-year intervals between the Olympics.

The world governing body is the Fédération Internationale des Sociétés d'Aviron.

The peak of competitive rowing is represented by the eights.

RUGBY

Rugby football was developed in England, where it shared a common ancestry with Association Football. Legend says that the split with soccer happened in 1823, when William Webb Ellis 'first took the ball in his arms and ran with it' at Rugby School. When the Football Association was formed in 1863, clubs who preferred the handling game remained aloof, and the Rugby Football Union was formed in 1871. In 1895, 21 northern clubs, who wished to pay players compensation for lost wages at work left the Union to form the Northern Union, which became the Rugby Football League in 1922. Rugby union and rugby league football have since developed separately and are distinct games.

RUGBY UNION

This game has remained, in principle, amateur. It is played on a rectangular grass pitch: at each end there are a pair of high goal posts joined together by a crossbar 3.05 m (10 ft) high. Rugby union is played with a leather oval ball by two sides of 15 players a side. Players pass, kick or run with the ball in an attempt to ground it over their opponents' goal line which scores a try. A try is followed by an attempt at conversion, i.e. kicking the ball from a place-kick between the posts and over the crossbar. A converted try is a goal. Other methods of scoring are from a penalty goal and a dropped goal from open play. Points values have varied, but

Positions in rugby union are fluid but rough positions for the 15 players are shown: 1 and 3 prop forwards, 2 hooker, 4 and 5 lock forwards, 6 left flank forward, 7 right flank forward, 8 No 8 forward, 9 scrum half, 10 outside half, 11 left wing threequarter, 12 left centre threequarter, 13 right centre threequarter, 14 right wing threequarter, 15 full back.

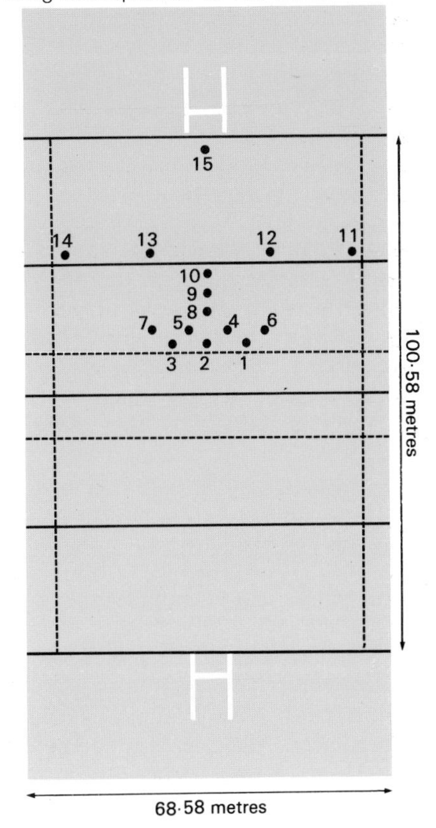

currently are: goal 6 points, unconverted try 4, penalty goal and dropped goal 3 points each.

The main rugby union nations are England, Ireland, Scotland, Wales, France, New Zealand, South Africa and Australia, with numerous other countries, particularly Argentina and Romania developing rapidly.

In Britain, many clubs encourage youngsters by organizing mini-rugby games for boys under the age of 12, often on Sunday mornings. Mini-rugby is for nine players a side and is played for 15 minutes each half, on a small pitch. It is the best possible introduction to the real game and a schoolboy should enquire at his local rugby clubs about playing.

RUGBY LEAGUE

This is played similarly to rugby union. The markings on the pitch are different, there are 13 players instead of 15, and various rules in play differ. The scoring values also differ: a goal counts five points, a try three, penalty goals two and drop goals one. It is played by amateurs and professionals and is confined mostly to the north of England, Australia, France and New Zealand. In England there is a very competitive professional league, and a Challenge Cup, the final of which is the showpiece of the season. Clubs which have built strong traditions include Wigan, St Helens, Warrington, Widnes, Huddersfield and Leeds. Test matches and a World Cup competition are held.

RUGBY LEAGUE – POSITIONS AND NUMBERS

These are usually as follows:

1 full back
2 right wing threequarter
3 right centre threequarter
4 left centre threequarter
5 left wing threequarter
6 stand off half
7 scrum half
8 front row prop forward
9 hooker
10 front row forward
11 second row forward
12 second row forward
13 loose forward

RUGBY UNION – POSITIONS AND NUMBERS

These are usually as follows:

1 prop forward
2 hooker
3 prop forward
4 lock forward
5 lock forward
6 flank forward
7 flank forward
8 No 8 forward
9 scrum half back
10 stand off or outside half back
11 left wing threequarter back
12 left centre threequarter back
13 right centre threequarter back
14 right wing threequarter back
15 full back

RUGBY UNION

International Championship (since 1946)

1946–7 Wales and England

1947–8 Ireland
1948–9 Ireland
1949–50 Wales
1950–1 Ireland
1951–2 Wales
1952–3 England
1953–4 England, France and Wales
1954–5 Wales and France
1955–6 Wales
1956–7 England
1957–8 England
1958–9 France
1959–60 England and France
1960–1 France
1961–2 France
1962–3 England
1963–4 Scotland and Wales
1964–5 Wales
1965–6 Wales
1966–7 France
1967–8 France
1968–9 Wales
1969–70 France
1970–1 Wales
1971–2 Wales
1972–3 All five countries finished level
1973–4 Ireland
1974–5 Wales
1975–6 Wales
1976–7 France
1977–8 Wales
1978–9 Wales
1979–80 England
1980–1 France
1981–2 Ireland
1982–3 Ireland and France
1983–4 Scotland
1984–5 Ireland
1985–6 France and Scotland
1986–7 France
1987–8 France and Wales

RUGBY LEAGUE

Challenge Cup Winners (since 1946)

1946–7 Bradford Northern
1947–8 Wigan
1948–9 Bradford Northern
1949–50 Warrington
1950–1 Wigan
1951–2 Workington Town
1952–3 Huddersfield
1953–4 Warrington
1954–5 Barrow
1955–6 St Helens
1956–7 Leeds
1957–8 Wigan
1958–9 Wigan
1959–60 Wakefield Trinity
1960–1 St Helens
1961–2 Wakefield Trinity
1962–3 Wakefield Trinity
1963–4 Widnes
1964–5 Wigan
1965–6 St Helens
1966–7 Featherstone Rovers
1967–8 Leeds
1968–9 Castleford
1969–70 Castleford
1970–1 Leigh
1971–2 St Helens
1972–3 Featherstone Rovers
1973–4 Warrington
1974–5 Widnes
1975–6 St Helens
1976–7 Leeds
1977–8 Leeds
1978–9 Wigan
1979–80 Hull Kingston Rovers
1980–1 Widnes
1981–2 Hull
1982–3 Featherstone Rovers
1983–4 Widnes
1984–5 Wigan
1985–6 Castleford
1986–7 Halifax
1987–8 Wigan
1988–9 Wigan

SQUASH

Squash derived from the older game of rackets, and was first played at Harrow School in England, around 1850. Now, it is played throughout the world, especially in Britain, Australia, New Zealand, India, Pakistan, USA, Canada and Egypt.

Squash is a racket game played by two players on an indoor court in which the walls are used in play. A small rubber or composition ball is used.

A standard squash rackets court measures 9.75 by 6.4 m (32 by 21 ft) and all four walls of the enclosed court are used. Service starts from the right-hand service 'box' on to the front wall above a 2-m (6-ft) line, so that the ball will fall into the left hand 'box' if allowed to bounce (the receiver may volley it). The ball may strike the side and back walls before landing in the box. Points are won only by the server when an opponent fails to reach the ball before it bounces twice or when he fails to return the ball to the front wall above a line 48 cm (19 in) from the floor. Matches usually consist of five games.

The first major international competition – the British Open – began in 1930. The first world amateur championships were in 1967, with Australia's Geoff Hunt winning the individual title and his country winning the team title.

View of a squash court.

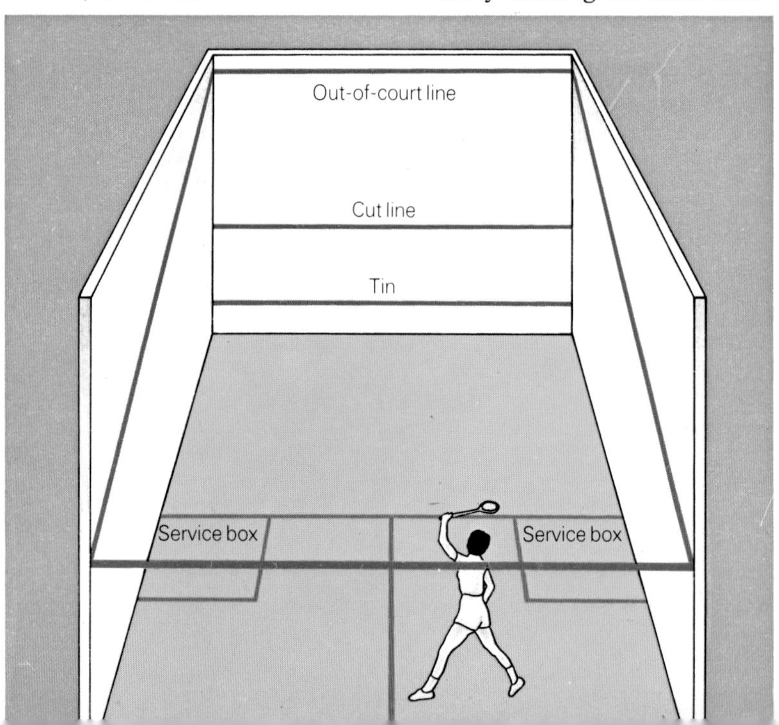

SWIMMING AND DIVING

SWIMMING

Swimming consists of four recognized styles in competitive events: the freestyle, butterfly, breaststroke and backstroke. Apart from freestyle races, in which competitors may use any stroke they prefer, the other strokes are governed by strict definitions. Races are of various distances, the Olympic programme including the following: men: 100 m, 200 m, 400 m and 1500 m freestyle, 100 m and 200 m butterfly, 100 m and 200 m breaststroke, 100 m and 200 m backstroke; women: 100 m, 200 m, 400 m and 800 m freestyle, 100 m and 200 m butterfly, 100 m and 200 m breaststroke, 100 m and 200 m backstroke. There are also 100 m and 200 m medley races for men and women, in which all four strokes are used. Relay races are also included in the Olympics.

Swimming is a sport that gives endless pleasure in itself, and it is also something that should be learned before any other sport connected with water is enjoyed.

Most instructors prefer to teach the breaststroke first. Many people learn to swim without proper instruction and can get around very well in the water and enjoy themselves without performing any of these strokes elegantly or well, but you will be a better swimmer if you learn the strokes properly from the beginning with a qualified instructor to teach you. And remember that if Olympic results are anything to go by, the best swimmers are young.

There is nothing difficult about learning to swim, and once learned, like walking or riding a bicycle, it is never forgotten.

WORLD RECORDS – SWIMMING

Event	*Time*	*Holder*	*Nation*	*Year*
50-m freestyle	22.14 sec	M Biondi	USA	1988
100-m freestyle	48.42 sec	M Biondi	USA	1988
200-m freestyle	1 min 47.25 sec	D Armstrong	Australia	1988
400-m freestyle	3 min 46.95 sec	U Dassler	E Germany	1988
800-m freestyle	7 min 50.64 sec	V Salnikov	USSR	1986
1500-m freestyle	14 min 54.76 sec	V Salnikov	USSR	1983
100-m backstroke	54.51 sec	D Berkoff	USA	1988

Event	*Time*	*Holder*	*Nation*	*Year*
200-m backstroke	1 min 54.14 sec	I Poljanski	USSR	1985
100-m breaststroke	1 min 01.65 sec	S Lundquist	USA	1984
200-m breaststroke	2 min 13.34 sec	V Davis	Canada	1984
100-m butterfly	52.84 sec	P Morales	USA	1986
200-m butterfly	1 min 56.24 sec	M Gross	W Germany	1986
200-m medley	2 min 00.17 sec	T Darnyi	Hungary	1988
400-m medley	4 min 14.75 sec	T Darnyi	Hungary	1988
4 × 100-m medley	3 min 36.93 sec	National team	USA	1988
4 × 100-m freestyle	3 min 16.53 sec	National team	USA	1988
4 × 200-m freestyle	7 min 12.51 sec	National team	USA	1988

DIVING

Diving is a sport in which competitors spring from an elevated board into a pool, performing, in turn, compulsory and chosen dives which are marked by a set of judges. The winner is the competitor with the highest total marks after a series of dives. There are springboard and highboard events. Springboards are flexible boards at heights of 1 m (3.2 ft) or 3 m (10 ft), and highboards are more rigid boards at heights of 3 m (10 ft), 5 m (16 ft), 7.5 m (24 ft) or 10 m (33 ft).

Men's springboard events consist of five required dives and six chosen dives; women's consist of five of each. The required dives for both men and women are: a forward dive, a backward dive, a reverse dive, an inward dive, and a forward dive with a half twist. Men's highboard events consist of four chosen dives with a maximum difficulty of 7.5, and six chosen dives without limit; women's consist of four of each. For all dives, the mark is a combination of the difficulty of the dive and how well it is done.

In the Olympics, the USA has been the most successful nation overall. The governing body is the Fédération Internationale de Natation Amateur (International Federation of Amateur Swimming).

TENNIS

Until recently, tennis was properly known as lawn tennis, but few major tournaments are now played on grass and progressively the word 'lawn' has been dropped. The game is played indoors or outdoors, by two sides of one or two players, on a court, usually of asphalt, clay, grass or shale, across the centre of which is a net. It is a racket game in which players return the ball into their opponents' court. The ball can be played after the bounce or on the volley. Matches are divided into a maximum of five sets for men and three for women, a set being won by the first side to win six games while holding a two-game lead. Points are not called as one, two, three but 15, 30, 40. Should the score reach six games all, a tie-break game is usually played. A tie-break game is won by the first side to win seven points, unless each wins six, when the game continues until one side is two points ahead.

The major tournaments are Wimbledon, which is still played on grass, the French championships at Roland-Garros, the US championships at Flushing Meadow and the Australian championships played at various venues. These tournaments are known as the 'Grand Slam'. The principal team events for nations are the Davis Cup, for men, and the Federation Cup, for women, while the Wightman Cup is contested by British and American women.

The rules for the game as we know it today were laid down by the All England Croquet Club, Wimbledon, who staged the first tournament in 1877 – a men's singles event, won by Spencer W. Gore. Wimbledon's success with tennis spread to the rest of the world and now over 100 national lawn tennis associations make up the Lawn Tennis Federation.

Although it began as an amateur game, tennis soon developed professional ranks, with players like the great Rod Laver becoming dollar millionaires. But amateurs and professionals didn't play together until the first Open Tournament in 1968 at Bournemouth. Now players can earn vast prize money, playing in American-organized World Championship Tennis and World Team Tennis tournaments, as well as at the major competitions of countries such as Australia, Italy and France.

All you need to play tennis are a racket, suitable clothing and footwear, an opponent similarly equipped, a court and a supply of tennis balls.

When buying a racket, try some practice swings in the shop before making your choice. Buy the best you can afford. Choose a well-known make, and a racket which feels comfortable and is not too heavy. A wooden frame is probably best for the beginner, and the grip should be square and as large as can be handled with comfort.

Most of the shots played in tennis (nearly all those played by beginners) are ground shots, which are shots played after the ball has bounced. Most of these shots are played just as the ball is beginning to drop after bouncing. Swing the racket 'through' the ball in a full arc and follow through with the racket. Do not stab at the ball. Both forehand and backhand shots are easy to play if you and your feet are in the right position. Getting into the right position is the most difficult part of the shot for many beginners. You can practise this art on your own by knocking a ball against a wall at various angles and speeds. Always watch the ball right on to the racket and concentrate all the time on the shot.

Each point in tennis begins with a service, so it is important to learn to serve well. As your racket is on its back swing, reach as high as you can with your 'free' hand, and try to put the ball exactly in the path of the racket as it swings through. It might help if you imagine you are throwing the racket – with practice, you should be able to serve the ball as accurately as if you were

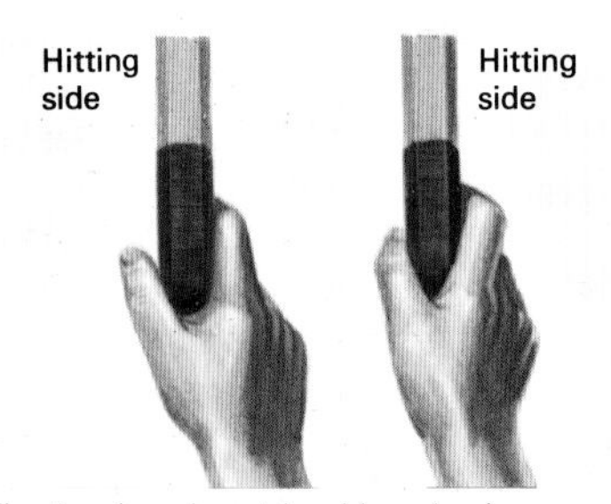

The forehand and backhand grips.

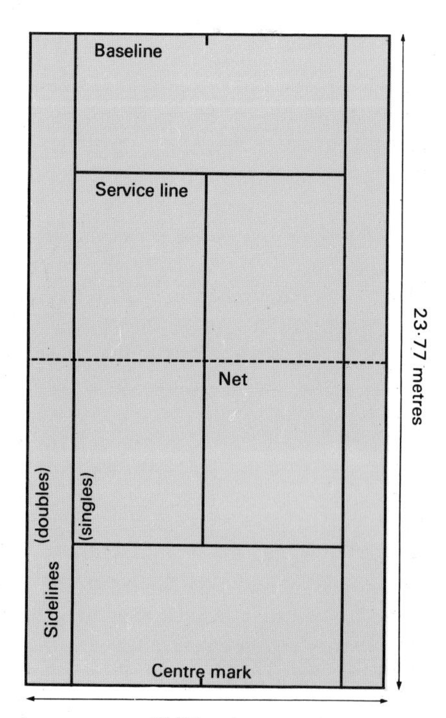

A tennis court.

throwing it. The overhead smash shot, so necessary to world champions, is played in a similar way to the service. Throw the racket at the ball, and watch the ball right on to the racket.

Volleys are shots played before the ball bounces. They are played with more of a punching action than a swing of the racket and are mostly played close to the net. Ask a friend to throw balls at you at around shoulder height, and jab them straight back at him or her.

When you can play these shots well, try lobbing and putting top spin and back spin on the ball. The best way to develop tennis skills is to find a friend willing to learn and practise with you. When you have reached a reasonable standard, you can join a club and play against other players. Do not worry too much about being beaten at first. Concentrate on your technique rather than on getting points at any price, work on your weaknesses, and eventually success will come.

WIMBLEDON MEN'S SINGLES CHAMPIONS

1877	S.W. Gore	1912	A.F. Wilding	1955	T. Trabert
1878	P.F. Hadlow	1913	A.F. Wilding	1956	L.A. Hoad
1879	J.T. Hartley	1914	N.E. Brookes	1957	L.A. Hoad
1880	J.T. Hartley	1915–18	*No competition*	1958	A.J. Cooper
1881	W. Renshaw	1919	G.L. Patterson	1959	A. Olmedo
1882	W. Renshaw	1920	W.T. Tilden	1960	N.A. Fraser
1883	W. Renshaw	1921	W.T. Tilden	1961	R. Laver
1884	W. Renshaw	1922	G.L. Patterson	1962	R. Laver
1885	W. Renshaw	1923	W.M. Johnston	1963	C.R. McKinley
1886	W. Renshaw	1924	J. Borotra	1964	R. Emerson
1887	H.F. Lawford	1925	R. Lacoste	1965	R. Emerson
1888	E. Renshaw	1926	J. Borotra	1966	M. Santana
1889	W. Renshaw	1927	H. Cochet	1967	J.D. Newcombe
1890	W.J. Hamilton	1928	R. Lacoste	1968	R. Laver
1891	W. Baddeley	1929	H. Cochet	1969	R. Laver
1892	W. Baddeley	1930	W.T. Tilden	1970	J.D. Newcombe
1893	J. Pim	1931	S.B. Wood	1971	J.D. Newcombe
1894	J. Pim	1932	H.E. Vines	1972	S.R. Smith
1895	W. Baddeley	1933	J.H. Crawford	1973	J. Kodes
1896	H.S. Mahony	1934	F.J. Perry	1974	J.S. Connors
1897	R.F. Doherty	1935	F.J. Perry	1975	A.R. Ashe
1898	R.F. Doherty	1936	F.J. Perry	1976	B. Borg
1899	R.F. Doherty	1937	J.D. Budge	1977	B. Borg
1900	R.F. Doherty	1938	J.D. Budge	1978	B. Borg
1901	A.W. Gore	1939	R.L. Riggs	1979	B. Borg
1902	H.L. Doherty	1940–45	*No competition*	1980	B. Borg
1903	H.L. Doherty	1946	Y. Petra	1981	J.P. McEnroe
1904	H.L. Doherty	1947	J. Kramer	1982	J.S. Connors
1905	H.L. Doherty	1948	R. Falkenburg	1983	J.P. McEnroe
1906	H.L. Doherty	1949	F.R. Schroeder	1984	J.P. McEnroe
1907	N.E. Brookes	1950	B. Patty	1985	B. Becker
1908	A.W. Gore	1951	R. Savitt	1986	B. Becker
1909	A.W. Gore	1952	F. Sedgman	1987	P. Cash
1910	A.F. Wilding	1953	V. Seixas	1988	S. Edberg
1911	A.F. Wilding	1954	J. Drobny		

THE INTERNATIONAL TENNIS CHAMPIONSHIP (Davis Cup)

1900	USA	1930	France	1962	Australia
1901	USA	1931	France	1963	USA
1902	USA	1932	France	1964	Australia
1903	British Isles	1933	Great Britain	1965	Australia
1904	British Isles	1934	Great Britain	1966	Australia
1905	British Isles	1935	Great Britain	1967	Australia
1906	British Isles	1936	Great Britain	1968	USA
1907	Australasia	1937	USA	1969	USA
1908	Australasia	1938	USA	1970	USA
1909	Australasia	1939	Australia	1971	USA
1910	Australasia	1940–45	*No competition*	1972	USA
1911	Australasia	1946	USA	1973	Australia
1912	British Isles	1947	USA	1974	South Africa
1913	USA	1948	USA	1975	Sweden
1914	Australasia	1949	USA	1976	Italy
1915–18	*No competition*	1950	Australia	1977	Australia
1919	Australasia	1951	Australia	1978	USA
1920	USA	1952	Australia	1979	USA
1921	USA	1953	Australia	1980	USA
1922	USA	1954	USA	1981	USA
1923	USA	1955	Australia	1982	USA
1924	USA	1956	Australia	1983	Australia
1925	USA	1957	Australia	1984	Sweden
1926	USA	1958	USA	1985	Sweden
1927	France	1959	Australia	1986	Australia
1928	France	1960	Australia	1987	Sweden
1929	France	1961	Australia	1988	West Germany

OLYMPIC GAMES

The Olympic Games are the greatest international festival of sport. They are a revival of the ancient games of Olympia, the first Olympiad dating from 776 BC, although games had been held in Olympia for hundreds of years before then. The ancient games were in honour of the god Zeus and, like today's, were held every four years, the last being in AD 393, after which they were banned by the Roman emperor, Theodosius, and Olympia declined rapidly.

The revival of the Olympics was the inspiration of Baron Pierre de Coubertin, a Frenchman, and the first of the modern games was held in Athens in 1896. The first separate Winter Olympics were held at Chamonix in 1924.

Athletics has always been the principal sport at the Olympics. The modern games include a variety of other sports, from association football, boxing, gymnastics and swimming to those less widespread such as shooting, volleyball and weightlifting. Other sports have been included and discarded: among them cricket, croquet, rugby and polo.

The Olympic ideal has been very important, the words of Coubertin appearing now on the electronic scoreboards: 'The most important thing in the Olympic Games is not winning but taking part.' All competitors must be amateurs, but the definition of amateurism is causing great concern nowadays. The games are confined to amateurs, in order to show that the athlete competes for honour and not financial interest. The strict International Olympic Committee (IOC) rules for defining an amateur have inspired criticism. Coubertin himself saw loyalty to sport as the only essential requirement of an Olympic athlete. The amateur ideal is tarnished nowadays by certain practices; American universities offer scholarships and the best facilities to sportsmen; communist countries provide intensive coaching for selected athletes for the purpose of winning medals; and potential gold medal winners arrange film contracts and future sponsorships before they actually compete.

However, despite arguments, the games have always provided excitement, and over the years the best performers in the world have captured the imagination of the public with their deeds in the Olympics. Some performances have become legendary. In London in 1908, for instance, an Italian named Dorando Pietri was on the programme as just Dorando, by which name he became famous. He led the marathon field into the stadium, but went the wrong way round the track, and then fell from exhaustion. Doctors and officials went to his aid and he was helped over the line. Of course, he was disqualified because of the help he received. However, the Queen presented him with a special gold cup for his bravery, songs were composed in his honour, and Dorando is better remembered than any of the actual winners.

The name of Jesse Owens will always be associated with the 1936 Olympics in Berlin, which the German Chancellor Hitler tried to use to show the might of Nazism. The black American won four gold medals. They were in the 100 and 200 metres, the sprint relay and the long jump, and it is alleged that Hitler was so angry that he refused to shake Owens' hand. In 1948, again in London, a Dutch housewife with two children, Fanny Blankers-Koen, stole the headlines. She too won four gold medals, in the sprints, the sprint relay and the 80 metres hurdles. Also in 1948 the great distance runner from

Czechoslovakia, Emil Zatopek, won his first gold medal, in the 10 000 metres. In 1952, in Helsinki, he won the race again, together with the 5000 metres and the marathon.

The sensation of the 1960 Olympics in Rome was Abebe Bikila of Ethiopia. The first athletics gold medalist from black Africa, he won the marathon running barefoot over the cobble stones of Rome. It was only his third marathon. In 1964, in Tokyo, he won again, five weeks after undergoing an operation to remove his appendix!

In the Mexico Olympics of 1968, Bob Beamon of the United States put up the best single athletic performance of all time. The long jump world record was 8.35 metres (27 feet 5 inches), having risen by only 23 cm (9 inches) in 30 years. Experts wondered how long it would be before anybody jumped 8.5 metres (28 feet). Beamon, in his first leap in the final, jumped 8.9 metres (29 feet 2½ inches)! Of all world records, this is certainly the best, and will probably remain unbeaten for many years.

These days, every Olympic Games appears to contain at least one astounding performance. In 1972 at Munich, for instance, Mark Spitz of the United States won seven gold medals in the swimming events. This is the most anybody has won at a single games. Lasse Viren, a village policeman from Finland, won the 5000 and 10 000 metres, beating the world record in the longer race despite falling at half-way.

Viren amazed the world again when the 1976 Olympics were held in Montreal. He put himself into history books by winning the same two races again. However, the undoubted star of 1976 was a 14-year-old girl, the Romanian gymnast Nadia Comaneci. She won three gold medals and a bronze in the individual events, but more remarkably, was six times given the perfect score of 10. She won on the asymmetric bars with a maximum 20 points. Others who made their mark included two Cubans, the tall Alberto Juantorena, called 'White Lightning,' who strolled home in the 400 and 800 metres, and Teofilio Stevenson, who won the heavyweight boxing gold medal for the second time. A 17-year-old East German schoolgirl, Kornelia Ender, took four gold medals in the swimming pool.

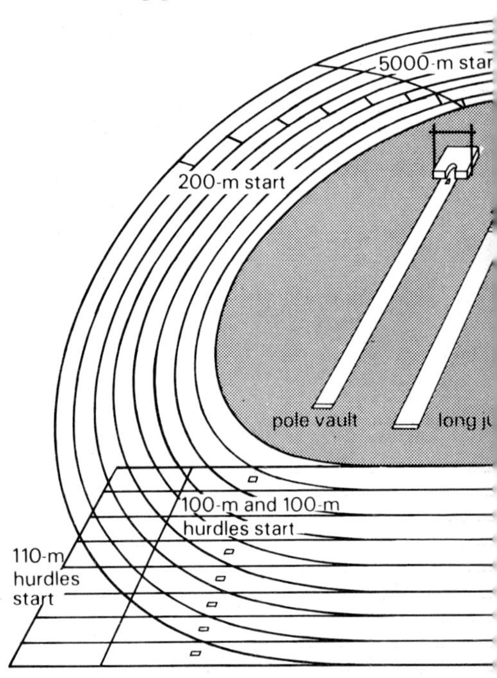

Notable performances in the 1980 Olympics included Nelli Kim from the USSR, who won the gymnastics floor event; and Romanian Nadia Comaneci, who won the gymnastics beam event and came equal second in the combined exercises with Maxi Gnauck of West Germany.

In 1984 at Los Angeles, the American Carl Lewis equalled Jesse Owens' 1936 achievement by gaining gold medals in the 100 m, 200 m, 4 × 100 m relay and long jump.

At the Winter Olympics, events include skiing, ice skating, tobogganing and ice hockey. They are held at a different time and place to the main Olympics as obviously the right weather is essential.

SITES OF THE OLYMPIC GAMES

When the Olympic Games were revived in 1896, they took place in Athens, and Greece hoped that they would always continue to do so, but this was not to be. Since then, the games have been held in many different countries. Nowadays the cities where the Olympic Games will be held are chosen years in advance.

1896 Athens
1900 Paris
1904 St Louis
1908 London
1912 Stockholm
1920 Antwerp
1924 Paris
1928 Amsterdam

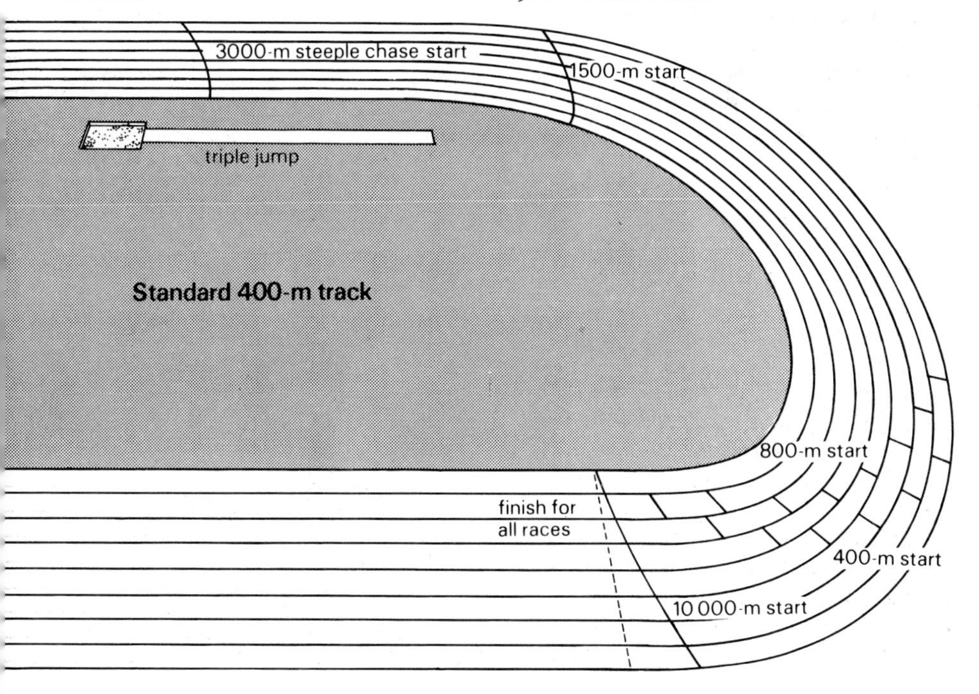

1932	Los Angeles	1960	Rome	1980	Moscow
1936	Berlin	1964	Tokyo	1984	Los Angeles
1948	London	1968	Mexico City	1988	Seoul
1952	Helsinki	1972	Munich	1992	Barcelona
1956	Melbourne	1976	Montreal		

TOTAL NUMBER OF MEDALS WON AT SUMMER OLYMPIC GAMES 1896–1988

USA	1782	Italy	406	Belgium	133
USSR	987	Japan	246	Norway	109
UK	607	Australia	235	Austria	87
West Germany	593	Canada	176	Spain	26
France	506	Switzerland	170	Ireland	14
Sweden	443	Netherlands	158		
East Germany	408	Denmark	152		

OLYMPIC GOLDS

Nowadays, an Olympic gold medal is one of the most coveted prizes in all sport. When the modern games began in 1896, the winners of each event won a silver medal, and the second a bronze. Gold medals were first awarded in 1908, with the silver going to the second and bronze to the third.

The current design of the medals was the work of an Italian, Professor Giuseppe Cassioli, and it depicts victory, fraternity and universality. All medals now bear the name of the appropriate sport, and are attached to a removable chain or ribbon. The first six events also get a diploma. The names of all winners are inscribed upon the walls of the stadium.

COMMONWEALTH GAMES

Originally called the British Empire Games, these games are held at four-year intervals, midway between the Olympic Games, which they resemble. The first Commonwealth Games were held in Hamilton, Canada, in 1930. The principal events are athletics and swimming, with a changing selection of other sports. The games are known as the 'friendly games' because of their relaxed atmosphere. Although England, Australia and Canada usually do best, around 30 Commonwealth countries have had medal winners.

FAMOUS SPORTSMEN

ALI, MUHAMMAD

Muhammad Ali (1942–) was born Cassius Clay in Louisville, Kentucky. He became heavyweight boxing champion of the world when he beat Sonny Liston in February 1964. As a brash young boxer who predicted, in verse, the round in which he would win, he became known as the 'Louisville Lip'. He joined the Black Muslims, changed his name, refused to be drafted for the Vietnam war, and in 1967 lost his boxing licence and his title. After three years out of the ring, he regained the title in 1974, knocking out George Foreman. He lost and regained his title in fights with Leon Spinks, retired, and then failed to gain the title for the fourth time when unsuccessfully challenging Larry Holmes.

ALLCOCK, TONY

Tony Allcock (1955–) began playing bowls aged ten, his parents being good players (his mother was an international). He soon became a good player himself, and won the British Junior Outdoor title three times. He won his first world title in 1980 – the triples with Jimmy Hobday and David Bryant. He won the world outdoor fours in 1984. Indoors, he won the world singles and pairs in both 1986 and 1987. With the game becoming popular on television, Tony, arguably the world's most successful player, turned professional in 1987 and his expert comments are heard on ITV (when he isn't actually engaged in winning).

BALLESTEROS, SEVERIANO

The golfer Severiano Ballesteros (1957–) was born in Santander, Spain. When he won the Open Golf Championship at Royal Lytham St Annes in 1979, he confirmed himself as one of the greatest-ever European players, being at 22 the youngest for a century to hold the title. He had already won the Dutch Open in 1976 and the French and Swiss Opens in 1977. After other good wins, he won the US Masters title in 1980 and again in 1983. He won his second Open in 1984 and was prominent as Europe won the Ryder Cup in 1985 and 1987, before winning a third Open in 1988.

BANKS, GORDON

The footballer Gordon Banks (1937–) was voted the best goalkeeper in the 1966 World Cup in which he won a winners' medal with England. When he made a fantastic save from Pelé in the 1970 World Cup finals, it was repeated on television playbacks around the world, and he was universally considered the world's best. In 1972 he suffered an eye injury in a car crash that cut short his career, but a goalkeeping record of 73 caps for England and his World Cup feats ensure his reputation as one of the best ever.

BANNISTER, SIR ROGER

Sir Roger Bannister (1929–) was born in London, and earned fame on 6 May 1954 when he became the first to run a mile in under four minutes. He was unbeaten in 1953 and 1954, and retired after winning the European championship in 1954, returning to the medical profession.

BEAUMONT, BILL

Bill Beaumont (1952–) led the England and British Lions rugby teams, and inspired the English rugby revival of 1980. Born in Liverpool, he made his England debut in 1975 and was captain in 1978. He led England 21 times and achieved victory over all the other major countries. In 1979–80, under his captaincy, England won the Grand Slam (beat Scotland, Wales, Ireland and France in the International Championship) for the first time in 23 years. After 33 appearances for his country, he received a bad knock on the head in 1982 and decided to retire. He has become popular in television's *A Question of Sport*.

BECKER, BORIS

Boris Becker (1968–) inspired a revival in German tennis when he burst upon the scene by winning the Wimbledon singles championship in 1985 aged 17. He is the youngest ever winner. A strong, well-built athlete, he played a very energetic game and his acrobatic diving returns and quick recoveries made him a great favourite with the spectators. Then a grass court specialist, he repeated his win in 1986, but had a leaner period thereafter. He disappointingly lost in the 1988 Wimbledon final, but had by then acquired an all-court game and won the Masters tournament in 1988. At the end of the year he led West Germany to a first-ever Davis Cup victory and looked set to become a world force for years to come.

BEST, GEORGE

George Best (1946–) never played in the World Cup finals, but he is still recognized as one of the best post-war footballers. Born in Belfast, he made his first appearance for Manchester United when 17 in 1962 and was immediately seen to be a footballing genius. He was afforded pop-star status and the pressure of his popularity led to a life-style which frequently caused him trouble with his club. On the field he won a European Cup winners' medal and 37 caps for Northern Ireland.

BOTHAM, IAN

Ian Botham (1955–) was born in Heswall, Cheshire, England, and made his debut for Somerset in 1973 (one-day matches) and 1974 (first-class). He first played for England in 1977, and began a series of feats which established him as one of cricket's greatest-ever all-rounders. He was the first to score 3000 runs and take 300 wickets in Test cricket, and in 1986 he passed Lillee's record total of 355 Test wickets. His two centuries against the Australians in 1980 and his double century against India in 1982 will be long remembered, and his bowling performance of 5 wickets for 58 runs and 7 for 48 and 114 runs against India in 1980 is unsurpassed in Test cricket.

BOYCOTT, GEOFFREY

Geoffrey Boycott (1940–) was a cricketer who was determined to become a great run-getter. So dedicated was he to his single purpose that he was frequently at odds with his fellow players, committee and critics. He was given the captaincy of Yorkshire, but had it taken away, and captained England only in emergency. His greatest moment was scoring his hundredth 100 in a Test match – against Australia at his home ground, Headingley. His greatest achievement was to top the list of Test match run-getters with a career total of 8114 runs, since passed. He is the only Englishman to average over 100 runs in a season, which he did twice.

BRADMAN, SIR DONALD

Don Bradman (1908–) has a record that suggests he was the greatest batsman of all time. Born in Cootamundra, Australia, he made his debut for New South Wales aged 19, and scored a century (100 runs). Throughout a long career, lasting from 1927 to 1949, he averaged a century in every three innings. He created many records, his 29 Test centuries and Test average of 99.94 being unchallenged. (His Test average is 50 per cent higher than the next best). He captained Australia in five Test series, winning four and tying the other. He was knighted in 1947.

CHARLTON, BOBBY

Bobby Charlton (1937–) survived the Munich air disaster of 1958 which killed so many of his colleagues in the great Manchester United side. He became one of England's best-loved footballers and a great ambassador for the game all round the world. An attacking midfield player, his most famous asset was a thundering shot, which brought him a record 49 goals for England in 106 internationals. Apart from 1974–5 as player-manager of Preston, he played only for Manchester United with whom he won a European Cup winners' medal in 1968 to add to his 1966 World Cup winners' medal.

COE, SEBASTIAN

Sebastian Coe (1956–) is one of the greatest middle distance runners of all time, and his battle for supremacy with fellow Briton, Steve

Ovett, thrilled athletics fans throughout the late 1970s and 1980s. Born in London, Coe emerged from promise to fulfilment in 1977, and had a brilliant spell in 1979, in which from 5 July to 15 August he broke the world records for 800 m, 1500 m and the mile, to become the first to hold all three records simultaneously. In 1980 he then broke the 1000 m world record to hold four world records, and reduced his 800 m time. He won the Olympic 1500 m gold medal, and a silver in the 800 m behind Ovett. He had another brilliant spell in 1981, reducing his 800 m time on 5 June, his 1000 m time on 11 July, and breaking the mile record twice in August. In 1984 he became the first to win a second 1500 m Olympic gold medal, and he won the silver at 800 m. He at last won 800 m gold in the European Championships in 1986.

COMPTON, DENIS

Denis Compton (1918–) was a first-class cricketer and footballer. He was one of England's best postwar batsmen and played for Middlesex at 18 and England at 19. His finest season was 1947, when he made the record total number of runs for a season (3816) and scored a record 18 centuries. In 78 Tests he made 5807 runs (average 50.06), but his figures cannot reflect the genius or charm of his style. As a footballer, he won Championship and Cup medals with Arsenal and played in 14 wartime internationals for England.

COOPER, HENRY

Henry Cooper (1934–) became one of Britain's best-known boxers. One of twin boxing brothers, Henry overcame a bad start to his career, and frequent bad eye injuries, to reign as British, Empire and European heavyweight champion for over a decade: 1959–69 and 1970–71. He then lost his titles to Joe Bugner after a questionable decision. He kept a record three Londsdale Belts (awarded to a boxer who becomes British Champion in any division, and who keeps the belt after three wins), and fought Muhammad Ali for the world title.

CRUYFF, JOHAN

Johan Cruyff (1947–) was born near the Ajax stadium in Amsterdam, Holland, where he won many honours, including three European Cup medals. On the retirement of Pelé, he was accepted as the world's best footballer. He was a marvellous attacking forward with amazing ball control and acceleration. He was part of a football renaissance in Holland and captained the national team in the World Cup Final of 1974. Although Holland lost, it was arguably the best footballing nation in the world at this time.

DAVIS, STEVE

Steve Davis (1957–) established himself at the top in snooker in

1981, when he suddenly improved so much that he took the World Championship and so many other tournaments that he was undoubtedly the world's number one. This position was consolidated when he won the title again in 1983 and 1984, reached the final in 1985 and 1986 and resumed winning ways in 1987, 1988 and 1989.

EDWARDS, GARETH

Gareth Edwards (1947–) was born in Gwaun-Cae-Gurwen, Wales, and became one of Wales's most popular rugby players. A scrum-half of all-round gifts, from his debut for Wales in 1967 till his retirement in 1978 he played 53 consecutive matches, the first Welshman to top 50. He was Wales's youngest captain at 20, but was not a regular captain. He formed two legendary half-back partnerships, with Barry John and Phil Bennett, and in his 12 years of internationals Wales won many championships and Triple Crowns (beat England, Scotland and Ireland in the International Championship) and three Grand Slams (beat all the other teams in the International Championship). He made three tours with the British Lions, in 1968, 1971 and 1974.

FALDO, NICK

Nick Faldo (1957–) was the most consistent golfer in the world in 1988, agonisingly running up a string of near misses in the top tournaments on both sides of the Atlantic. An outstanding amateur, he became the youngest English champion eight days after his 18th birthday. Five professional wins in 1983 took him to the top of the money-winning list, and next year he won the Heritage Classic in America. He then decided to alter his swing, and struggled for three years, but his striving for perfection paid off, and he won the 1987 Open championship and consolidated a place among the world's best when he won the 1989 US Masters.

GAVASKAR, SUNIL

Sunil Gavaskar (1949–) was the greatest run-scorer in Test cricket history. Sunny made his Test debut in 1970 and assumed the captaincy of India in 1978. A small opening batsman, he was the first to pass 10000 runs in Test cricket, a record unlikely to be surpassed for some years. He also scored 34 Test centuries, another record.

GRACE, W.G.

W.G. Grace (1848–1915) was the first cricketer to become an immortal figure, and a century after his greatest feats, he is still the best-known. He so dominated the sport, that he was named 'The Champion'. From 1865 to 1908 he scored 54896 runs (average 39.55), including 117 centuries, took 2876 wickets (average 17.99) and held 871 catches.

HENDRY, STEPHEN

Stephen Hendry (1969–) became a professional snooker player in 1985 – at 16 the youngest to join the paid ranks. He had already been the youngest national champion (Scottish Amateur champion at 15), and at 17 he was to become the youngest winner of a professional event, and at 18 the youngest winner of a ranking tournament (the 1987 Rothmans Grand Prix). He says he wants to retire a millionaire at 27, and certainly will have no bother earning the money. Ranked fourth in the world in 1988, he can only go upwards, and is after the very top spot.

HICK, GRAEME

Graeme Hick (1966–) was born in Salisbury in what was then Rhodesia and is now Zimbabwe. A useful all-round cricketer, but principally a batsman, he came to England on a Zimbabwe Cricket Union scholarship and made his debut for Worcestershire in the last match of 1984, at the Oval. Batting number nine, he scored 82 not out. In succeeding seasons he established himself as a great batsman, and in 1988 assumed the mantle of the best in the world. In this season he scored 2,713 runs, the highest since the reduction of Championship matches in 1969. It included 40 sixes, ten centuries and a score of 405 not out against Somerset – the highest score made in England since 1895. Under present regulations he could play Test cricket for England in 1991, and might become the best batsman the world has seen.

IMRAN KHAN

Imran Khan (1952–), the cousin of another Pakistan Test cricketer Majid Khan, made his debut for Pakistan in 1971. He played much of his cricket in England, for Worcestershire, Oxford University and Sussex. He is a genuine all-rounder and one of the best and fastest bowlers in the world. He had superb tours of England in 1982 and 1987, as captain, and on the second occasion Pakistan won the series in England for the first time. He is one of three players to top 3000 Test runs and 300 Test wickets.

JACKLIN, TONY

Tony Jacklin (1944–) had a magnificent golfing year from the middle of 1969, playing as well as anybody ever has. He seemed to be inspired as he won the Open Championship, the first British golfer to win it since 1951. He helped Britain halve the Ryder Cup, their best performance for 12 years, and then won the US Open, the second British golfer to do so, and the first since 1920. He might have achieved more Open victories, but desperate luck robbed him in both 1970 and 1972, after which he lost his touch and appetite for the game at the highest levels. However he found all his old inspiration again as a popular non-playing captain of the victorious European Ryder Cup teams of 1985 and 1987. He was awarded the OBE for his services to golf.

KAPIL DEV

Kapil Dev (1959–) is perhaps the best Indian fast bowler of all, and also one of the world's best all-round cricketers. He made his Test debut against Pakistan in 1978–9. In the Test year 1979–80 Kapil took 78 wickets and scored 677 runs. In January 1987, he became the second man in Test history to score 3000 runs and take 300 wickets.

LAVER, ROD

Rod Laver (1938–), an Australian tennis player, nicknamed the 'Rocket', was one of the great modern players. He won all the major championships, beginning with the Australian in 1960. He turned professional in 1963, having won Wimbledon the previous two years, and returned to win in 1968 and 1969 when Wimbledon went 'open'. He returned to the Davis Cup in 1973 and won all his matches, his third successful Davis Cup campaign.

LEONARD, RAY

Sugar Ray Leonard (1956–) was a good-looking charismatic boxer who won an Olympic gold medal in 1976, turned professional, became world champion and looked like succeeding Muhammad Ali as the 'golden boy' of boxing. A detached retina then forced him to retire, but so much was boxing in his blood that after having had only one fight in over five years he came back in 1987 to challenge Marvin Hagler, the outstanding middleweight champion. In the world's richest fight Leonard amazingly won, and nearly two years later he fought again to win the light-heavyweight championship. He could claim to be the outstanding boxer of the 1980s.

LILLEE, DENNIS

Dennis Lillee (1949–) became the greatest wicket-taker in Test cricket. An aggressive fast bowler with a superb action, he began his career with Western Australia in 1969–70, and made his Test debut the following season. He took a record 31 Test wickets for Australia on the tour of England in 1972, and in harness with Jeff Thomson in 1974–5 demolished England with his speed and penetration. In 1981–2 he passed Lance Gibbs' record aggregate of Test wickets of 309, and by the time he retired in early 1984, he had taken a total of 355 Test wickets.

LYLE, SANDY

Sandy Lyle (1952–) is an immensely gifted golfer who for many years seemed too amiable to succeed at the highest level. He found the necessary steel in 1985, when he squeezed home to win the Open Championship at Royal St George's, Britain's first Open Champion since 1969. From then on his game seemed to acquire authority, and he rapidly became recognised as Ballesteros' rival as the best in the world. He broke through in America when he won the 1986 Greater Greensboro Open, and in 1987 he took the US Tour's most important title – the Tournament Players' Championship. Next year came the prestigious US Masters. His performances in the triumphant Ryder Cup sides of 1985 and 1987 confirm his eminence.

MATTHEWS, SIR STANLEY

Sir Stanley Matthews (1915–) is perhaps the most famous of pre-war footballers. He made his debut for Stoke in 1931 and was nicknamed the 'Wizard of Dribble' for his trickery on the right wing. A fitness fanatic, he continued playing till 1964–5, when he was 50. Perhaps the highlight of his career came in 1953 when, playing for Blackpool, he was brilliant in a 4–3 Cup Final win in a match known as 'Matthews' match'. He played 698 league matches and won 54 full caps plus making 26 wartime appearances for England. He was knighted in 1965.

MOORE, BOBBY

Bobby Moore (1941–) had an almost perfect football career, joining West Ham United from school, leading them to FA Cup and European Cup-winners Cup successes. In 1966, at the age of 25, he captained England's winning side in the World Cup. He played on the left-hand side of the defence, rarely lost a tackle and led his teams by example, with cool constructive play. He went on to win a record 108 caps for England.

NICKLAUS, JACK

Jack Nicklaus (1940–) has had one of the longest careers at the top of golf, and could claim to be the greatest-ever player. Born in Columbus, Ohio, USA, he was a brilliant amateur before turning professional in 1962. He has won all the major championships, beginning with the US Open in 1962. When he won the US Masters in 1986 he was winning his 18th major title (20 if two US Amateur titles are included), easily the most in history. He has always been a popular ambassador for his sport.

NORMAN, GREG

Greg Norman (1955–) took up golf seriously aged 17, became a scratch player in two years, came to Europe to polish his game, and was soon a power in Europe, the Far East and his native Australia. In 1983 he decided to conquer America, and in 1986 was top of the prize-money list. He won the Open Championship that year, and astonishingly was poised to win the other three major tournaments of the world, only to be foiled at the last. However he confirmed himself as one who will always be in contention in the top tournaments.

OVETT, STEVE

Steve Ovett (1955–) swapped world records in the middle distances, in the late 1970s and early 1980s, with Sebastian Coe, and the pair established themselves as the best runners in the world. In 1980 Ovett equalled Coe's world record in the 1500 m. He won the 800 m gold medal in the 1980 Olympics and the bronze behind Coe in the 1500 m. In August he took the 1500 m world record. In 1981 he gained the mile record, and then in nine days lost it to Coe, regained it and lost it again. A leg injury curtailed his activities in 1982 but in 1983 he returned to lower his 1500 m time.

OWENS, JESSE

Jesse Owens (1913–1986) was born in Alabama, USA. He will always be remembered for his four gold medals in the 1936 Olympics: 100 m, 200 m, 4 × 100 m relay and long jump. He had on 25 May 1935 already set five world records and equalled a sixth: 100 yds, long jump, 220 yds, 200 m, 220 yds hurdles, 200 m hurdles. He also held world records in the 100 m and 4 × 100 m relay.

PALMER, ARNOLD

Arnold Palmer (1929–) did more than anybody to establish a world circuit in golf, beginning the trend which led to the top golfers travelling all over the world for the big tournaments. Born in Pennsylvania, USA, he won the US Amateur Championship at 24 and went on to over 60 wins on the professional circuit, including the US Open, two British Opens and four Masters. A fighter rather than a stylist, he drew crowds everywhere, and he was the first golfing dollar millionaire.

PELÉ

Pelé (1940–), perhaps the most famous footballer of all, was born Edson Arantas do Nascimento in Tres Coracoes, Brazil. A complete attacking player, he was first noticed by the world when he scored a brilliant goal in the 1958 World Cup Final, when only 17. He played in the World Cup finals of 1962 and 1966, and had another brilliant tournament in Brazil's win in 1970. He won numerous medals with his club, Santos, played at the end of his career for New York Cosmos, and, in all, scored over 1200 goals; 97 in 110 matches for Brazil.

RICHARDS, VIV

Viv Richards (1952–) was born in Antigua. He was persuaded to come to England to play cricket for Somerset in 1974, and became a West Indian Test player in 1974–5. A magnificent stroke-playing batsman, he enjoyed a fantastic year in 1976, scoring 1710 Test runs in eight months in three countries – a record for a calendar year. For a long time in the 1980s he was regarded as the world's leading batsman, and by the end of the 1988 season he had scored 7,268 Test runs at an average of 52.66, and was captain of West Indies.

ROBSON, BRYAN

Bryan Robson (1957–) has been England's outstanding footballer of the 1980s. He began his career with West Bromich Albion, and was so commanding in the midfield that Manchester United paid £1½ million for his services in 1981. He was already an England player, and went on to lead club and country. He scored the fastest goal of the 1982 World Cup finals, but sadly was injured during the 1986 finals. He scored twice for United in the 1983 FA Cup final replay, and it is his ability to score brilliant surging goals as well as to rule the midfield that makes him one of the world's most valuable players.

SOBERS, SIR GARY

Sir Gary Sobers (1936–) is generally considered to be the best all-round cricketer the world has even seen. Born in Barbados, he made his Test debut in 1954, aged 17. He was a great left-handed batsman, a bowler who could open with fast-medium balls or bowl varieties of slow balls, an excellent fielder, a good captain and a universally liked sportsman. He played in 93 Tests, 19 as captain, scoring 8032 runs, (a record, until passed by Boycott) averaging 57.78, took 235 wickets, (second to Lance Gibbs among West Indians), and held 109 catches. He also captained the Rest of the World side in the 1970s. He holds the record Test score, 365 not out against Pakistan.

THOMPSON, DALEY

Daley Thompson (1958–) has claims to be Britain's greatest all-round athlete. Born in London, he won the Olympic gold medal for the decathlon in 1980, setting a world record for the event. Having seen it surpassed, he established his supremacy by winning the European Championship in 1982. He won the gold again at the 1984 Olympics, and the European Championship in 1986. He finished fourth in the 1988 Olympics.

TYSON, MIKE

Mike Tyson (1966–) exploded onto the boxing scene in 1985, aged 18, and in 18 months had destroyed 27 opponents, all but two inside the distance. Nobody had seen such devastating punching from such a young boxer. It earned him a WBC world title shot with Trevor Berbick, whom he knocked out to become the youngest ever world heavyweight champion. By beating James Smith and Tony Tucker, the claimants of other authorities, he became undisputed champion. He then disposed of unbeaten Michael Spinks, a contest which earned him $20 million.

THE WORLD AROUND US

The world we live in is a very complicated place, but the tables, charts, diagrams and pictures included in this section will give you all the facts at your fingertips. You will be able to settle many school and family arguments if you study this information carefully.

Let us start with our place in space. We live on a planet called earth, which is one small planet in a group of planets called the solar system. The nine planets in the solar system all revolve around a central star, the sun. (The difference between a star and a planet is that stars give off heat and light whereas planets do not.)

Our sun is just one of many millions of stars in a huge system called a galaxy. The sun is not even one of the biggest stars in our galaxy. Compared to some stars it is quite small. Astronomers estimate that there are about 100 000 million stars in our galaxy, and that there may be as many as 10 000 million galaxies. All the galaxies, together with the space between them, make up the universe.

THE SOLAR SYSTEM

	Planet	*Average distance from sun (million km, followed by million miles)*	*Diameter (km, followed by miles)*
1	Mercury	57.9 (36)	4 880 (2 950)
2	Venus	108.2 (67.2)	12 100 (7 500)
3	Earth	149.6 (93)	12 756 (7 920)
4	Mars	227.9 (141.5)	6 790 (4 200)
5	Jupiter	778.3 (483.6)	142 200 (88 700)
6	Saturn	1 427 (886.6)	119 300 (75 100)
7	Uranus	2 870 (1 782)	51 800 (32 000)
8	Neptune	4 497 (2 794)	49 500 (30 000)
9	Pluto	5 900 (3 666)	3 000* (1 865)*

	Planet	*Circles sun in*	*Turns on axis in*	*Known moons*
1	Mercury	88 days	58.7 days	0
2	Venus	224.7 days	243 days	0
3	Earth	365.25 days	23.56 hours	1
4	Mars	687 days	24.37 hours	2
5	Jupiter	11.9 years	9.50 hours	16
6	Saturn	29.5 years	10.14 hours	17
7	Uranus	84 years	20 hours*	5
8	Neptune	165 years	18.5 hours*	2
9	Pluto	248 years	153 hours	1

* means data uncertain

THE SOLAR SYSTEM

The solar system is spread in a disc shape over 90 000 light years. (Each light year is more than 9 million million kilometres/5.6 million million miles.) It includes the planets Mercury, Venus, the earth, Mars, Jupiter, Saturn, Uranus (only discovered in 1781), Neptune (discovered in 1846) and Pluto (1930), in that order of increasing distance from the sun. The earth is at an average distance of 150 million kilometres (9 million miles) from the sun.

The planets move around the sun at different rates. Pluto takes 248 years to complete its circuit. Neptune 165 years and Mars 687 days.

The first Mariner spacecraft from the USA flew past Mars in 1969, and Viking I went into orbit and sent down a small landing craft in 1976. More is now known about Mars as a result of these recent events, but no evidence of advanced forms of life has been found, and it is doubtful that any exists.

Much more is known about the moon than Mars. The moon is not a planet; it is a satellite of the earth. It is only 380 000 kilometres (237 500 miles) away from the earth and travels in orbit around the earth once every 29 days. As the moon travels in its orbit, light from the sun shines on it making it visible from earth. The size of the moon as we see it varies according to the time of the month. When it lies between earth and sun we cannot see it, but as it moves in its orbit, it seems to grow and change shape as the sun illuminates more and more of it. Then it gets smaller again, and disappears. Thus we see the different *phases* of the moon.

The earth travels round the sun in an elliptical orbit every $365\frac{1}{4}$ days. Each year lasts 365 days, and the quarters add up to make an extra day every fourth year, or leap year.

As well as revolving around the sun, the earth also rotates on its own axis once every 24 hours. Half of the earth faces the sun and receives daylight whilst the other

The earth's movements produce day, night and the seasons.

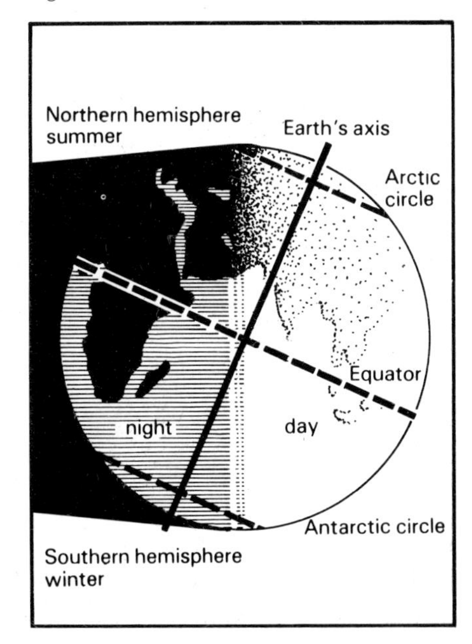

half faces away and is in darkness. On earth we get the impression that the sun rises in the east, travels across the sky during the day and sets in the west, but in reality it is not the sun which is moving, but the earth. Easterly locations receive daylight first, and their clock time is therefore earlier. For example, Australia receives light 10 to 11 hours before Britain.

The earth revolves through 360° in 24 hours. Every 15° of longitude (lines of longitude are the north to south lines which run from the North Pole to the South Pole) represent a difference of one hour in time, because of the movement of the earth on its own axis. This movement causes time differences each day, whilst the movement of the earth around the sun every year causes the seasons. The earth's axis is tilted at $23\frac{1}{2}$° and therefore in its journey around the sun, there is a period in June when the northern hemisphere is tilting towards the sun. This gives rise to the northern summer, while winter is occurring south of the equator. Six months later, the southern hemisphere is tilting towards the sun, and so experiences summer, whilst winter is in progress north of the equator.

Standard time is normally taken to be the 0° meridian which runs through Greenwich in London. If the time was midday on a Monday in London, the time would be 1300 hours at 15°E or 1100 hours at 15°W. 180°E would be 12 hours ahead of Greenwich, i.e. midnight on Monday, whereas 180°W would be 12 hours behind Greenwich, i.e. midnight on Sunday. But 180°E and

World standard times at noon Greenwich Mean Time.

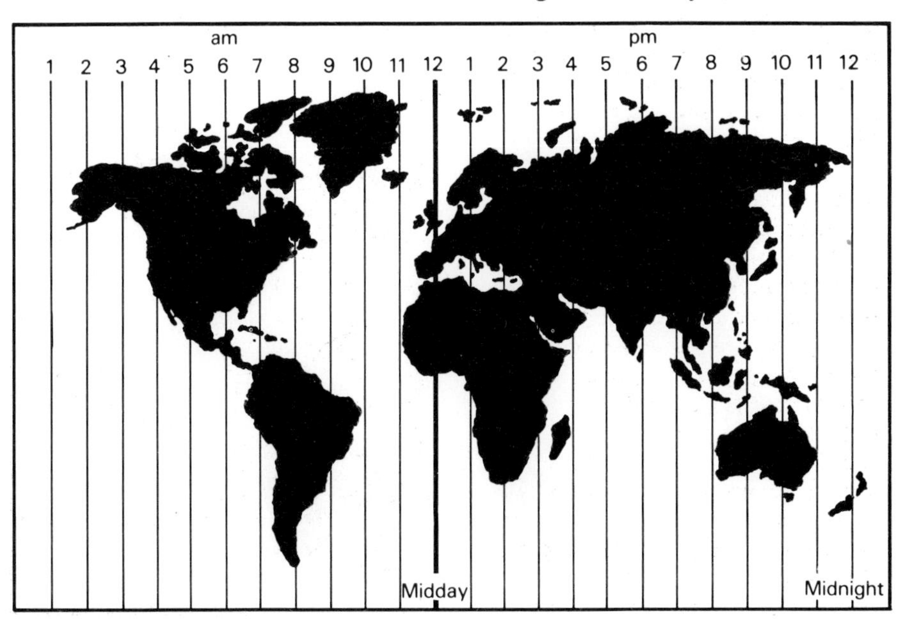

180°W are actually the same line of longitude. We call this imaginary line the *International Date Line*. A person travelling from east to west goes ahead 24 hours upon crossing the line, while a person travelling in an easterly direction goes back 24 hours. The International Date Line diverges from the 180° meridian in a few places such as Fiji and the Aleutian Islands. *See* p. 65 for world standard times at noon Greenwich mean time.

Other time problems are solved by having time zones. Large countries endeavour to regulate time and reduce confusion by having set zones with standard times. The

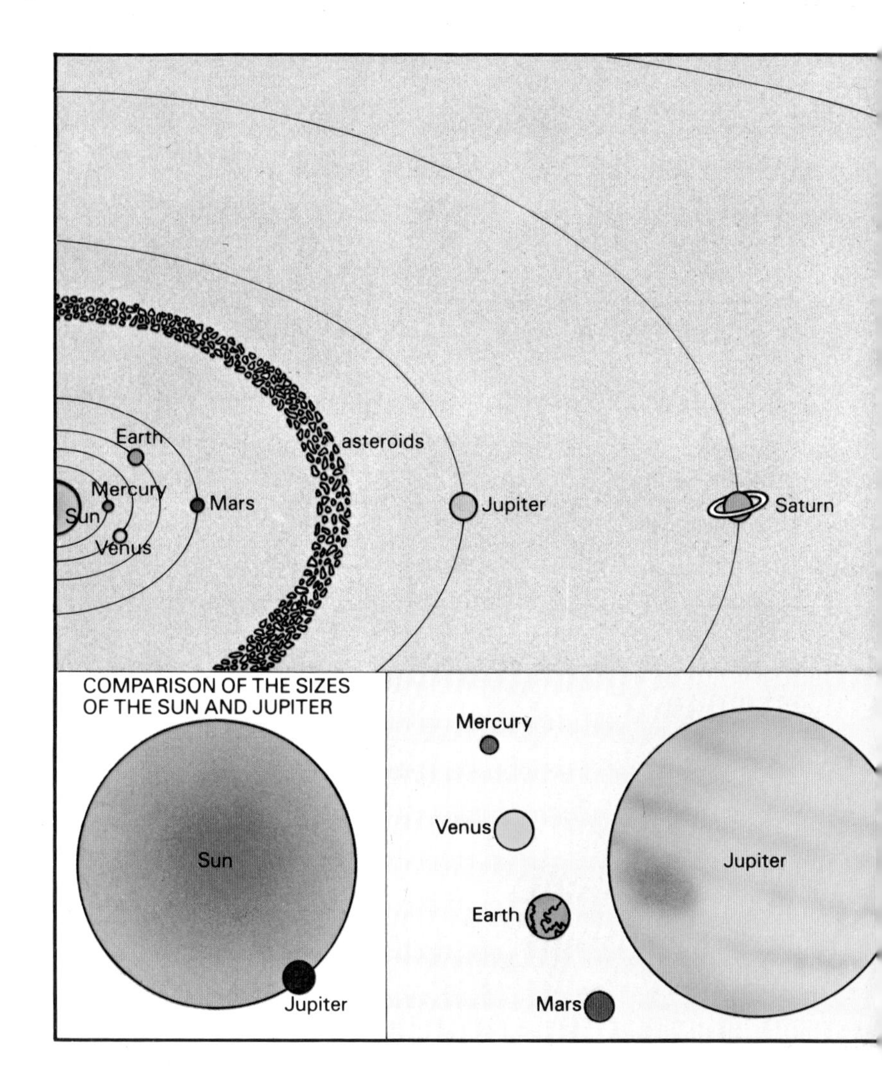

USA, has seven time zones.

Lines of longitude are much wider on the equator than at the North and South poles, where they all converge on a point. Lines of latitude on the other hand are all equidistant, about 110 kilometres (68 miles) apart.

Planets of the solar system in order of their distance from the sun (not to scale). Asteroids are mini planets and boulders which orbit in a belt between Mars and Jupiter. Note that Pluto's orbit crosses that of Neptune.

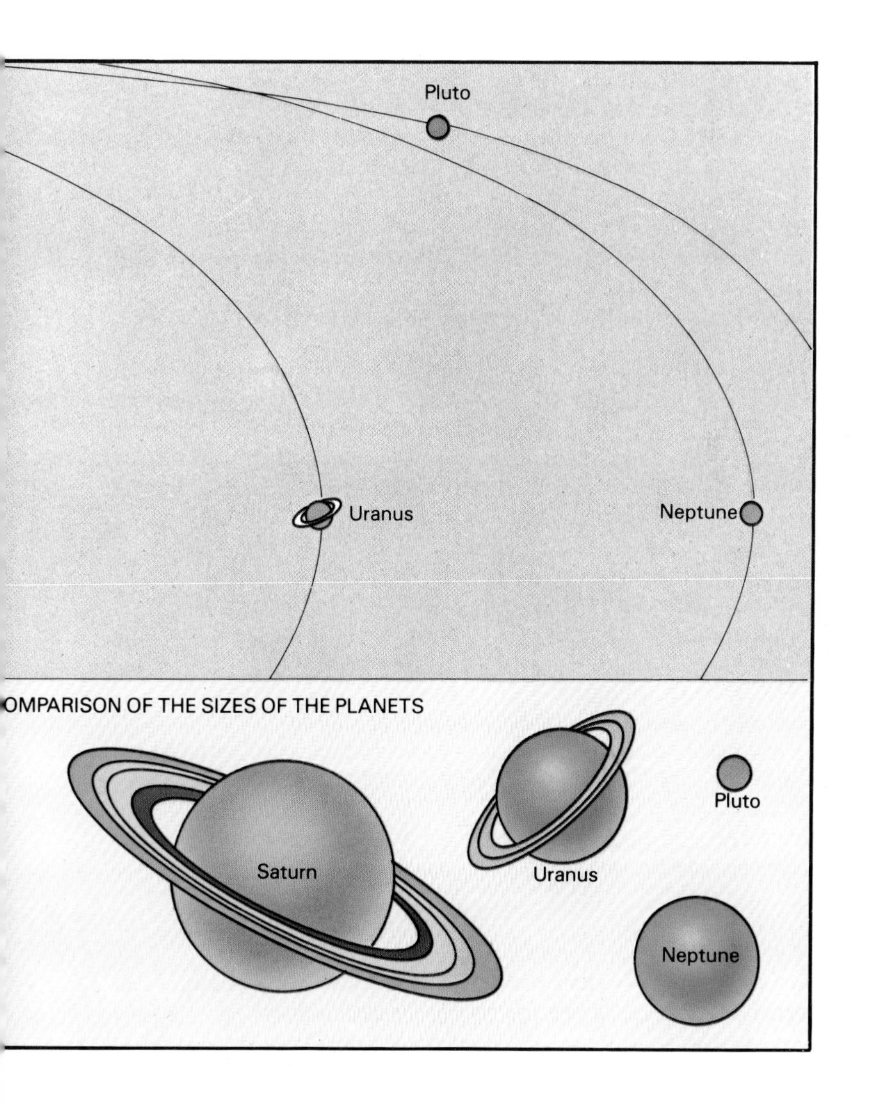

COUNTRIES OF THE WORLD

Asia occupies nearly one-third of the world's land, and contains more than half the people. It is clearly bordered by ocean in the north, east and south. The western boundary in the USSR is generally considered to be the Ural mountains. The Caucasus mountains also separate European Russia from Asia, and the Straits of Bosphorus form part of the boundary. The Sinai Peninsula is a transitional area between Asia and Africa.

Asia is a very hot continent in summer, but much of it is very cold in winter. It extends from the heights of Everest to below sea level in the Dead Sea, and contains tropical forests, jungles, tundra and ice caps.

Asia is a continent of extremes in more ways than its weather and climate: there are some very ancient civilizations in both China and Mesopotamia, highly industrialized areas as in Japan, and some extreme poverty in India and elsewhere.

Africa is the second largest continent, and extends an equal distance both north and south of the equator. It is a warm continent, as no land is more than 36° north or south.

There are forests on the equator and vast expanses of tropical grassland all around the tropical forest area. The Sahara and Kalahari deserts occupy large areas. The Sahara is much larger than the Kalahari because Africa is wider in the north and it is drier.

Africa was virtually unknown to the outside world until the 19th century. Many African countries are still quite poor, though there is much wealth in the Republic of South Africa.

North America is the third largest continent, and is surrounded by oceans. The southern tip contains the *Central American* republics which link North to South America.

The islands of the West Indies are east of Central America.

North America contains large expanses of forest, grassland and desert. Much of the continent is sparsely populated, and although inhabited for a long time by the native Indians, has been settled by white people during the last 400 years. Canada and the USA are rich countries, but Central America contain areas of poverty.

South America is broadest in the tropics and therefore is a fairly warm and wet continent. It does, however, contain the Atacama desert which is the driest area in the world. It also contains the longest range of mountains in the world, the Andes, which run from the north to the south of South America.

The countries of South America are now independent, with the exception of French Guiana. Spain originally colonized most of the continent, though Portugal settled Brazil.

There has been much intermarriage between Indians, negroes imported as slaves to work the plantations, and the Europeans, As a result, the people of the South American countries are very mixed and there are few racial problems.

Antarctica is a large land mass almost completely covered by ice, and surrounded by the great Southern Ocean. There are no real settlements in this continent, but a few scientific research stations are situated there. The climate is so inhospitable that normal life would be impossible.

The Arctic is a region of sea almost completely surrounded by land. It is so cold that the sea around the North Pole is permanently frozen.

Europe consists of many fairly small countries, but is well populated and well developed. The Mediterranean and Baltic Seas enable oceanic influences to extend far inland, and thus it is a climatically mild continent. It is really a large peninsula protruding from Asia, and is broken up by many mountain ranges such as the Alps, Carpathians and Harz mountains.

Australasia consists of Australia, New Zealand and the thousands of islands in the Pacific Ocean. These islands can be divided into three main groups – Melanesia, Micronesia and Polynesia. Islands to the north represent a transitional area with Asia.

New Zealand has a maritime climate, as nowhere is far from the coast, but Australia is a very dry country. It is in an area of latitude known as the horse latitude and the Great Dividing Ranges in the east prevent any wet weather from extending far inland. Because of this, Australia is sparsely populated in the interior and likely to remain so.

Australian settlement was mainly from Britain and began in the nineteenth century.

More than half of all the land in the world is uninhabitable – because it is rock, desert, tundra (treeless Arctic plain), dense jungle, swamp or is covered with ice.

Nearly one-half of the world's population lives on one-thirtieth of the total area of land. There are immense areas which are very sparsely populated – such as the Northern Territory of Australia; other areas – such as Japan and India – are very densely populated.

THE OCEANS

Water covers more than 70 per cent of the earth's surface, and the average depth of the world's oceans is nearly 4000 m (13 000 ft); some parts are over 11 000 m (36 000 ft) deep.

The oceans are shallowest around the edges of the land. These areas, where the water is less than 200 m (650 ft) deep, are called the continental shelves. The deep ocean floors have a landscape as varied as the land above the water. There are trenches much deeper than the Grand Canyon in the USA, and vast plains of sand and mud.

The oceans and seas of the world have salty water. About 3.5 per cent of the total volume of this water is actually made up of salts which are dissolved in the water.

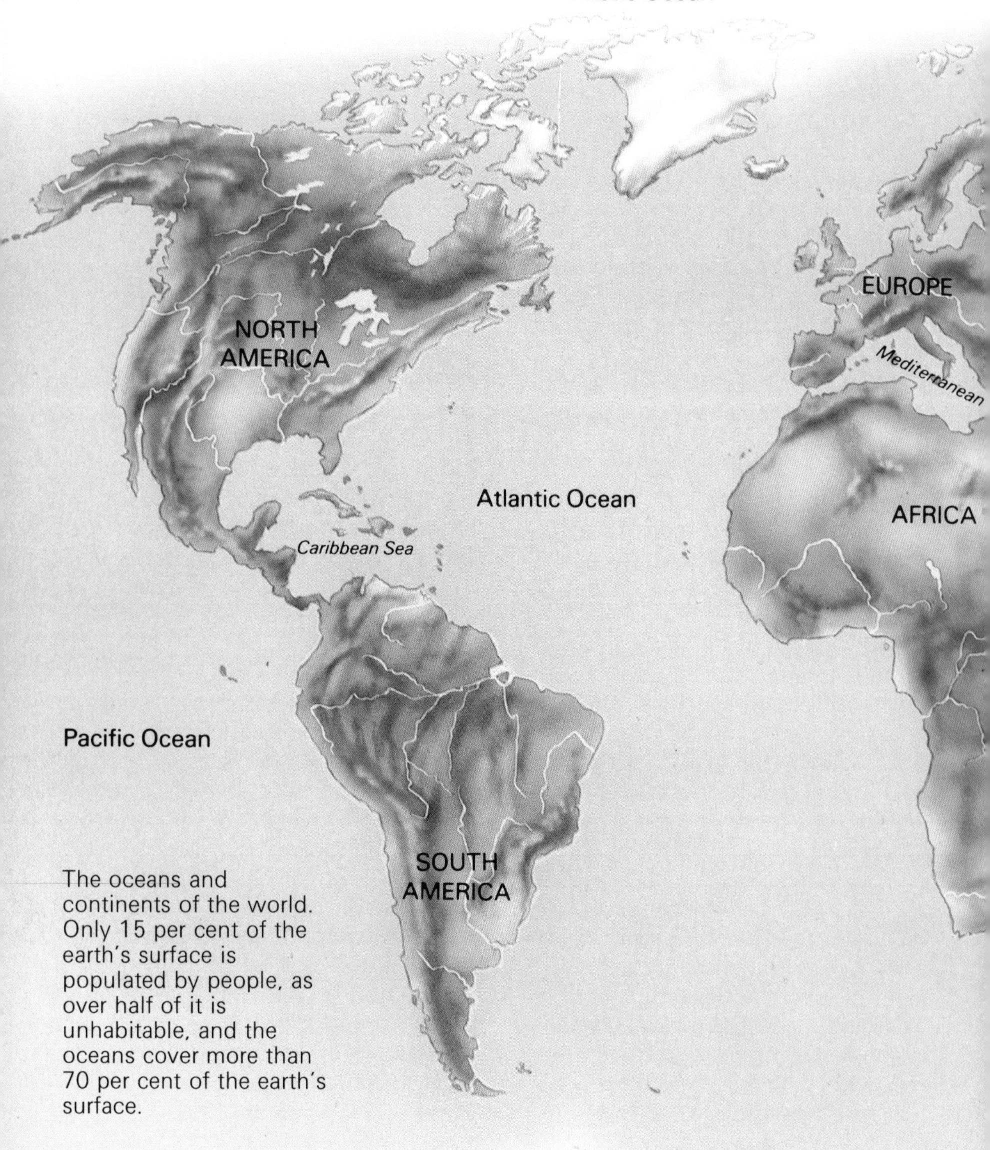

The oceans and continents of the world. Only 15 per cent of the earth's surface is populated by people, as over half of it is unhabitable, and the oceans cover more than 70 per cent of the earth's surface.

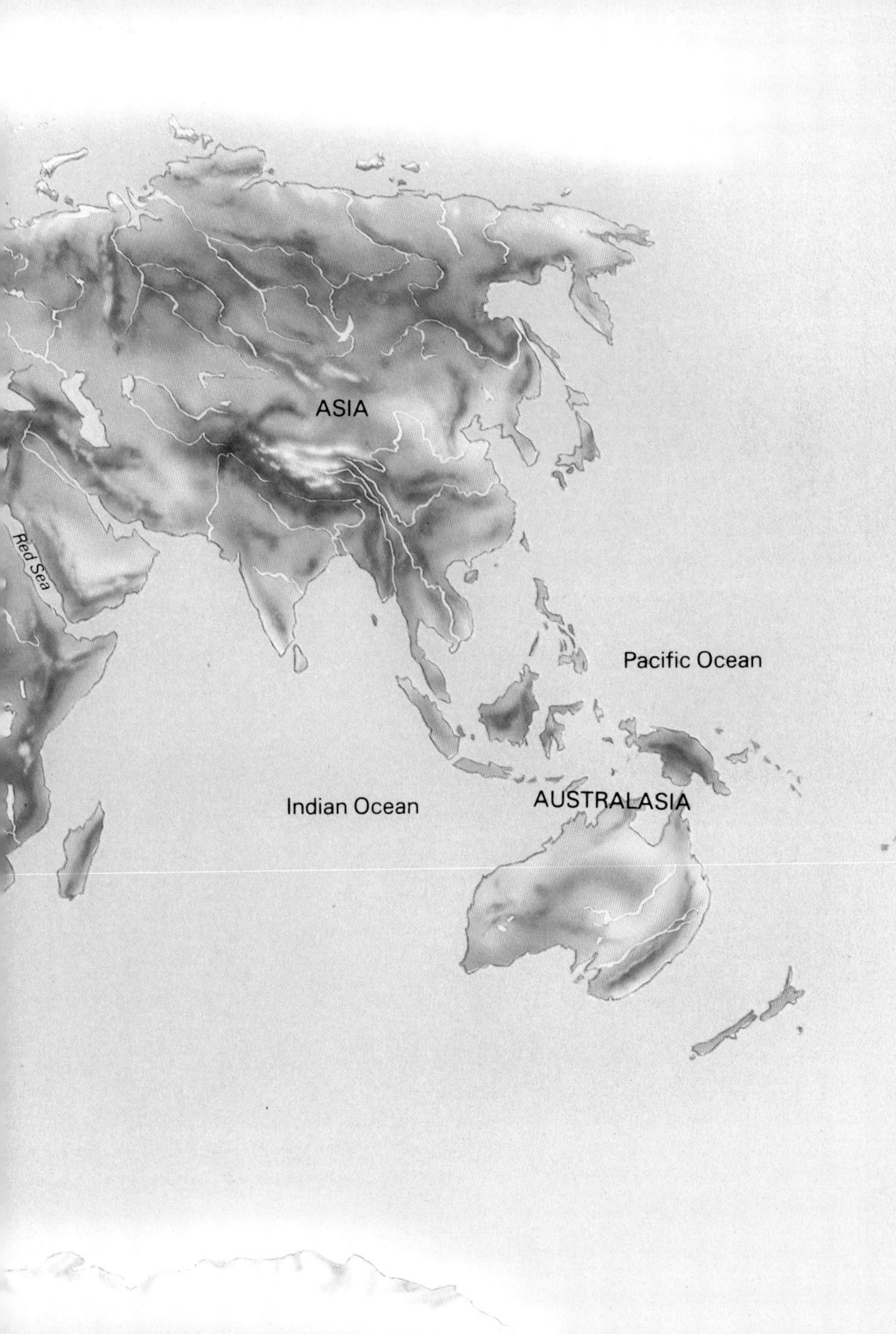
ASIA
Red Sea
Pacific Ocean
Indian Ocean
AUSTRALASIA

COUNTRIES OF THE WORLD: FACTS AND FIGURES

AFRICA

Country	*Population*	*Capital*	*Area sq km*	*Area sq miles*
Algeria	22600000	Algiers	2214400	855000
Angola	8960000	Luanda	1263900	488000
Benin	4150000	Porto Novo	121730	47000
Botswana	1130000	Ouagadougou	259000	100000
Burkina Faso	8330000	Gaborone	569800	220000
Burundi	4920000	Bujumbura	27700	10700
Cameroon	9880000	Yaounde	474000	183000
Cape Verde Islands	350000	Praia	3900	1516
Central African Rep.	2780000	Bangui	606000	234000
Chad	5240000	N'djaména	1263900	488000
Comoros	422500	Moroni	1862	
Congo	2180000	Brazzaville	336600	129960
Côte d'Ivoire	10600000	Abidjan	328900	127000
Djibouti	470000	Djibouti	23300	9000
Egypt	49280000	Cairo	997100	385000
Equatorial Guinea	384000	Malabo	28500	11000
Ethiopia	46000000	Addis Ababa	1036000	400000
Gabon	1220000	Libreville	262600	101400
The Gambia	698817	Banjul	10360	4000
Ghana	12210000	Accra	238500	92100
Guinea	6340000	Conakry	251200	97000
Guinea Bissau	935000	Bissau	36260	14000
Kenya	20030000	Nairobi	582700	225000
Lesotho	1630000	Maseru	30300	11700
Liberia	2500000	Monrovia	111400	43000
Libya	3960000	Tripoli	2097900	810000
Madagascar	10570000	Antananarivo	590500	228000
Malawi	7100000	Lilongwe	117600	45400
Mali	8730000	Bamako	1204300	465000
Mauritania	2010000	Nouakchott	1085200	419000
Mauritius	1041000	Port Louis	2090	805
Morocco	23000000	Rabat	466200	180000
Mozambique	14540000	Maputo	771800	298000
Niger	6600000	Niamey	1188800	459000
Nigeria	105000000	Lagos	924600	357000
Réunion	564600	St Denis	2590	1000
Rwanda	6320000	Kigali	26340	10169
St Helena	5895	Jamestown	122	47
Ascension Is.	1708	Georgtown	88	34
Tristan da Cunha	325	Edinburgh	98	38
S. Tomé and Príncipe	113000	Saõ Tomé	963	372
Senegal	6700000	Dakar	202000	78000
Seychelles	67000	Victoria	324	125
Sierra Leone	3600000	Freetown	72520	28000
Somalia	6110000	Mogadishu	637100	246000
South Africa	23390000	Pretoria	1222500	472000
S.W. Africa (Namibia)	1184000	Windhoek	823600	318000
Sudan	25550000	Khartoum	2504500	967000
Swaziland	676049	Mbabane	17350	6700
Tanzania	23200000	Dodoma	940200	363000

Country	Population	Capital	Area sq km	Area sq miles
Togo	3 160 000	Lomé	54 400	21 000
Tunisia	7 320 000	Tunis	164 200	63 380
Uganda	16 790 000	Kampala	235 700	91 000
Zaïre	3 178 000	Kinshasa	2 343 000	905 000
Zambia	7 210 000	Lusaka	753 700	291 000
Zimbabwe	8 640 000	Harare	390 600	150 820

ASIA

Country	Population	Capital	Area sq km	Area sq miles
Afghanistan	9 000 000	Kabul	647 500	250 000
Bahrain	416 275	Manama	600	231
Bangladesh	104 100 000	Dacca	142 780	55 126
Bhutan	1 300 000	Thimphu	46 620	18 000
Brunei	221 900	Bandar Seri Begawan	5 770	2 226
Burma	37 850 000	Rangoon	678 030	261 789
Cambodia	6 230 000	Phnom Penh	181 300	70 000
China				
Mainland	1 072 200 000	Peking	9 583 000	3 700 000
Taiwan (Formosa)	19 500 000	Taipei	35 980	13 890
Hong Kong	5 590 000		1 050	404
India	748 000 000	Delhi	3 268 600	1 262 000
Indonesia	172 000 000	Jakarta	1 903 600	735 000
Iran	49 860 000	Tehran	1 626 700	628 060
Iraq	17 090 000	Baghdad	445 480	172 000
Israel	4 330 000	Jerusalem	20 720	8 000
Japan	121 670 000	Tokyo	369 720	142 748
Jordan	2 850 000	Amman	97 640	37 700
Korea				
North	20 550 000	Pyongyang	124 320	48 000
South	41 800 000	Seoul	99 720	38 500
Kuwait	1 770 000	Kuwait	19 430	7 500
Laos	3 670 000	Vientiane	233 100	90 000
Lebanon	3 500 000	Beirut	11 140	4 300
Malaysia	16 500 000	Kuala Lumpur	331 520	128 000
Maldive Islands	189 000	Malé	300	115
Mongolia	1 970 000	Ulan Bator	1 567 000	605 022
Nepal	16 630 000	Katmandu	139 860	54 000
Oman	1 200 000	Muscat	310 800	120 000
Pakistan	102 200 000	Islamabad	803 940	310 403
Philippines	57 360 000	Manila	297 850	115 000
Qatar	371 863	Doha	10 360	4 000
Saudi Arabia	11 520 000	Riyadh	2 401 000	927 000
Singapore	2 590 000	Singapore	590	226
Sri Lanka	15 800 000	Colombo	65 610	25 332
Syria	10 960 000	Damascus	183 890	71 000
Thailand	52 500 000	Bangkok	512 820	198 000
Turkey (in Asia)	50 670 000	Ankara	755 688	292 000
United Arab Emirates	1 770 000	Abu Dhabi	82 880	32 000
USSR (in Asia				
RSFSR (Asia)	*see Europe*			
Armenia	3 400 000	Erevan	30 000	11 500
Azerbaijan	6 800 000	Baku	87 000	33 500

(*continued on page 76*)

Some national flags of countries around the world.

Argentina

Australia

Austria

Belgium

Brazil

Canada

China

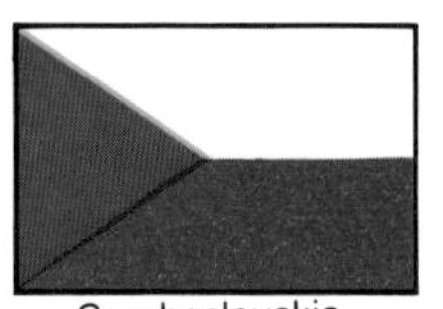
Czechoslovakia

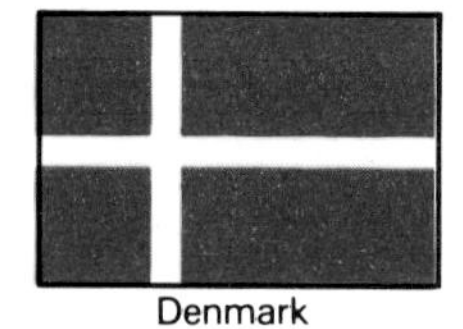
Denmark

Egypt

Finland

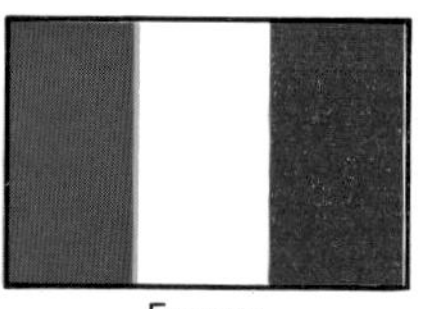
France

German Federal Republic

Greece

India

Indonesia

Irish Republic

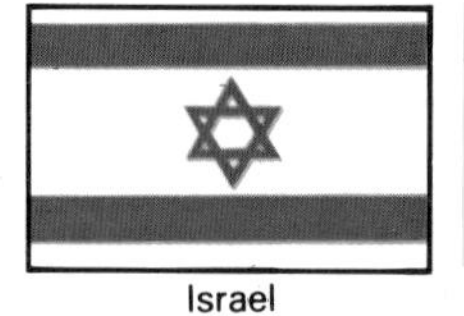
Israel

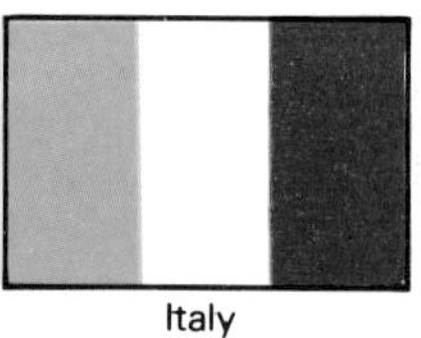
Italy

Jamaica

Japan

Malaysia

Mexico

Netherlands

New Zealand

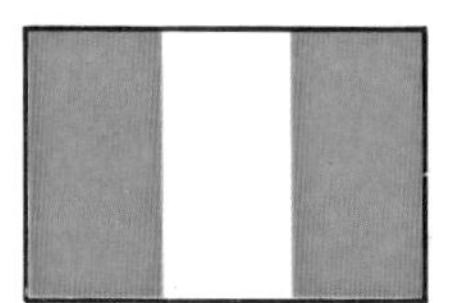
Nigeria

Norway

Pakistan

Peru

Poland

Portugal

Switzerland

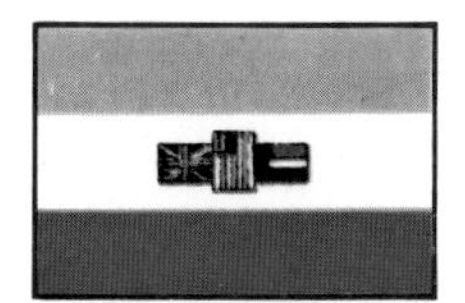
South Africa

Spain

Turkey

U.S.S.R.

United Kingdom

U.S.A.

Zaire

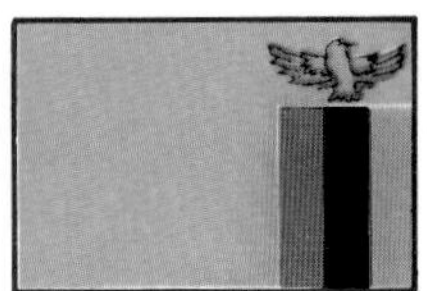
Zambia

ASIA *cont.*

Country	*Population*	*Capital*	*Area sq km*	*Area sq miles*
USSR (in Asia) (*cont*)				
Georgia	5 300 000	Tbilisi	70 000	27 000
Kazakhstan	16 200 000	Alma Ata	2 717 000	1 048 000
Kirghizia	4 100 000	Frunze	199 000	74 000
Tadzhikistan	4 800 000	Dushanbe	143 000	54 000
Turkmenistan	3 400 000	Ashkahabad	488 000	188 000
Uzbekistan	19 000 000	Tashkent	447 000	172 000
Vietnam	61 950 000	Hanoi	334 110	129 000
Yemen	6 530 000	San'a	194 250	75 000
Yemen PDR	2 300 000	Aden	466 200	180 000

EUROPE AND THE MEDITERRANEAN

Country	*Population*	*Capital*	*Area sq km*	*Area sq miles*
Albania	3 080 000	Tirana	27 000	10 700
Andorra	42 712	Andorre-la-Vieille	470	180
Austria	7 570 000	Vienna	83 850	32 376
Belgium	9 860 000	Brussels	30 560	11 800
Bulgaria	8 950 000	Sofia	111 370	43 000
Cyprus	673 100	Nicosia	9 070	3 500
Czechoslovakia	15 500 000	Prague	127 950	49 400
Denmark	5 120 000	Copenhagen	44 030	17 000
Finland	4 930 000	Helsinki	336 700	130 000
France	55 620 000	Paris	551 670	213 000
Germany				
West	61 000 000	Bonn	248 590	95 980
East	16 600 000	E. Berlin	108 180	41 768
Gibraltar	29 216	Gibraltar	5	2
Greece	9 970 000	Athens	132 610	51 200
Hungary	10 620 000	Budapest	93 240	36 000
Iceland	244 009	Reykjavik	104 900	40 500
Irish Republic	3 540 000	Dublin	68 890	26 600
Italy	57 300 000	Rome	339 290	131 000
Liechtenstein	27 400	Vaduz	168	65
Luxembourg	369 500	Luxembourg	2 590	1 000
Malta	343 334	Valetta	313	121
Monaco	27 063	Monaco-ville	2	$\frac{2}{3}$
Netherlands	14 620 000	Amsterdam	34 960	13 500
Norway	4 200 000	Oslo	323 750	125 000
Poland	37 600 000	Warsaw	313 390	121 000
Portugal	10 290 000	Lisbon	89 360	34 500
Romania	22 700 000	Bucharest	237 240	91 600
San Marino	22 638	San Marino	60	23
Spain	38 900 000	Madrid	510 230	197 000
Sweden	8 400 000	Stockholm	448 070	173 000
Switzerland	6 500 000	Berne	41 440	16 000
Turkey (in Europe)	*see Asia*	Ankara	23 764	9 200
United Kingdom	55 780 000	London	240 940	93 026
USSR (in Eur.)				
RSFSR (Eur.)	145 300 000	Moscow	17 075 000	6 591 000
Byelorussia	10 100 000	Minsk	208 000	80 000
Estonia	1 600 000	Tallinn	45 000	17 000
Latvia	2 600 000	Riga	64 000	25 000
Lithuania	3 600 000	Vilnius	65 000	25 000

Country	Population	Capital	Area sq km	Area sq miles
Moldavia	4200000	Kishinev	34000	13000
Ukraine	51200000	Kiev	604000	233000
Vatican City	1000	Vatican City	44 hectares	109 acres
Yugoslavia	23270000	Belgrade	256410	99000

NORTH AND CENTRAL AMERICA; THE WEST INDIES

Country	Population	Capital	Area sq km	Area sq miles
Anguilla	7000	The Valley	155	60
Antigua and Barbuda	81500	St John's	440	170
Bahamas	235000	Nassau	13900	5380
Barbados	253055	Bridgetown	430	166
Belize	171000	Belmopan	23100	8900
Bermuda	57145	Hamilton	54	21
Canada	25400000	Ottawa	9976139	3851787
Cayman Islands	22900	George Town	260	100
Costa Rica	2660000	San José	50900	19653
Cuba	10190000	Havana	114000	44000
Dominica	94191	Roseau	751	290
Dominican Rep.	6600000	Santo Domingo	50000	19300
Grenada	88000	St. George's	344	133
Guadeloupe	335300	Basse-Terre	1780	688
Guatemala	8990000	Guatemala City	108800	42000
Haiti	5300000	Port-au-Prince	27700	10700
Honduras	4300000	Tegucigalpa	111400	43000
Jamaica	2300000	Kingston	11400	4400
Martinique	328500	Fort-de-France	1040	400
Mexico	76000000	Mexico City	1972400	761530
Montserrat	11802	Plymouth	101	39
Netherlands Antilles	183000	Willemstad	1 020	394
Nicaragua	3500000	Managua	147600	57000
Panama	2280000	Panama City	77082	29761
Puerto Rico	3196520	San Juan	8810	3400
St Christopher-Nevis	47000	Basseterre	262	101
St Pierre and Miquelon	6300	St Pierre	241	93
St Lucia	143600	Castries	616	238
St Vincent	138000	Kingstown	388	150
El Salvador	5480000	San Salvador	21240	8200
Trinidad and Tobago	1220000	Port-of-Spain	5130	1980
Turks and Caicos Is.	7436	Grand Turk	499	193
United States	238700000	Washington, D.C.	9160400	3536855
Virgin Islands:				
British	12034	Road Town	153	59
US	110800	Charlotte Amalie	344	133

OCEANIA

Country	Population	Capital	Area sq km	Area sq miles
American Samoa	32297	Fagatogo	197	76
Australia	15970000	Canberra	7687000	2968000
New South Wales	5378500	Sydney	800300	309000
Northern Territory	136800	Darwin	1347500	520280
Queensland	2488000	Brisbane	1727500	667000

OCEANIA *cont.*

Country	*Population*	*Capital*	*Area sq km*	*Area sq miles*
South Australia	1347000	Adelaide	984200	380000
Tasmania	434700	Hobart	67340	26000
Victoria	4053400	Melbourne	227900	88000
Western Australia	1373700	Perth	2527800	976000
Fiji	714000	Suva	18390	7100
French Polynesia	184600	Papeete	6480	2500
Guam	115756	Agaña	541	269
Kiribati	66250	Tarawa	683	264
Micronesia	123298	Kolonia	893	341
New Caledonia	153500	Nouméa	18650	7200
New Zealand	3300000	Wellington	269400	104000
Cook Islands	17745	Avarua	293	113
Niue	2442	Alofi	258	100
Northern Marianas	19635	Saipan	477	184
Palau	15000	Koror	497	192
Papua New Guinea	3480000	Port Moresby	461700	178260
Solomon Islands	270000	Honiara	29780	11500
Tonga	94535	Nuku'alofa	746	288
Tuvalu	8229	Funajuti	26	10
Vanuatu	141400	Vila	15670	6050
Western Samoa	163000	Apia	2840	1097

SOUTH AMERICA

Country	*Population*	*Capital*	*Area sq km*	*Area sq miles*
Argentina	31060000	Buenos Aires	2797100	1079965
Bolivia	6250000	Sucre	1074800	415000
Brazil	143100000	Brasilia	8518500	3289000
Chile	12070000	Santiago	751100	290000
Colombia	29500000	Bogotá	1139600	440000
Ecuador	9640000	Quito	585300	226000
Falkland Islands	1916	Stanley	12170	4700
Guiana, French	89000	Cayenne	90650	35000
Guyana	812000	Georgetown	215000	83000
Paraguay	3790000	Asunción	406600	157000
Peru	20200000	Lima	1375300	531000
Pitcairn Island	57	Adamstown	5	2
Suriname	370000	Paramaribo	139900	54000
Uruguay	2950000	Montevideo	186500	72000
Venezuela	17320000	Caracas	916900	354000

FORMER NAMES OF COUNTRIES

Bangladesh	East Pakistan
Belize	British Honduras
Botswana	Bechuanaland
Burkina Faso	Upper Volta
Burundi	Part of (1) German East Africa, (2) Ruanda-Urundi
Central African Republic	Ubangi-Shari
Congo (People's Republic)	Middle Congo (French)
Côte d'Ivoire	Ivory Coast
Democratic Kampuchea	Cambodia
Djibouti	Afars & Issas, Tty. of; French Somaliland
Equatorial Guinea	Spanish Guinea
Ethiopia	Abyssinia
Ghana	Gold Coast
Guinea	part of French West Africa
Guinea-Bissau	Portuguese Guinea
Guyana	British Guiana
Iran	Persia
Lesotho	Basutoland
Malawi	Nyasaland
Malaysia	Malaya, Sabah (North Borneo), and Sarawak
Mali	French Sudan
Netherlands Antilles	Dutch East Indies
Pakistan	West Pakistan
Rwanda	Part of (1) German East Africa, (2) Ruanda-Urundi
Somalia	Somaliland (Brit. & Ital.)
Sri Lanka	Ceylon
Suriname	Dutch Guinea
Tanzania	Tanganyika and Zanzibar
Thailand	Siam
Togo	Togoland
United Arab Emirates	Trucial States
Yemen (People's Democratic Republic of)	Southern Yemen (incl. Aden)
Zäire	Belgian Congo
Zambia	Northern Rhodesia
Zimbabwe	Rhodesia

THE WORLD'S LARGEST COUNTRIES

	Country	Area sq km	Area sq miles	Population in millions
1	USSR	22 276 000	8 600 000	279
2	Canada	9 976 139	3 851 787	25
3	China	9 583 000	3 700 000	1 072
4	USA	9 160 400	3 536 855	239
5	Brazil	8 518 500	3 289 000	143
6	Australia	7 687 000	2 968 000	16
7	India	3 268 000	1 262 000	784
8	Argentina	2 797 000	1 079 965	31
9	Sudan	2 504 500	967 000	25
10	Saudi Arabia	2 401 000	927 000	11
11	Zaire	2 343 900	905 000	32
12	Algeria	2 214 000	855 000	22
13	Greenland	2 175 000	839 782	0.049

THE WORLD'S SMALLEST COUNTRIES

	Country	Area sq km	Area sq miles	Population
1	Vatican City	0.44	$\frac{1}{6}$	1 000
2	Monaco	2	$\frac{2}{3}$	27 063
3	Pitcairn Island	5	2	57
4	Tuvalu	26	10	8 229
5	San Marino	60	23	22 638
6	Liechtenstein	168	65	27 400
7	Maldives	300	115	189 000
8	Seychelles	324	125	67 000
9	Malta	313	121	343 334
10	Grenada	344	133	88 000

THE WORLD'S LEAST POPULATED COUNTRIES

	Country	Population
1	Pitcairn Island	57
2	Vatican City	1 000
3	Tuvalu	8 229
4	San Marino	22 638
5	Monaco	27 063
6	Liechtenstein	27 400

	Country	Population
7	Andorra	42472
8	Kiribati	66250
9	Seychelles	67000
10	Grenada	88000

THE WORLD'S MOST POPULATED CITIES

	City	Population
1	Mexico City, Mexico	12932116
2	Buenos Aires, Argentina	9927404
3	Calcutta, India	9166000
4	Moscow, USSR	8815000
5	Paris, France	8706963
6	Tokyo, Japan	8354000
7	Bombay, India	8227000
8	São Paolo, Brazil	7033529
9	Shanghai, China	6980000
10	London, England	6775200

GREAT OCEANS OF THE WORLD

	Ocean	Area millions of sq km	Area millions of sq miles
1	Pacific	165	64
2	Atlantic	81.5	31.5
3	Indian	73.5	28.35
4	Arctic	14.25	5.5

OCEAN DEEPS

	Position	Name	Depth metres	Depth ft
1	Mariana Trench	Challenger Deep	11 520	37 800
2	Tonga Trench	—	10 630	34 885
3	Philippine Trench	Galathea Deep	10 540	34 580
4	Kuril Trench	Vityaz Deep	10 375	34 045
5	Japanese Trench	Ramapo Deep	10 372	34 035
6	Kermadec Trench	—	9 995	32 788
7	Guam Trench	—	9 632	31 614
8	Puerto Rico Trench	Milwaukee Deep	9 200	30 246
9	New Britain Trench	Planet Deep	9 140	29 987

GREAT SEAS

	Name and location	Area sq km	Area sq miles
1	Mediterranean Sea (Southern Europe, Africa, Asia Minor)	2 850 000	1 100 000
2	South China Sea (China, East Indies)	2 486 000	960 000
3	Bering Sea (Alaska, Siberia)	2 274 000	878 000
4	Caribbean Sea (Central America, West Indies)	1 942 000	750 000
5	Gulf of Mexico (USA, Mexico)	1 855 000	716 000
6	Sea of Okhotsk (Siberia)	1 525 000	589 000
7	Hudson Bay (Canada)	1 230 000	475 000
8	Sea of Japan (Japan, USSR, Korea)	1 007 500	389 000
9	North Sea (North-western Europe)	572 400	221 000
10	Red Sea (Africa, Saudi Arabia)	461 000	178 000
11	Caspian Sea (USSR, Iran)	440 300	170 000
12	Black Sea (USSR, Turkey, Eastern Europe)	430 000	166 000
13	Baltic Sea (Scandinavia, USSR)	422 000	163 000
14	Aral Sea (USSR)	67 340	26 000

GREAT RIVERS

	River	Outflow	Length km	Length miles
1	Nile	Mediterranean	6695	4160
2	Amazon	Atlantic	6520	4050
3	Mississippi-Missouri-Red Rock	Gulf of Mexico	5970	3710
4	Yangtze	North Pacific	5470	3400
5	Yenisei	Arctic	5310	3300
6	Mekong	China Sea	4500	2800
7	Zaire	Atlantic	4375	2710
8	Amur	North Pacific	4345	2700
9	Ob	Arctic	4345	2700
10	Lena	Arctic	4310	2680
11	Mackenzie	Beaufort Sea	4240	2635
12	Niger	Gulf of Guinea	4185	2600

The development of river scenery:
1 young river with steep valleys,
2 mature river cuts successive terraces,
3 senile river forms meanders.

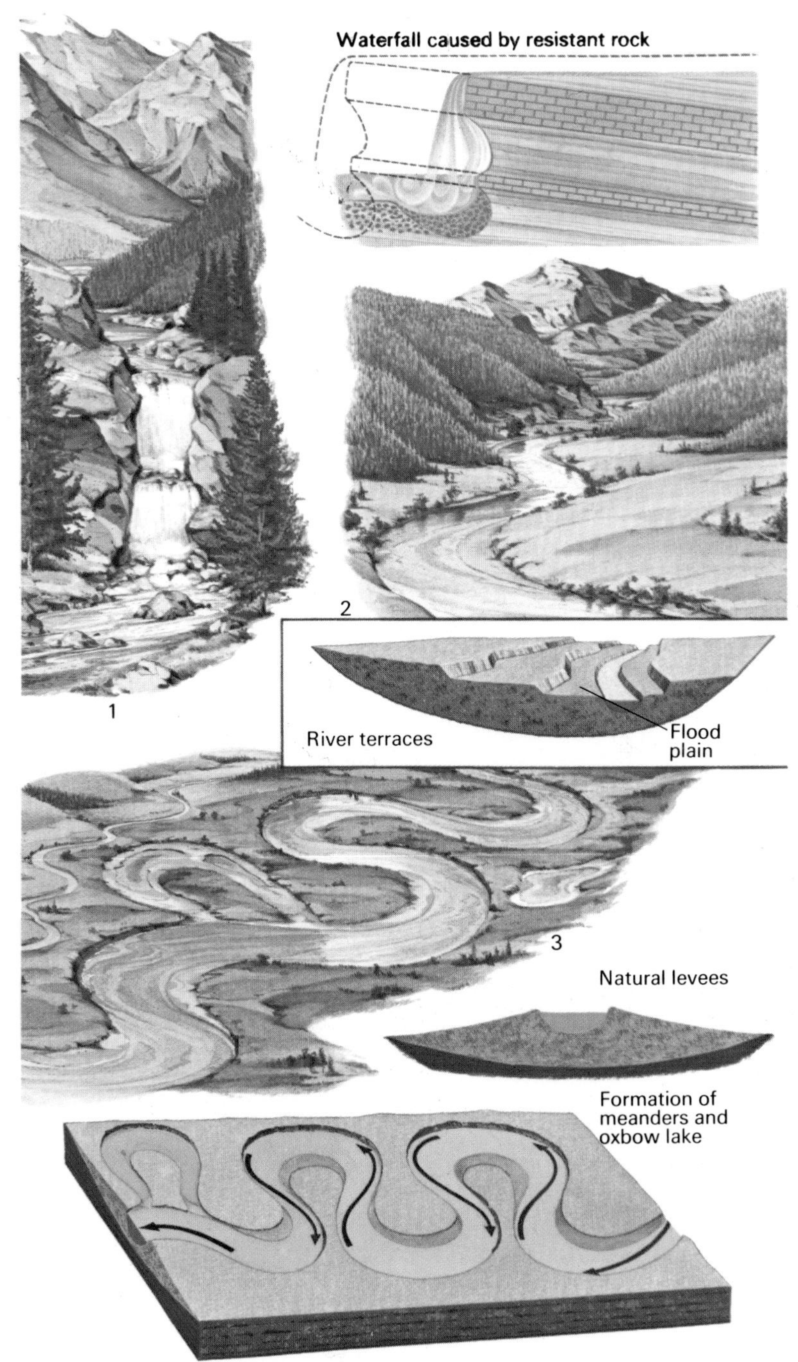
Waterfall caused by resistant rock
1
2
River terraces
Flood plain
3
Natural levees
Formation of meanders and oxbow lake

THE WORLD'S LARGEST ISLANDS

	Island	*Area sq km*	*Area sq miles*
1	Australia	7 687 000	2 968 000
2	Greenland	2 175 030	839 782
3	Papua New Guinea	820 670	316 861
4	Borneo	738 150	285 000
5	Baffin Island	611 240	236 000
6	Madagascar	589 840	227 737
7	Sumatra	418 570	161 612
8	Honshu	230 300	88 919
9	Great Britain	218 040	84 186

THE WORLD'S HIGHEST MOUNTAINS

	Name	*Height metres*	*Height ft*
1	Mount Everest	8848	29 028
2	K2 (Chogori)	8610	28 250
3	Kangchenjunga	8597	28 208
4	Lhotse	8511	27 923
5	Yalung Kang, Kangchenjunga West	8502	27 894
6	Yalung Kang, Kangchenjunga South Peak	8488	27 848
7	Makalu 1	8481	27 824
8	Kangchenjunga Middle Peak	8475	27 806
9	Lhotse Shar	8383	27 504
10	Dhaulargiri 1	8167	26 795

THE WORLD'S HIGHEST ACTIVE VOLCANOES

	Volcano	*Height metres*	*Height ft*
1	Cotopaxi, Ecuador	5978	19 613
2	Popocatapetl, Mexico	5452	17 887
3	Sangay, Ecuador	5410	17 749
4	Tungurahua, Ecuador	5033	16 512
5	Cotacachi, Ecuador	4937	16 197
6	Klyuchevskaya, USSR	4850	15 912
7	Purace, Colombia	4756	15 604
8	Wrangell, Alaska, USA	4269	14 005
9	Tajmulco, Guatemala	4210	13 812
10	Mauna Loa, Hawaii, USA	4168	13 675

GREAT LAKES

	Lake	Location	Area sq km	Area sq miles
1	Caspian Sea	Asia	440 300	170 000
2	Superior	North America	82 400	31 820
3	Victoria	Africa	69 480	26 820
4	Aral	USSR	67 340	26 000
5	Huron	North America	59 575	23 010
6	Michigan	North America	58 000	22 400
7	Tanganyika	Africa	32 890	12 700
8	Great Bear	Canada	31 600	12 200
9	Baikal	USSR	31 470	12 150
10	Great Slave	Canada	28 930	11 170
11	Nyasa	Africa	28 490	11 000
12	Erie	North America	25 740	9 940

HIGH WATERFALLS

	Falls	Country	Drop metres	Drop ft
1	Angel	Venezuela	807	2648
2	Cuquenan	Venezuela	610	2000
3	Ribbon	USA	490	1612
4	W. Mardalsfoss	Norway	467	1535
5	Upper Yosemite	USA	436	1430
6	Gavarnie	France	421	1385
7	Tugela	South Africa	421	1385
8	Glass	Brazil	403	1325
9	Krimml	Austria	381	1250
10	Takkakaw	Canada	366	1200
11	Silver Strand	USA	357	1170
12	Geissbach	Switzerland	350	1150
13	Wollomombie	Australia	335	1100
14	Cusiana	Colombia	300	984
15	Staubbach	Switzerland	300	984
16	E. Mardalsfoss	Norway	297	974
17	Helena	New Zealand	271	890
18	Vetisfoss	Norway	271	889
19	Chirombo	Zambia	268	880

The famous Victoria Falls (Zimbabwe, Zambia) has a drop of 108 metres (355 feet) and Niagara Falls (USA, Canada) has a drop of 59 metres (193 feet).

THE STRUCTURE OF THE EARTH

Most of us think of the planet as a sphere, although it is more accurately described as an *oblate spheroid*, being flattened at the poles and bulging at the Equator. The earth and its atmosphere is rather like an onion – that is a ball made up of layers, although, unlike an onion, each layer is made of a different material.

The *inner core* of our planet is thought to be made of an alloy of nickel and iron at a pressure some four million times greater than that which we experience at the surface. Surrounding this inner core is an *outer core* which seems to be liquid and is made of nickel and iron together with a lighter element such as silicon or sulphur.

It is very difficult to discover what it is like within the earth. Information has been collected from the study of earthquake waves, which react differently in rocks of different densities and different degrees of solidity. Volcanoes also provide evidence as they throw up to the surface materials from great depths. There is one other source of information – meteorites which fall from space and are thought to represent the composition of the universe as a whole.

Outside the core is the *mantle*. The evidence we have from the way in which earthquake waves pass through the mantle suggest that it is solid but it is likely that the upper part is more plastic in consistency.

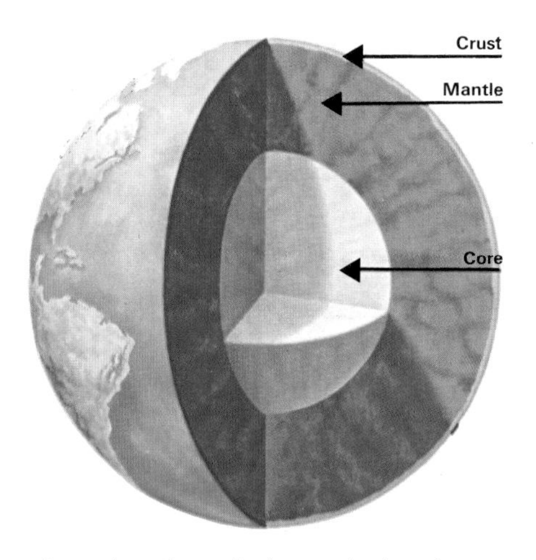

A section through the earth showing the different layers which lie beneath the crust.

The composition of the mantle seems to be similar to that of a rock found at the earth's surface called *peridotite* which contains iron, magnesium, silicon, and oxygen.

Finally, surrounding the mantle, the earth has a very thin skin known as the *crust* which is probably nowhere more than 50 km (30 miles) thick. The crust is thickest under mountain belts.

THE ATMOSPHERE

Surrounding the solid ball of the earth itself is a thin envelope of gases and water vapour which we call the *atmosphere* – this is the air we breathe. The earth has not always had an atmosphere like the one which we enjoy today and, of course, most planets do not have a breathable atmosphere at all.

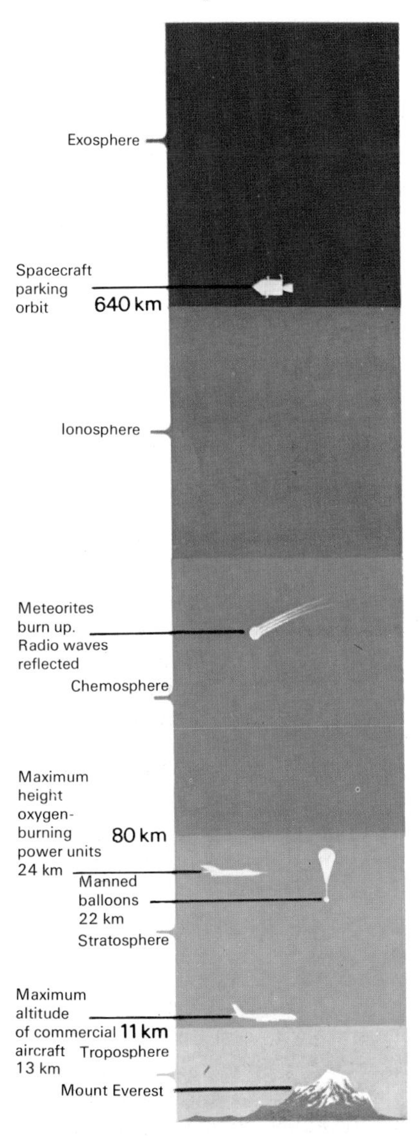

The earth's atmosphere can be divided into layers with different properties.

The heating that took place as the earth was formed meant gases were set free from the evolving planet but we would certainly not think of this first atmosphere as 'air'. It was probably composed of the gases hydrogen and carbon monoxide, plus water vapour. The carbon monoxide together with some carbon dioxide which was also present may then have reacted with the hydrogen leaving an atmosphere of methane and hydrogen. Later, other volcanic gases were added so that the earth's atmosphere gradually became like it is today.

It was the spread of plants which made the final difference, providing sufficient oxygen to support animal life. By a process called *photosynthesis*, green plants use the sun's energy to convert carbon dioxide from the air, and water from the soil, into the sugars and starches that provide the energy to make them grow.

Photosynthesis produces oxygen as a by-product, so as plant life spread, the excess carbon dioxide in the air was replaced by oxygen. At present there is a state of balance: plants take in carbon dioxide and release oxygen, animals breathe in oxygen and expel carbon dioxide.

The air is now made up of 78 per cent nitrogen, 21 per cent oxygen, 0.9 per cent of the inert gas, argon, 0.03 per cent carbon dioxide (although there are fears that this is increasing as a result of industrial pollution and the removal of huge areas of forest), and smaller amounts of other gases. Of course, there is also water vapour in the air but this varies in amount.

WEATHER AND CLIMATE

The earth is kept warm by the energy it receives from the sun as sunshine, but temperatures vary from place to place and from season to season.

TEMPERATURE VARIATIONS

Rays of sunlight travel from 150 million km (93 million miles) away, and when they reach the earth they are parallel rays. The curve of the earth means that the rays are vertical at the Equator but at quite a low angle when they reach temperate latitudes. As the rays lose heat passing through the atmosphere, the more direct the journey, the greater the heat which penetrates through to the surface of the earth. The vertical rays in equatorial latitudes mean it is much hotter at the Equator than it is in the regions where the sun's rays strike at a low angle. It is these variations in temperature that are largely responsible for the changes in the weather.

AIR PRESSURE

Although we do not notice it, the air is really quite heavy and exerts a considerable pressure on the earth. On average, a column of air from sea-level to the top of the atmosphere, and measuring about a square centimetre, would weigh about a kilogram (average air pressure could also be expressed as 14 pounds per square inch). The air pressure is not uniform all over the earth – if it was, we would not have weather as we know it. Nor is the pattern a simple one. Where the earth is warmest – at the Equator – air rises and creates a low pressure region known as the *equatorial low pressure* or *doldrum belt*. The main mass of air which rises from the doldrums falls near the tropics, creating regions of high pressure which are known as the *tropical highs* or *horse latitudes*. The falling air near the tropics cannot just disappear, but travels across the surface of the earth. Some of the major planetary winds have their origin in this falling air.

In addition to the falling air of the tropics there is also falling air in the Arctic and Antarctic because it is so cold. From these two high pressure areas, winds blow out into temperate latitudes and meet air blowing out from the tropical highs. Where the tropical air meets the cold polar air, friction creates a whirling air mass which will eventually form a *depression*.

As a general rule it is true to say that winds blow from areas of high pressure to areas of low pressure, but this is complicated by the rotation of the earth which means that in the northern hemisphere winds are deflected to the right and in the southern hemisphere to the left. In fact, the circulation of the atmosphere is even more complicated because the earth is not warmed uniformly. This warming is affected by such factors as the water content of the air, how much dust or other pollution is present, what sort of surface the sunshine is falling on to and so on.

CLOUDS AND RAIN

Various different things happen to the rays of sunlight that reach the earth. Some of the sun's radiation causes water to evaporate from the oceans and rivers and from growing plants, giving rise to water vapour. When this water vapour cools, it condenses to form the various types of clouds that you will have seen at one time or another.

There are two main types of cloud: cumulus, which results from the cooling of a rising column of air and water vapour, and stratus, which occurs when there is a pocket of cool air between layers of warm air. The drops of water that make up a cloud are so small that they are light enough to float in the air.

Before it can rain, water droplets in a cloud have to join together to form large enough drops to fall. If the temperature at cloud level is below freezing point and the air temperature beneath this is low enough, the water will freeze and fall as snow or, under certain conditions, particularly during thunderstorms, the water will freeze into small lumps of ice that are called hailstones. Hailstones the size of golf balls have been reported but a diameter of about 6 mm (0.25 in) is normal.

THUNDER AND LIGHTNING

One particular weather phenomenon which many people find very frightening is thunderstorms in which lightning flashes across the sky accompanied by loud claps of thunder. It should be remembered that the thunder claps are not caused by clouds banging together as is sometimes thought. If you observe a storm carefully, you will notice that the thunder always follows the flash of lightning. The lightning is like a huge spark caused by an electrical discharge within a thunder cloud. You can imagine that a spark on this grand scale would be very hot and it is the sudden expansion and contraction of the air caused by the heating and cooling effect that produces the bang. When forked lightning is a long way away or is hidden by the cloud, it is seen as a brief flash of light; this is called sheet lightning.

Lightning, like all electricity, tends to be drawn to earth and is attracted by conductors such as a tall tree, so you should never hide under one during a storm – you would be safer in the open.

WEATHER MAPS AND FORECASTING

The weather maps that you may see during the weather forecast on television or in the daily newspapers, in the synoptic charts as they are called, look very confusing. They are not quite so complicated as they seem, however.

(continued on page 92)

Major Winds of the World

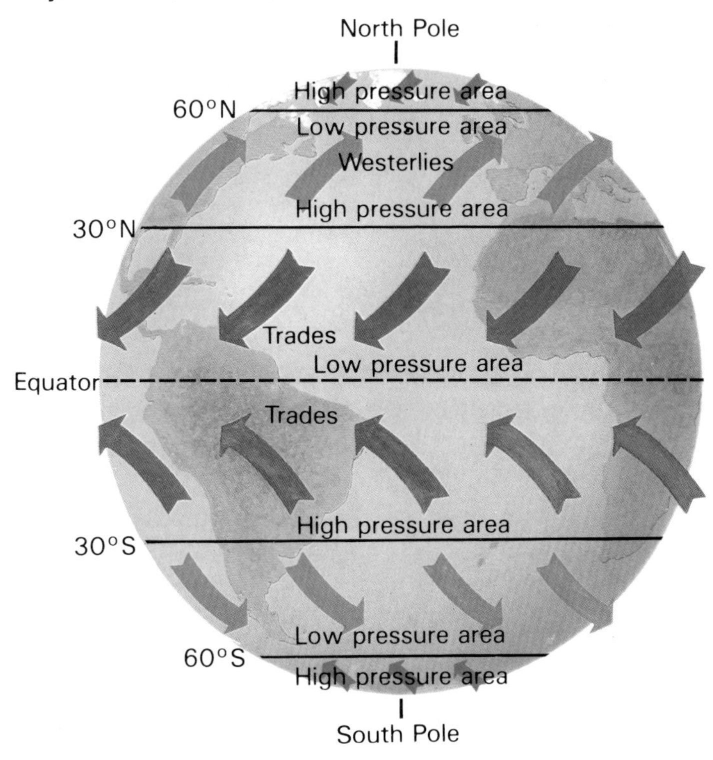

The major winds of the world are the result of air moving from areas of high pressure to areas of low pressure.

Illustrated below are some of the main cloud formations.

Cirrus

Cirrocumulus

Altocumulus

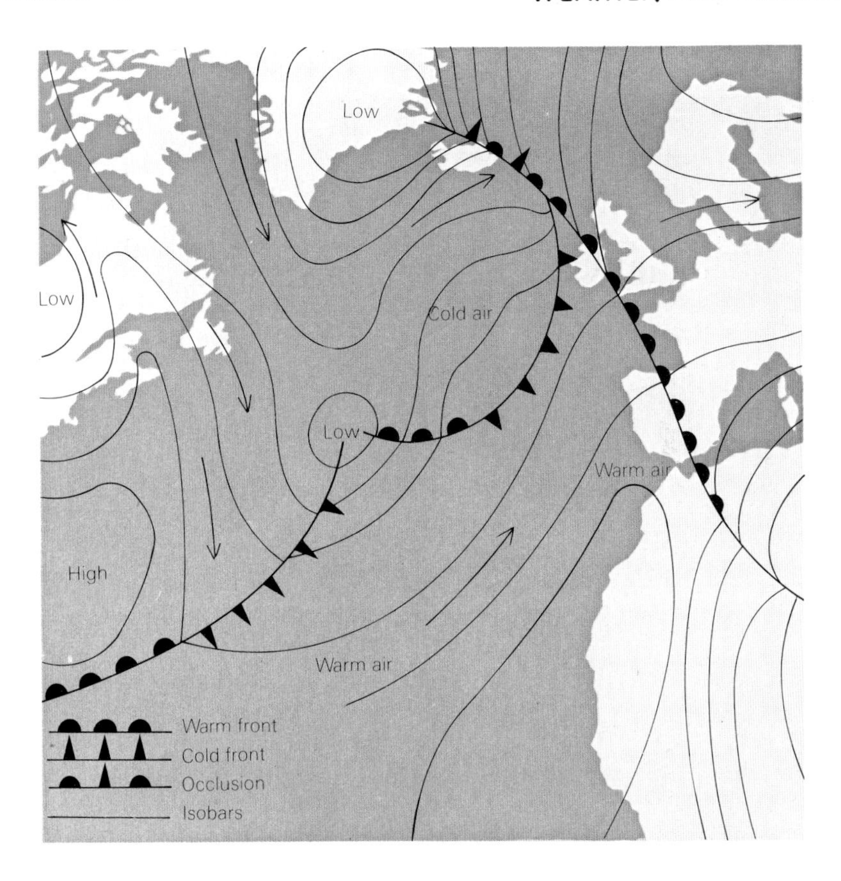

A typical synoptic weather chart for the northern hemisphere.

Stratus

Cumulus

Cumulonimbus

The first thing you might notice are the lines that look like contour lines on an ordnance survey map. These are called isobars, and they indicate lines of equal air pressure. The shapes they form are areas of high and low pressure, or anticyclones and depressions. Winds blow from high to low pressure, but the rotation of the earth diverts them, and in fact they blow almost parallel to the isobars, crossing them at a small angle. In the northern hemisphere the winds blow anti-clockwise around depressions and clockwise around anti-cyclones. It is vice versa in the southern hemisphere.

The lines with points or semicircles on them indicate cold fronts and warm fronts, that is, the boundaries between different masses of air. Cold fronts usually give cool, showery weather, whereas warm fronts bring a wide belt of

CLOUDS

Name	Description	Weather
Cirrus	hair-like and wispy	fine weather but rain is due if the clouds thicken
Cirrocumulus	thick and fluffy	rain is on its way
Cirrostratus	a thin white layer	bad weather to come
Altocumulus	patches of small clouds	when positioned high they usually indicate good weather, if they are low then rain can be expected
Altostratus	uniform grey sheet of cloud	rain, especially if changing to Nimbostratus
Stratocumulus	rolling bank of thick cloud	fine weather
Stratus	pale grey in thin layers	if they clear in the morning fine weather is likely, but if they remain then rain can be forecast
Nimbostratus	dark grey layer at low level	rain or snow
Cumulus	fluffy, like cotton wool	during the day an indication of continuing fine weather; seen early morning could indicate thunder; seen late evening means a fine day tomorrow
Cumulonimbus	towering, dense and dark	heavy rain is due

continuous rain, perhaps followed by finer weather.

Sometimes, a warm front and a cold front join together, resulting in what is known as an occluded front. At an occluded front the weather may be rain, followed quickly by a period of clear weather and then showers.

So a weather chart can tell us a lot about the weather to come.

WEATHER LORE

You have probably heard the expression, 'Red sky at night, shepherd's delight; red sky in the morning, shepherd's warning'. This suggests that if there is a red sunset then the following day will bring fine weather, whereas if the dawn is accompanied by a red sky then the day will not be very pleasant.

Then there is the saying, 'The north wind doth blow and we shall have snow'. This is not always true, of course, but it does indicate quite correctly that bad weather often accompanies a wind from the north.

If you see a halo around the moon on a clear night this is said to be an infallible sign that there is wet weather to come. Of course, in Britain and Europe, this is very likely to be true because the weather is so variable anyway. In fact, the halo around the moon occurs when there is a certain type of cloud present that often precedes rain.

WEATHER RECORDS (°C)

The highest temperatures recorded were 56.6 in Death Valley, California in 1913;
58.5 in the shade at Al Aziziyah, Libya in 1922.
The hottest place in the world is Dallol, Ethiopia, where the annual mean temperature is 34.4.
The lowest temperatures recorded were – 68 at Oimyakon, Siberia in 1892;
– 68 at Verkoyansk, Siberia in 1933;
– 87 at Vostok, Antarctica in 1950;
– 73 at the South Pole in Antarctica in 1957.
The coldest place in the world is Polus Nedostupnosti, or the Pole of Cold, Antarctica, where the annual mean temperature is −57.8.
The heaviest rainfall was 31 mm (1.2 in) in 1 minute in Maryland, USA in 1956;
1870 mm (73.6 in) in 24 hours in Reunion, Indian Ocean in 1952;
9200 mm (362 in) in a month at Cherrapunji, Assam in 1861;
26 400 mm (1 039 in) in a year at Cherrapunji, Assam in 1861.
The heaviest snowfall was 25 800 mm (1 015 in) of snow on Mt Rainier in Washington, USA in 1972.
The biggest hailstone was 0.75 kg (26 oz), 18 cm (7 in) in diameter, in Kansas, USA in 1970.
The driest place in the world is the Atacama desert in Chile, where the annual mean rainfall is nil.
The windiest place in the world is Commonwealth Bay, George V Coast, Antarctica, where gales reach 320 km/h (200 mph).
The sunniest place in the world is the eastern Sahara desert, which averages over 4300 hours of sunshine per year.

THE BEAUFORT SCALE

The force of the wind is measured according to the Beaufort Scale, illustrated below. This was devised by the Admiral, Sir Francis Beaufort, who lived from 1774 to 1857. He wanted a scale of wind speeds that would indicate simply and quickly the effect of wind of any given force on sailing ships and on the sea itself.

This scale is still used today, but it has been adapted to indicate the

Force	0	1	2	3	4	5
Description	Calm	Light air	Light breeze	Gentle breeze	Moderate	Fresh
Effect						
Weather symbol						

Force 0 Calm weather

Force 1 Smoke is moved by the wind but it is not strong enough to move a weather vane.

Force 2 Weather vanes begin to move and leaves rustle; wind is felt on face.

Force 3 Leaves and small twigs are in constant motion.

Force 4 Loose paper blows about and dust is raised.

Force 5 Ripples appear on expanses of water; small trees sway.

Force 6 Large branches sway; whistling is heard in telegraph wires.

effects upon things on dry land. For example, at force 1 or light air, a column of smoke would be diverted, but the wind would not be strong enough to cause a change in the direction of a wind vane. On the other hand, a wind of speed force 9 or a strong gale would be powerful enough to damage the roof of a house. These terms are commonly used in shipping forecasts. It can be fun to keep a record of wind speeds using this system.

6	7	8	9	10	11	12
Strong	Moderate gale	Gale	Strong gale	Whole gale	-	-

Force 7 Extremely blustery; whole trees sway; walking is difficult.

Force 8 Gale force; the wind is strong enough to break twigs off trees.

Force 9 Strong gale; slates can be dislodged from roofs.

Force 10 Whole gale; seldom occurs on land but when it does trees can be torn up by the roots.

Force 11 Causes great damage but, luckily, does not occur very often.

Force 12 Hurricane; occurs mainly in tropical areas.

CLIMATE AND VEGETATION ZONES

Climates are often referred to as hot and wet, or mild and damp, but these words are not very precise. When you look at actual temperature and rainfall figures, you can see exactly what is meant by these vague words. The terms tropical, sub-tropical and temperate climates are also slightly confusing. Tropical climates are really those within the tropics – that is, between $23\frac{1}{2}^\circ$ north and $23\frac{1}{2}^\circ$ south. Temperate climates are those which never experience excessive heat. In between the temperate and tropical regions are areas such as parts of India and the Mediterranean lands where summers can be very hot. These lands are called sub-tropical.

The map below shows a generalized division of the world into climatic and vegetation regions. It is very difficult to decide where a forest ends and grassland begins, as there may be many kilometres of grassland with scattered trees in between the true forest and the true grassland. A similar problem applies to locating the edge of the desert. Boundary lines have been drawn for clarity on the map, but they are

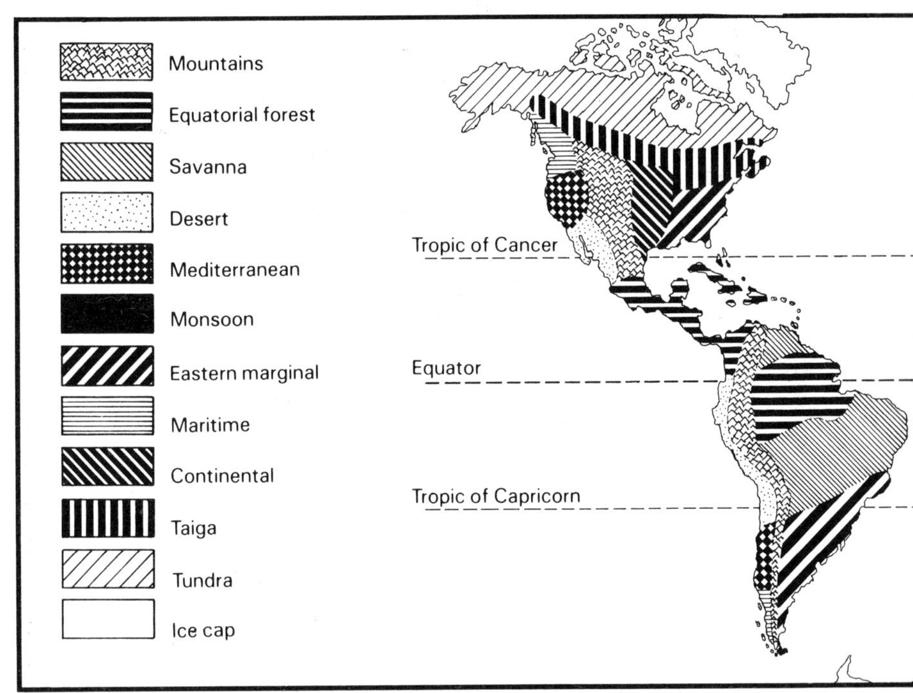

The chief climate and vegetation zones of the world.

really zones of transition and not sharp dividing lines.

The equatorial forest region receives rain throughout the year and this is why trees grow. To the north and south of these equatorial forests are the lands which receive rainfall for only part of the year, in the summer months, and here trees do not survive. Grass is the main vegetation, so this land is called savanna or tropical grassland. Moving further from the equator are high pressure belts which bring dry weather and cause the deserts.

Outside the tropics the climatic regions are the Mediterranean, maritime, continental, taiga, tundra and ice cap. Both within tropical latitudes and in temperate lands are the monsoon and mountain climates. Monsoons occur on the eastern sides of continents in all latitudes from 0°–60° north and 0°–40° south, and mountain climates occur wherever a large mountain range is high enough to cause climatic variations.

Mediterranean lands are like deserts in summer, and maritime regions in winter, with thorny scrub and grass. Maritime regions are wet all the year round and so forests can survive. The continental regions have only sufficient rainfall for grassland, and here are found the main temperate grasslands of the northern hemisphere. Taiga and tundra are cold forms of continental, and support coniferous forest and poor Arctic type vegetation, respectively.

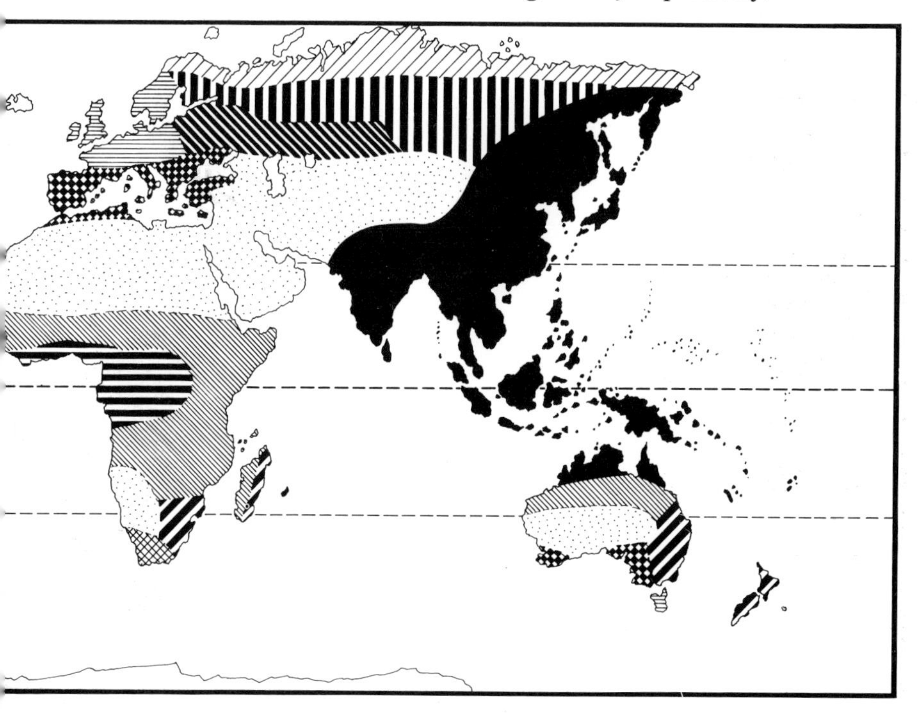

TIDES AND WAVES

On most shores you will notice that the level of the sea changes throughout the day. These ups and downs of the seas are called tides.

Why should tides occur?

Everything on the earth's surface is attracted towards the earth by a force called *gravity*. The moon and the sun also have a gravitational pull of their own. As the moon passes around the earth it attracts the waters of the oceans on the side facing it, pulling them away from the earth, and causing them to bulge.

On the opposite side from this 'tidal bulge', there is another bulge, because on that side, the land is nearer the moon than the waters, and the land is pulled away from the seas, leaving a bulge behind.

These two bulges remain in the same position in relation to the moon, but the rotation of the earth means that each of them appears to move around the earth.

As a result, a tidal bulge passes the same place on earth about every 12 hours. These bulges are called high water, and the gaps between them are called low water.

There are two other factors which help in the formation of the tides. You know that if you cause the water in your bath to rock, it may rise and fall against the side of the bath for some time after you have stopped rocking it.

In the same way, once the tides have begun, the waters tend to continue to rock up and down, and they are given an extra push by the attraction of the moon.

The sun also tends to attract the earth's oceans towards itself, but because it is so much further away the attraction is less important.

At certain times of the year, however, the sun, the moon, and the earth are all in a straight line. When this happens, the attraction of the sun is added to the attraction of the moon and tides are extra high. These are called spring tides. If the sun and the moon are neutralizing each other, tides are much lower, and are called neap tides.

Waves are almost wholly the result of wind blowing across the surface of the water. The wind drags the water to form waves which move slowly forward, and get larger. Although the wave shape moves forward, each particle of water moves round in circles and does not change its average position.

The height of a wave depends on three factors: how hard the wind is blowing, how long the wind has been blowing, and the fetch. The word fetch means the length of the stretch of open water over which the wind is blowing.

The diagrams opposite show the effects of the moon and the sun on the earth's oceans.

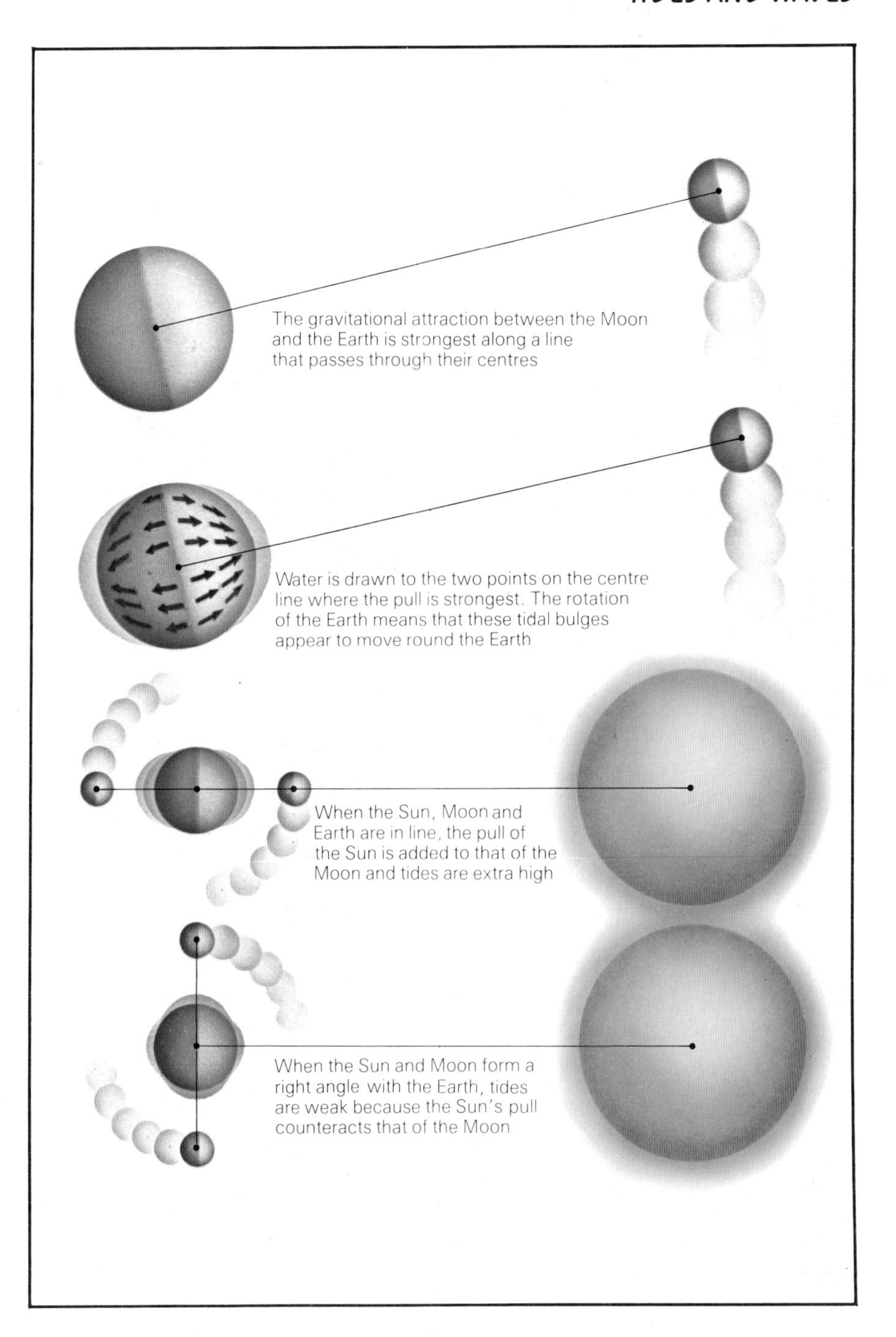
The gravitational attraction between the Moon
and the Earth is strongest along a line
that passes through their centres
Water is drawn to the two points on the centre
line where the pull is strongest. The rotation
of the Earth means that these tidal bulges
appear to move round the Earth
When the Sun, Moon and
Earth are in line, the pull of
the Sun is added to that of the
Moon and tides are extra high
When the Sun and Moon form a
right angle with the Earth, tides
are weak because the Sun's pull
counteracts that of the Moon

CONSTELLATIONS

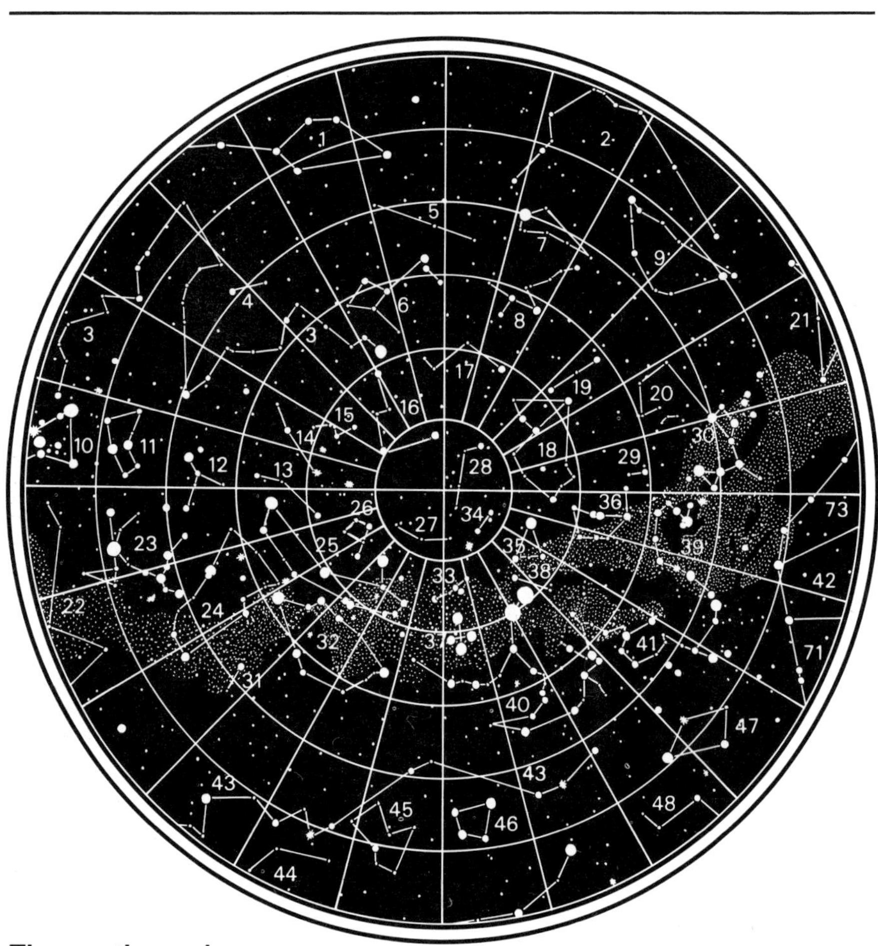

The southern sky

1 Cetus
2 Aquarius
3 Eridanus
4 Fornax
5 Sculptor
6 Phoenix
7 Piscis Austrinus
8 Grus
9 Capricornus
10 Orion
11 Lepus
12 Columba
13 Pictor
14 Dorado
15 Reticulum
16 Hydrus
17 Tucana
18 Pavo
19 Indus
20 Sagittarius
21 Aquila
22 Monoceros
23 Canis Major
24 Puppis
25 Carina
26 Volans
27 Chamaeleon
28 Octans
29 Telescopium
30 Corona Australis
31 Pyxis
32 Vela
33 Musca
34 Apus
35 Triangulum Australe
36 Ara
37 Crux
38 Circinus
39 Scorpius
40 Centaurus
41 Lupus
42 Ophiuchus
43 Hydra
44 Sextans
45 Crater
46 Corvus
47 Libra
48 Virgo

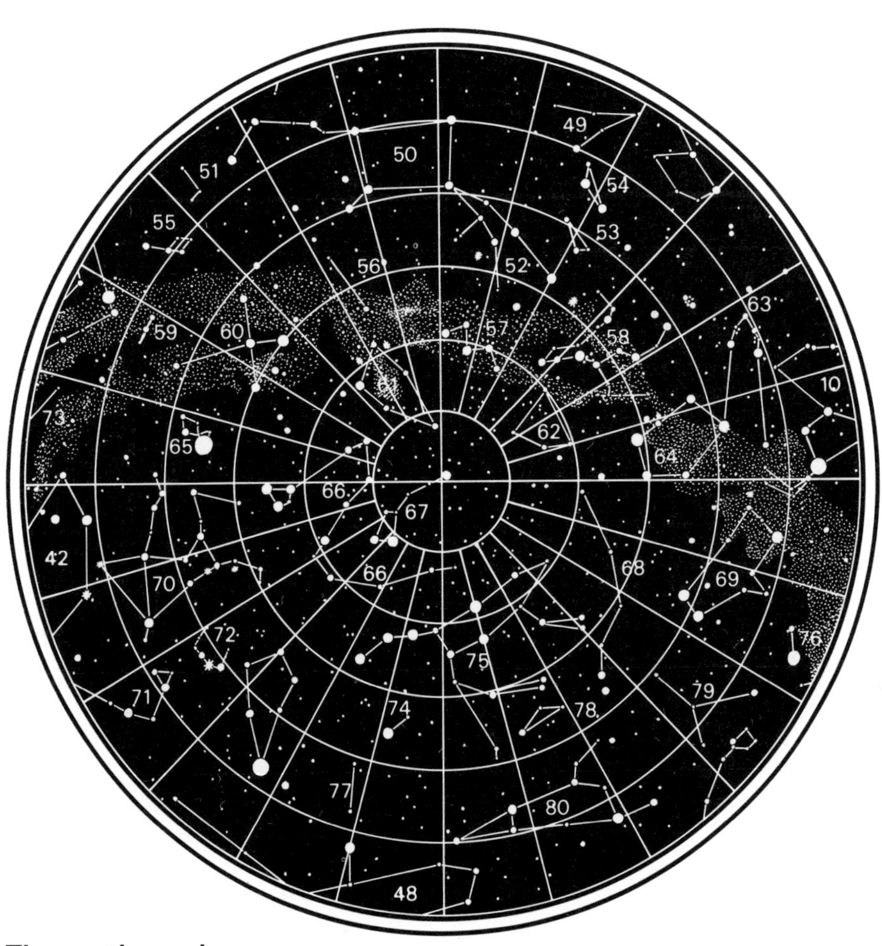

The northern sky

49 Pisces
50 Pegasus
51 Equuleus
52 Andromeda
53 Triangulum
54 Aries
55 Delphinus
56 Lacerta
57 Cassiopeia
58 Perseus
59 Sagitta
60 Cygnus
61 Cepheus
62 Camelopardalis
63 Auriga
64 Taurus
65 Lyra
66 Draco
67 Ursa Minor
68 Lynx
69 Gemini
70 Hercules
71 Serpens
72 Corona Borealis
73 Bootes
74 Canes Venatici
75 Ursa Major
76 Canis Minor
77 Coma Berenices
78 Leo Minor
79 Cancer
80 Leo

CONSTELLATIONS

Latin name	English name
Andromeda	Andromeda
Antlia	Air pump
Apus	Bird of paradise
Aquarius	Water carrier
Aquila	Eagle
Ara	Altar
Aries	Ram
Auriga	Charioteer
Boötes	Herdsman
Caelum	Chisel
Camelopardalis	Giraffe
Cancer	Crab
Canes Venatici	Hunting dogs
Canis Major	Greater Dog
Canis Minor	Lesser Dog
Capricornus	Sea-goat
Carina	Keel (of the *Argo*)
Cassiopeia	Cassiopeia
Centaurus	Centaur
Cepheus	Cepheus, the king
Cetus	Whale
Chamaeleon	Chameleon
Circinus	Compasses
Columba	Dove
Coma Berenices	Berenice's hair
Corona Australis	Southern crown
Corona Borealis	Northern crown
Corvus	Crow
Crater	Cup
Crux	Southern cross
Cygnus	Swan
Delphinus	Dolphin
Dorado	Goldfish
Draco	Dragon
Equuleus	Little horse or foal
Eridanus	Eridanus River
Fornax	Furnace
Gemini	Twins
Grus	Crane
Hercules	Hercules
Horologium	Pendulum clock
Hydra	Water-snake
Hydrus	Lesser water-snake
Indus	Indian
Lacerta	Lizard
Leo	Lion
Leo Minor	Lesser lion
Lepus	Hare
Libra	Scales
Lupus	Wolf
Lynx	Lynx
Lyra	Lyre
Mensa	Table mountain
Microscopium	Microscope
Monoceros	Unicorn
Musca	Fly
Norma	Level
Octans	Octant (old sextant)
Ophiuchus	Serpent-holder
Orion	Orion the hunter
Pavo	Peacock
Pegasus	Pegasus (winged horse)
Perseus	Perseus
Phoenix	Phoenix
Pictor	Painter's easel
Pisces	Fishes
Piscis Austrinus	Southern fish
Puppis	Stern (of the *Argo*)
Pyxis	Mariner's compass (of the *Argo*)
Reticulum	Net
Sagitta	Arrow
Sagittarius	Archer
Scorpius	Scorpion
Sculptor	Sculptor
Scutum	Shield
Serpens	Serpent
Sextans	Sextant
Taurus	Bull
Telescopium	Telescope
Triangulum	Triangle
Triangulum Australe	Southern triangle
Tucana	Toucan
Ursa Major	Grear bear (or plough)
Ursa Minor	Lesser bear
Vela	Sails (of the *Argo*)
Virgo	Virgin
Volans	Flying fish
Vulpecula	Fox

FAMOUS COMETS

		First recorded	*Orbital period in years*
1	Halley's Comet	240BC	76
2	Encke's Comet	1786	3.3
3	Biela's Comet	1806	6.7
4	Great Comet of 1811	1811	3 000
5	Pons-Winnecke Comet	1819	6.0
6	Great Comet of 1843	1843	512.4
7	Donati's Comet	1858	2 040
8	Schwassmann-Wachmann Comet	1925	16.2
9	Arend-Roland Comet	1957	10 000
10	Humason Comet	1961	2 900
11	Ikeya-Seki Comet	1965	880
12	Kouhoutek's Comet	1975	Unknown

INTRODUCTION

This section gives you lots of ideas for hobbies you can enjoy all the year round.

Cookery is fun for both girls and boys, and is a useful skill for everyone to learn.

Many children enjoy keeping pets, and here is helpful advice on what pet may suit you, and how to look after it.

Birdwatching and photography are both rewarding pastimes, and so are cycling, camping and fishing, which are good ways of enjoying yourself in the open air. Cycling allows you to see the countryside, and keep healthy, too.

Wherever you live, there will probably be some freshwater nearby, and the best place for a beginner to learn to fish is probably a pond or lake.

Horse riding and sailing are both enjoyable hobbies, and you will find riding schools and sailing clubs good places to learn the basic skills.

With any hobby or sport, accidents can happen and people can be hurt, sometimes badly. Study the first aid section carefully, then you will be prepared in an emergency.

Nearly all accidents can be avoided if you remember a few simple precautions when pursuing any sport or hobby:

This Tasar is a one-design class dinghy used for racing.

* follow the rules of the sport or hobby very carefully
* always use the proper equipment and make sure that it is in good order
* if protective clothing is recommended, wear it
* make sure you understand exactly what you ought to be doing
* if you are a beginner, make sure an instructor or responsible person is present
* keep your temper. Many accidents happen because someone loses their temper and does something silly or careless.

And last of all, remember – enjoy yourself!

COOKERY

Cookery is a useful skill for everyone to learn, and here are some simple recipes for different kinds of sandwiches, tasty sandwich fillings, main dishes which are suitable for lunch or supper, as well as simple cakes and a delicious pudding, for you to enjoy making and eating.

When you are cooking remember these simple rules:

Do's

Always wash your hands before starting to cook.

Tie back long hair

Wear an apron to keep your clothes clean.

Use a chopping board for cutting up fruit and vegetables – *never* the counter or table top.

Sift flour and icing sugar before using them.

Keep your working area as tidy as possible, cleaning up as you go along.

Wash up everything after you have finished and leave the kitchen clean and tidy.

Don'ts

Don't allow pets in the kitchen when you are cooking.

Don't guess at weights and measures – follow the recipe and measure carefully.

Don't handle food too much.

USEFUL FACTS AND FIGURES

Notes on metrication: In many cookery books quantities are given in metric and imperial measures. Exact conversion from imperial to metric measures does not usually give very convenient working quantities and so the metric measures have been rounded off into units of 25 grams. The table below shows the recommended equivalents.

Ounces	Approx grams	Recommended conversion	Ounces	Approx grams	Recommended conversion
1	28	25	11	312	300
2	57	50	12	340	350
3	85	75	13	368	375
4	113	100	14	396	400
5	142	150	15	425	425
6	170	175	16 (1 lb)	454	450
7	198	200	17	482	475
8	227	225	18	510	500
9	255	250	19	539	550
10	283	275	20 ($1\frac{1}{4}$ lb)	567	575

Note: When converting quantities over 20 oz first add the appropriate figures in the table on page 104, then adjust to the nearest unit of 25. As a general guide, 1 kg (1000 g) equals 2.2 lb or about 2 lb 3 oz. This method of conversion gives good results in nearly all cases, although in certain pastry and cake recipes a more accurate conversion is necessary to produce a balanced recipe.

Liquid measures

Imperial	Approx ml	Recommended ml	Imperial	Approx ml	Recommended ml
¼ pint	142	150 ml	1 pint	567	600 ml
½ pint	283	300 ml	1½ pints	851	900 ml
¾ pint	425	450 ml	1¾ pints	992	1000 ml (1 litre)

Spoon measures given in cookery books are usually level unless otherwise stated. At present, cans are marked with the exact (usually to the nearest whole number) metric equivalent of the imperial weight of the contents, so cookery books usually follow this practice when giving can sizes.

Oven temperatures: The table below gives recommended equivalents

	°C	°F	Gas Mark		°C	°F	Gas Mark
Very cool	110	225	¼	Moderately hot	190	375	5
	120	250	½		200	400	6
Cool	140	275	1	Hot	220	425	7
	150	300	2		230	450	8
Moderate	160	325	3	Very hot	240	475	9
	180	350	4				

Notes for American and Australian cooks: In America the 8 fl oz measuring cup is used. In Australia metric measures are now used in conjunction with the standard 250 ml measuring cup. The imperial pint, used in Britain and Australia, is 20 fl oz, while the American pint is 16 fl oz. It is important to remember that the Australian tablespoon differs from both the British and American tablespoons; the table below gives a comparison. The British standard tablespoon holds 17.7 ml, the American 14.2 ml and the Australian 20 ml. A teaspoon holds approximately 5 ml in all three countries.

British	American	Australian
1 teaspoon	1 teaspoon	1 teaspoon
1 tablespoon	1 tablespoon	1 tablespoon
2 tablespoons	3 tablespoons	2 tablespoons
3½ tablespoons	4 tablespoons	3 tablespoons
4 tablespoons	5 tablespoons	3½ tablespoons

Solid measures

Imperial	American
1 lb butter or margarine	2 cups
1 lb flour	4 cups
1 lb granulated or caster sugar	2 cups
1 lb icing sugar	3 cups
8 oz rice	1 cup

Liquid measures

Imperial	American
¼ pint liquid	⅔ cup liquid
½ pint	1¼ cups
¾ pint	2 cups
1 pint	2½ cups
1½ pints	3¾ cups
2 pints	5 cups (2½ pints)

Note: When making recipes in any book, only follow one set of measures as they are not interchangeable

Triple-decker sandwiches

All you need for a picnic

1. Spread four slices of bread with butter or soft margarine.
2. On the first put lettuce and grated cheese; on the second put sliced tomato; on the third put scrambled egg. Top with fourth slice, butter side down. For a supper dish – replace the bread with toast.

Open toasted sandwiches

A quick dish for a cold day

1. Toast bread on one side under the grill and turn over.
2. Cover the *untoasted* side with grated cheese. Put it back under the grill.
3. When the cheese begins to bubble, remove from grill and add chopped tomato.

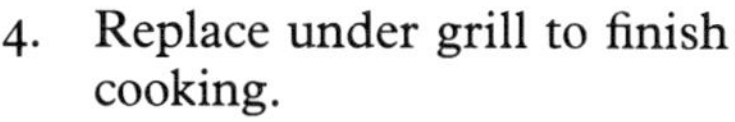

4. Replace under grill to finish cooking.

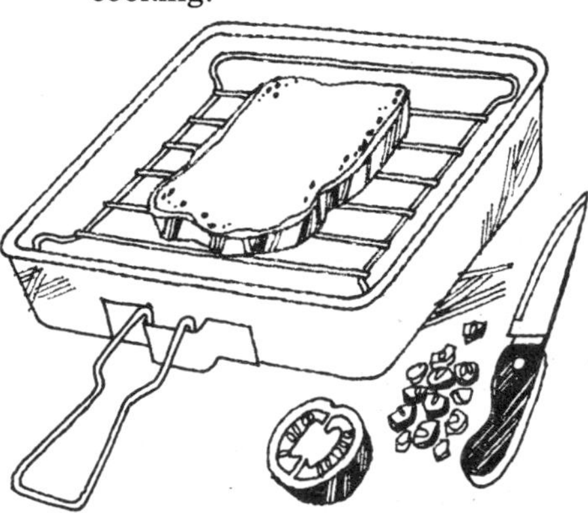

Fried sandwiches

For using up leftovers

1. Make a sandwich with any filling except lettuce.
2. Melt butter or margarine in the frying pan.
3. Fry the sandwich to a rich golden colour.
4. Serve with a fried egg on top.

Heroes

For a hungry day

1. Cut a small French loaf horizontally (one for each person).
2. Spread with butter or soft margarine.
3. Fill with lettuce, tomato and cucumber.
4. Put together as a sandwich. Eat when *really* hungry.

Buck rarebit

(for 4 people)

You will need:
225 g (8 oz) Cheddar cheese
6 tablespoons milk
pinch of dry mustard
pinch of cayenne pepper
1 teaspoon Worcester sauce
5 eggs
4 small slices of toast (trimmed)

How to make:
1. Grate the cheese into a pan.
2. Melt it over a very low heat.
3. As the cheese begins to melt gradually stir in the milk.
4. Add the mustard, cayenne and Worcester sauce and stir thoroughly.
5. Break 1 egg into a bowl, beat and add to the cheese mixture in the pan.
6. Stir until thick and creamy. Remove from heat and keep warm.
7. Poach four eggs.
8. Pour the rarebit over the pieces of toast, top each one with an egg and serve immediately.

Other ideas for sandwich fillings

Mashed banana and cream cheese; bacon and fried egg, coconut and lemon curd; grated chocolate and raisins or sultanas; sardine with tomato sauce; jam or jelly and peanut butter; chopped apple with chopped celery; salad cream with chopped hard-boiled egg.

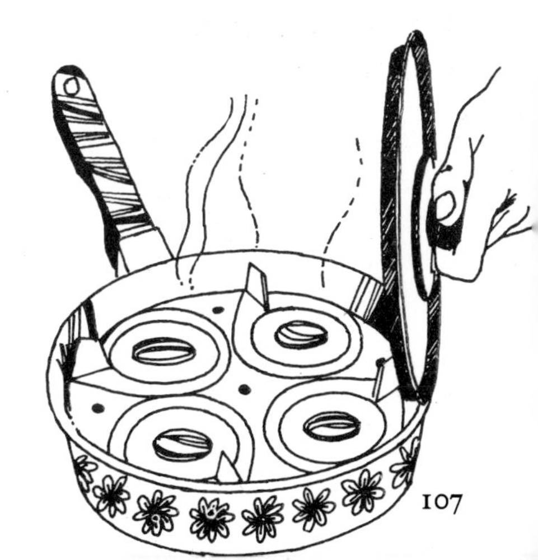

Lasagne

(for 4–6 people)

You will need:
1.25 litres (2 pints) water
1 teaspoon salt
175 g (6 oz) lasagne

Bolognese sauce:
2 onions
2 tablespoons cooking oil
or 50 g (2 oz) lard
225 g (8 oz) minced beef
salt, pepper, herbs (if available)
1 small (60 g/2¼ oz) can of tomato pureé
150 ml (¼ pint) stock or water

Cheese sauce:
6 oz cheese
1 oz margarine
1 oz flour
300 ml (½ pint) milk

To cook the lasagne:
1. Put the water, with salt, into a large pan and bring to the boil. Add the lasagne, pushing it in with a wooden spoon as it softens. Boil for 12 minutes, then remove from heat, drain, rinse in cold water and leave aside.

To make Bolognese sauce:
2. Chop onions.
3. Heat cooking oil or lard in a saucepan and fry the chopped onion until transparent (about 5 minutes).
4. Add the minced beef, and cook, stirring constantly, until brown.
5. Season with salt and pepper and add a sprinkling of herbs if available.

6. Pour off any excess fat.
7. Add tomato purée and stock or water.
8. Simmer gently for 20 minutes.
9. Turn on the oven. Set to Gas No. 7 – Electricity 220°C (425°F).

This meat sauce can be served with spaghetti to make Spaghetti Bolognese.

To make the cheese sauce:
10. Grate the cheese (or mix grated Cheddar and Parmesan)
11. Melt the margarine and stir in the flour. Cook for one minute. Remove from heat and add milk gradually, stirring to avoid lumps. Return to heat and cook, stirring for 3 minutes.
12. Remove from heat and add half the cheese. Stir well. Season with salt and pepper.
13. Grease an ovenproof dish and cover the bottom with lasagne.

14. Cover thinly with Bolognese sauce, then with cheese sauce.
15. Add a second layer of lasagne and again cover with Bolognese sauce and then with cheese sauce. Continue until all the sauce is used.

16. Top with a layer of lasagne and sprinkle on the remaining grated cheese.
17. Bake near the top of a hot oven (Gas No. 7 – Electricity 220°C [425°F]) for 20–25 minutes.

Savoury pancakes

(for 4–6 people)

You will need:
100 g (4 oz) flour
2 eggs
1 tablespoon cooking oil
150 ml (¼ pint) milk
2 tablespoons water
pinch of salt

Filling:
225 g (8 oz) of either cooked chicken, meat, sausages or vegetables
25 g (1 oz) margarine
25 g (1 oz) flour
12 tablespoons milk

Cheese sauce:
See Lasagne, previous page.

How to make:
1. Grease a frying pan with oil or lard.
2. Sift the flour into a bowl. Break the eggs into the centre. Add cooking oil and milk. Beat very thoroughly.
3. Add 1 tablespoon water and beat again.
4. Fry a small 'test' pancake. If the mixture flows too stiffly to form a thin pancake, add another tablespoon of water.
5. Fill a saucepan with hot water, put it on the stove and cover with an upturned plate. Put the cooked pancakes over the plate to keep warm.

6. Make the pancakes thin, frying until just set and lightly browned on each side.

To make the filling:

7. Chop the chicken. Season. Add any other chopped left-overs such as sausages, potato or vegetables.
8. In a small pan, melt the margarine, stir in the flour to form a 'roux', remove from the heat and stir in 8 tablespoons milk. Re-heat and stir until smooth. Stir in 4 further tablespoons milk over the heat. Cook for a further two minutes.
9. Add the chicken and other filling ingredients. Stir and heat through.
10. Lay each pancake flat, fill with filling and roll up.
11. If liked, serve with a cheese sauce (as used for Lasagne, see page 108).

Scotch eggs

(for 4 people)

You will need:

Oil for deep frying
5 eggs
4 sausages
2 tablespoons crisp breadcumbs

How to make:

1. Half fill a saucepan with cooking oil. Fit a frying basket into the pan and leave aside.
2. Bring a pan of water to the boil, put in 4 eggs, bring back to the boil and boil for 10 minutes. Remove, plunge eggs into cold water and remove shells.
3. Skin the sausages and cover each egg with the meat from one sausage, being careful to leave no cracks.
4. Break one egg into a deep plate and mix the yolk and white with a fork. Into a second deep plate put about 2 tablespoons crisp breadcrumbs.
5. Roll the eggs covered with sausagemeat, first in the egg, then in the breadcrumbs, until completely covered.

6. Heat the oil in the saucepan, still with the frying basket in place, until a square of bread thrown into it browns and rises to the top. *Ask a grown-up to help with deep-frying. Hot fat is dangerous.*

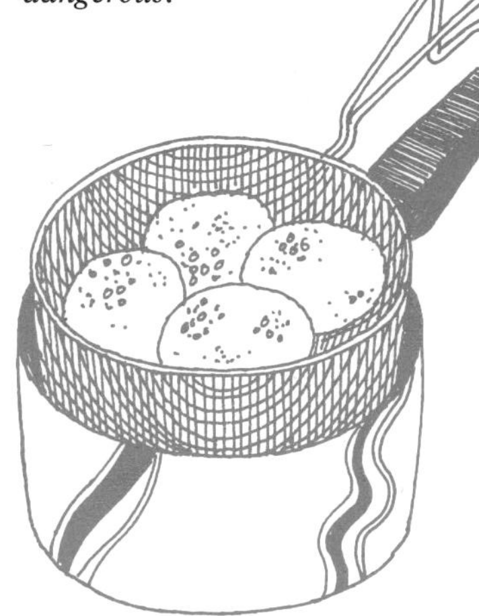

7. Put the four eggs into the basket and lower it into the fat. Cook until golden brown (2–3 minutes).
8. Remove, cut each Scotch egg in two and serve hot with mashed potato and peas, or cold with salad.

Old English gingerbread

You will need:

225 g (8 oz) plain flour
1 teaspoon ground ginger
good pinch of bicarbonate of soda
100 g (4 oz) soft brown sugar
150 ml ($\frac{1}{4}$ pint) milk
100 g (4 oz) butter or margarine
2 eggs
100 g (4 oz) black treacle.

How to make:

1. Turn on oven. Set to Gas No. 2 – Electricity 150°C (300°F).
2. Grease and flour an 18 × 28 cm (7 × 11 in) swiss-roll tin.
3. Sift together the flour, ginger, bicarbonate of soda, and sugar.
4. Warm the milk and dissolve the butter or margarine in it. *Do not boil.*
5. Beat the eggs.
6. Add the eggs and the treacle to the dry ingredients.
7. Add the milk and butter mixture. Beat well. The mixture should be really runny.
8. Pour into the prepared tin.
9. Bake for 35 minutes in the centre of a cool oven (Gas No. 2 – Electricity 150°C [300°F]) then lower the heat to very cool (Gas No. $\frac{1}{2}$–1 – Electricity 120–140°C [250–275°F]) for a further 25 minutes.
10. Allow to cool in the tin before turning out on to a cake rack.

Fruit buns

You will need:

50 g (2 oz) self-raising flour
50 g (2 oz) sugar
pinch of salt
50 g (2 oz) softened butter or margarine
1 egg
few drops vanilla essence
1 teaspoon water
50 g (2 oz) sultanas, raisins or mixed fruit

How to make:

1. Turn on oven. Set to Gas No. 5 – Electricity 190°C (375°F).
2. Grease and flour a tray of 12 bun tins or prepare 12 small paper cases.
3. Put all the ingredients into one bowl and beat together with a wooden spoon.

4. Put one heaped teaspoon of the mixture into each bun tin or paper case.
5. Bake in the top half of a moderately hot oven (Gas No. 5 – Electricity 190°C [375°F]) for 10–15 minutes.

Ginger buns:
Replace fruit and vanilla with 1 level teaspoon ground ginger and 25 g (1 oz) chopped crystallized ginger.

Lemon sorbet

(for 4–6 people)

You will need:

3 lemons
175 g (6 oz) loaf sugar
600 ml (1 pint) cold water
1 small egg

How to make:

1. Fill an 18 × 10 cm (7 × 4 inch) loaf tin with cold water and leave aside.
2. Peel the lemons very thinly, with a potato peeler or sharp knife.
3. Squeeze the juice out of the peeled lemons.

4. Put the rind into a pan with the sugar and water.
5. Heat gently to dissolve the sugar, then bring to the boil and boil *fast* for 6 minutes.
6. Remove from the heat and stand the pan in cold water to cool.
7. Separate the white from the yolk of the egg. Beat the white until stiff.
8. Add the lemon juice to the sugar mixture in the pan.

9. When cool, strain (to remove the rind) straight on to the white of egg.
10. Fold them together with a metal spoon. (If some of the white persists in rising to the top, don't worry – it will taste good and look pretty when frozen.)
11. Empty the loaf tin and pour the lemon mixture into the undried tin.

12. Set in the ice-making compartment of the refrigerator overnight.
13. If you want it sooner, turn the refrigerator to MAX, remembering to remove foods you do not want turned to ice!

KEEPING PETS

A lot of satisfaction can be obtained from keeping pets, but with it goes responsibility. Owning a pet is like keeping a bargain. Your pet will give you companionship and fun, and in return you must provide your pet with food, exercise, love, attention, shelter, and sometimes pay a vet's bill. For example, puppies and kittens will need injections when young.

You must choose your animal with care, being sure you can look after it properly. Consider what space you have, whether you can exercise your pet, what your family thinks of it joining the home, how long the animal will live, whether you will be able to arrange for its welfare while you are on holiday, and how much it costs to house and feed.

DOGS

You can buy a puppy from a friend whose dog has a litter, from advertisements in the newspapers, from a dogs' home or from a pet shop. But do not buy a puppy on impulse. First of all decide the kind of dog you want. Bear in mind how large it will grow. It is no good buying an appealing puppy with, say, a retriever in its ancestry, if you live in a town and will be unable to give it all the daily walks and exercise it will need in a few months' time. Similarly, do not buy a sad-looking puppy you feel sorry for – be sensible and buy a lively

A Golden Cocker Spaniel puppy with some common types of collars and leads.

one with a cold wet nose and alert clear eyes, like the Golden Cocker Spaniel opposite.

Puppies need a basket to sleep in out of draughts. It is best to have one with sides, raised off the ground. Put an old blanket inside for bedding. Other things you will need are a collar and lead (some examples are shown opposite), and separate bowls for its food and water. Other necessary items are a bath and especially if it is a long-haired puppy, a brush to keep his coat shining.

When you buy your puppy it will not be trained, especially where toilet habits are concerned, and you must be very patient, spreading newspapers for it and placing it on them whenever it shows signs of messing. Eventually you will be able to take it outside. Encourage it with kind words, which it will quickly recognize.

At first your puppy will require five meals a day, including plenty of moist food and occasional meat. At three months old it should have three meals a day, with more meat. Always make sure it has plenty of fresh water.

CATS

A warm place to sleep, enough food and drink and the freedom to come and go when it pleases will usually be enough to keep your pet cat happy. All cats will become very independent and not require much looking after.

Kittens are usually quite easy to come by, unless they are pedigrees. Most people know the lively Siamese and long-haired Persian, but the 'ordinary' black or tabby cat has no less intelligence or character. Shown here is an Abyssinian cat.

An Abyssinian cat with a common type of cat basket, and brush and comb.

Kittens should not be taken from their mothers until they are about two to three months old. Choose one that looks lively with good teeth and a good coat. Beware of a kitten with a runny nose, eyes or mouth or one that seems to have breathing troubles, as these problems are very difficult to cure.

When first brought home your new kitten will be very frightened and unhappy. Do not handle it too much. Show it its bed, and food and water bowls. If you regularly place your kitten in a dirt tray it will soon learn how to use it. In the early stages of its life, it should be fed little and often (three to four meals a day), and be allowed to sleep a great deal between meals.

If you have a garden, a cat flap can be cut into your door. A smallish hole with a light plywood flap which swings from the top will allow a cat to get in and out at will. But do not let a young kitten out unattended.

Cats require little food. Mashed cooked meat, boneless fish and proprietary foods are fine, but cats have individual tastes, so keep the diet varied. Offer both milk and water, but do not leave uneaten food or milk around. However, a bowl of water should always be available.

Cats soon learn to groom themselves. Long-haired breeds need daily brushing and combing; brush short-haired cats regularly too. Cats are very good at keeping themselves healthy, and a well-kept cat may live for 12 years or more.

RABBITS

Pet rabbits will usually live for five years, but can live twice that long. English or Dutch breeds are easier to keep than the larger or long-haired varieties. They can live in hutches out of doors if used to it – otherwise a light well-ventilated shed is best. Rabbits cannot tolerate draughts or damp and must have a hutch raised off the ground. The hutch should have an enclosed wooden compartment with plenty of hay for sleeping, and a larger area for running around with one side only of this area covered with chicken wire.

Proprietory rabbit food can be given twice a day, with cabbage or fresh-picked dandelion leaves and an occasional carrot given in the evening. You can offer potato peelings or a slice of bread, but dry them in the oven first. Water is best given in a special feeding bottle. Change the water daily and remove uneaten food. The hutch should be cleaned out at least once a week. Your rabbit will like a run in the garden, but be careful it cannot escape and dogs or cats cannot get in.

Dutch rabbits are among the easiest to keep.

There are about 300 species of parrot, all of which are excellent climbers.

Budgerigars are natives of Australia where they live in huge flocks.

CAGE BIRDS

Everybody is familiar with budgerigars and canaries, but more exotic birds can be kept as pets, such as finches, cockatoos, parrots, mynahs, macaws, love-birds and toucans. Whichever you prefer, it is best to buy the cage with the bird, as each species' requirements are different.

Budgerigars and mynahs can be taught a word or two of speech, canaries are prized for their song, the long-lived birds of the parrot family are kept for their plumage and character. The parrot is too big for small rooms, whereas budgerigars can sometimes be allowed to fly free.

Cage birds will need dishes or dispensers for seed and other food, a water container, and various perches, but take care not to clutter up all the space. All food containers must be easily and regularly cleaned. Cuttlefish, millet and greenstuff can vary most birds' usual diet. Take care that the bird's cage is not in a draught.

GUINEA PIGS

The correct name for a guinea pig is a cavy. The more hardy smooth-haired kinds are best for beginners to keep. Cavies like raised cages similar to rabbit hutches, with hay for sleeping and a run covered with sawdust. They eat little and often: fresh greens, carrots, turnips, apple peel, bread and special mix from the pet shop. In summer they can crop the grass in the garden – but enclose and protect them. They like a hot bran mash meal at night in winter, but do not let them get fat. They need plenty of water, changed each day, from a large water bottle. If well cared for, a cavy can live for up to eight years.

HAMSTERS

Hamsters are not hardy and will seldom live for more than a year or two. They must be kept alone, as they fight. An aquarium tank with a strong wire-mesh top for ventilation is probably the best home. The bottom should be covered with peat or sawdust, and hay should be provided, with which the hamster will make a nest. Give it a strong branch to climb and chew.

Your pet will need water from a bottle, and a food bowl. A small evening meal of seeds, cereal, fruits and nuts is enough for a hamster, but it will make a food hoard, which you should regularly remove, as food goes bad. A hamster should always be kept indoors, warm and dry, and not allowed to hibernate as it will seldom survive.

Hamsters are descended from the wild species of Syria.

The life expectancy of a mouse is about 18 months.

MICE

Pet mice can be bought in many colours and markings. The best home for them is like that described for a hamster, but they will chew through a wooden cage. Dampness is their worst enemy, so keep their cage in a dry place.

Mice are very lively and will use ladders, ropes, tunnels, and exercise wheels. You can keep one mouse on its own, but a small colony is more fun. However, this poses problems as a pair of mice will breed rapidly, and you must be able to dispose of surplus stock regularly as mice do not like to be overcrowded.

Provide your mice with hay or newspaper to make nests. They will eat the pet shop feeds and also small scraps such as stale bread, fruit, vegetables and meat. A little twice a day is best, but remove old food.

When handled, mice should be picked up by the base of the tail and held gently, as in the illustration.

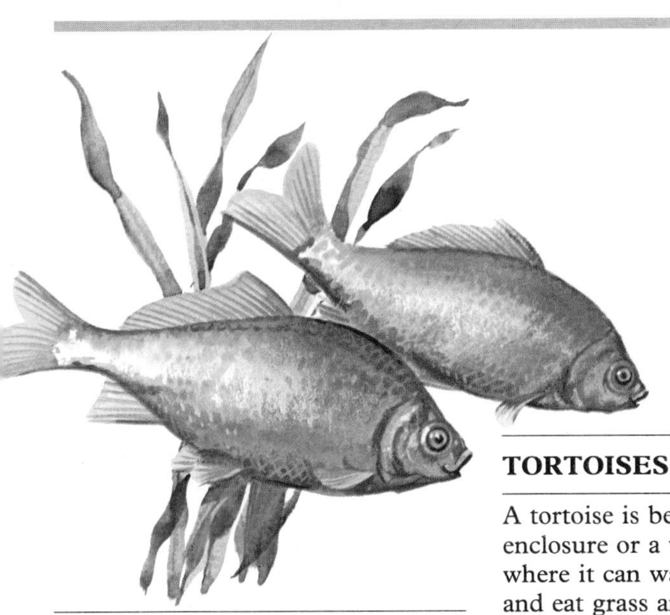

The Common Goldfish is the hardiest and the easiest to keep.

FISH

Fish are most attractive in garden ponds. If it is not possible to build a proper pond, buy one 'ready-made' in glass fibre. Look at other ponds to discover the best ways of using rocks and plants.

Fish can also be kept indoors in a glass tank, which must be kept away from direct sunlight. Goldfish are popular and easiest to keep. The bottom of the tank should be covered with gravel into which plants are inserted, all obtainable from the pet shop. Add a few stones, too. Everything should be thoroughly washed beforehand, and the tank should stand for a few days before the fish are added. A tropical aquarium is set up in the same way, but will need electric heaters, a thermostat, a thermometer, a filtration system and an aerating pump. The pet shop will sell a complete assembly to suit your tank.

TORTOISES

A tortoise is best kept in a secure enclosure or a well-fenced garden where it can wander in the summer and eat grass and plants. It will also enjoy eating soft fruits such as a slice of banana or tomato. It must have water and shade from the sun, and is best brought indoors at night. Feed it well in autumn, to last it through its winter hibernation. Tortoises should be allowed to hibernate in a large wooden box filled with hay or straw, away from frost and draughts. In spring the box can be moved to a warm place, and the tortoise should be allowed to wake up in its own time.

A Radiated Tortoise.

BIRDWATCHING

Birdwatching is a fascinating hobby, as long as you are quiet and patient. You will be amazed at how many species can be seen in a short time just by being observant.

A garden is a good place to start, since the passing birds can be tempted to stay a while if you put food out on a bird table. This can be of the most elementary kind, such as a platform set on top of a pole, upon which can be left bread, bacon rind, nuts, dried fruit, apple cores, etc. A more sophisticated table might have a roof to keep the food dry, and a very low roof will ensure that the smaller birds are untroubled by larger aggressive ones. Untippable water bowls can be added which, if constantly replenished, will attract birds in winter if ponds are frozen. Food can also be suspended from trees in hoppers of plastic-covered wire netting. In winter the food can be mixed in melted beef dripping which, when set hard, can also be suspended. This is popular with birds of the tit family.

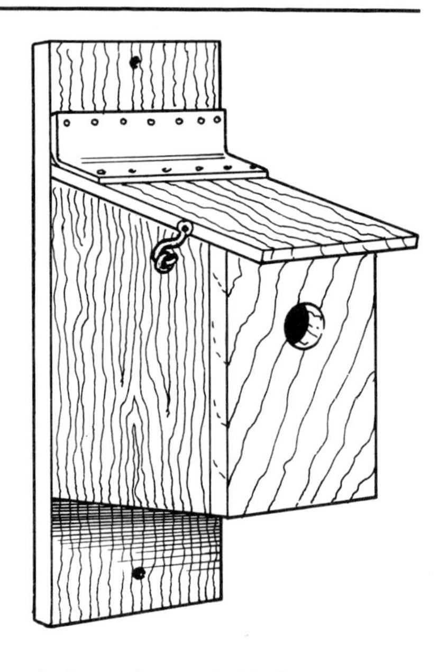

A typical nest box suitable for tits.

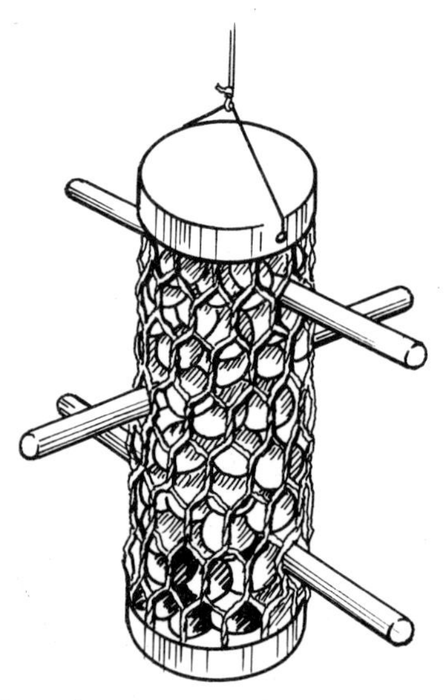

A nut hopper made from plastic-covered netting.

These small birds can also be attracted to the garden to nest if you provide nest boxes hung in trees. These can either be made or bought, and consist of a small wooden box, or sometimes a hollowed-out piece of tree trunk, with access by a small round hole just large enough for a tit to enter.

Finches, robins, sparrows,

blackbirds, wrens, thrushes and pigeons are often common in gardens, but the keen birdwatcher will soon wish to travel further afield to see other species. It is a good idea to buy a field guide to birds and carry it with you. Although you might not be able to find the right reference to a new bird seen while the bird sits conveniently before you, you can at least look the bird up while it is still clear in your mind, and then look for it again.

Many birds are so timid that it is virtually impossible to get close enough to them to identify them with certainty, and a pair of binoculars will bring new species closer.

Birds have favourite habitats, and a walk in woods will reveal many species not found on moorland, for example. Ponds and rivers will contain varieties of ducks, swans, grebes, etc, and if you are patient you might well see a kingfisher or tern diving into the water to find food then flying off with a flapping fish in its beak. At the seaside will be the various gulls and the birds of the sand-flats, such as oyster-catchers.

In many parts of the world there are clubs or societies you can join, such as the Royal Society for the Protection of Birds in Great Britain, and some will have bird sanctuaries you can visit. These might contain 'hides', in which keen naturalists hide to get closer to timid species.

When birdwatching, keep a notebook in which to record the date and place of sightings, and try sketching the birds you see.

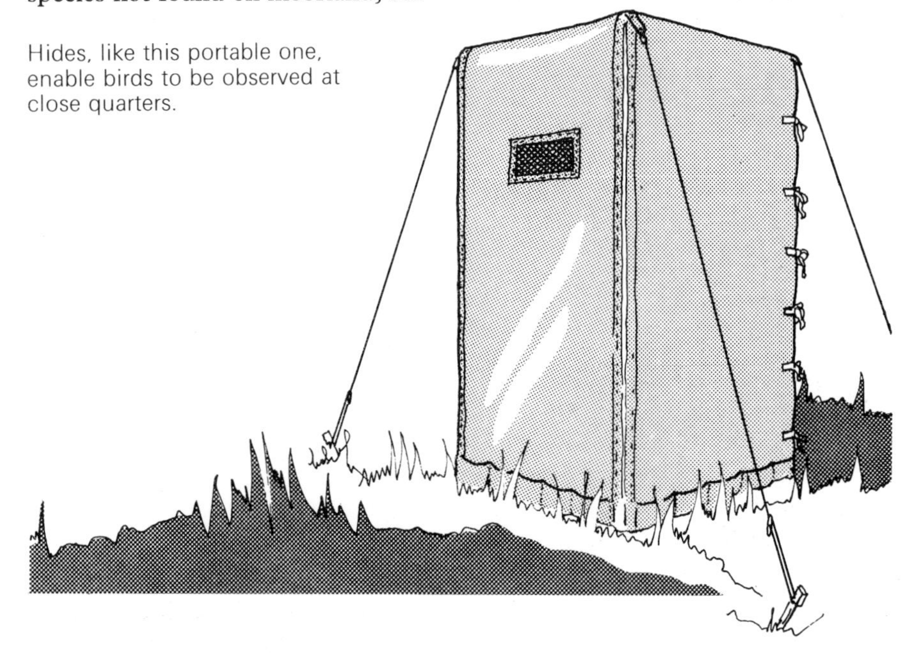

Hides, like this portable one, enable birds to be observed at close quarters.

PHOTOGRAPHY

Photography is a rewarding hobby since not only will it provide the pleasure of making a good picture in its own right, it will also enable you to keep a record of your friends, your holidays, your parties and the places you've visited.

There is more fun to photography than pointing the camera at a scene and 'snapping' away. If you are prepared to pay some attention to such things as light, composition and unusual angles, you will learn to see pictures that others miss, and will produce dramatic and unusual photographs.

While it is usually a good policy to buy the best equipment you can afford, do not worry if your camera must necessarily be of the cheaper kind. Ask youself first what its main use will be. If it is to photograph sports, you will need a fast shutter speed. If you wish to take close-up pictures of small objects, like butterflies, you will want a camera upon which you can fit a close-up lens. Seek advice first from a keen photographer friend, and buy your camera from a good dealer, who should also be willing to discuss your requirements and advise you. Do not be in too much of a hurry – consider all the alternatives carefully.

The illustration below shows the basic camera. The *viewfinder* allows you to see the picture you are

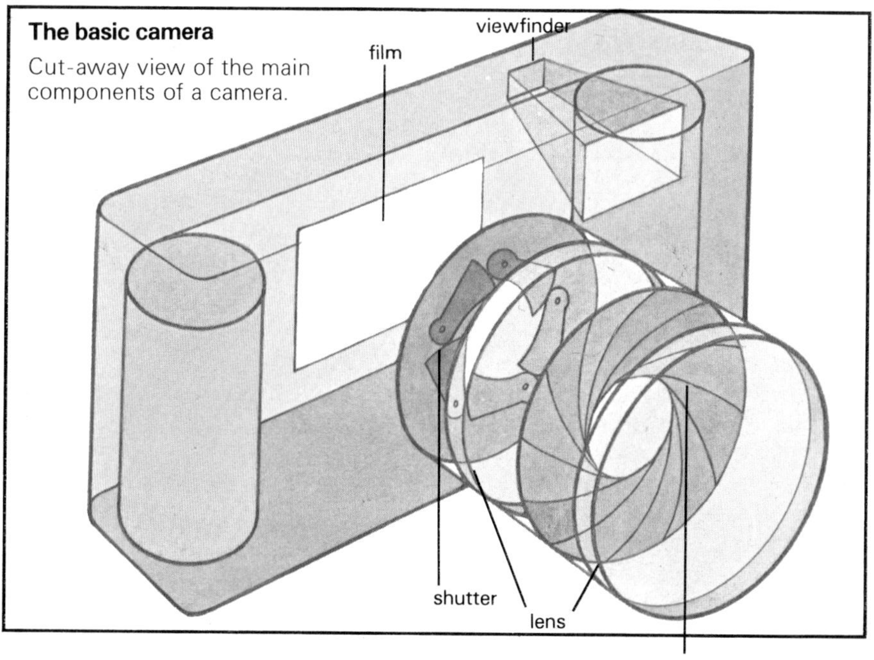

The basic camera

Cut-away view of the main components of a camera.

taking. You will notice that the viewfinder is not behind the lens, and therefore you do not take a picture of exactly what you see through the lens. This is called parallax error, and is only important when taking close-up shots, where the error is naturally greater. More sophisticated cameras get round this problem by means of a reflex viewfinding system. A single lens reflex (shortened to SLR) uses a mirror and prism to show the exact image that will appear on the film. This is probably the best system. A twin lens reflex viewfinder (TLR) uses two lenses, but does not entirely dispense with parallax error.

The *shutter* determines how much light falls on the film, by opening and shutting. On many cameras the speed of the shutter can be varied so that it can be opened for longer on a dull day than on a bright day.

The *lens* 'bends' the light coming into the camera to form the bright clear image on the film.

The *aperture*, like the shutter, regulates the amount of light falling on the film by altering the size of the hole through which the light passes, so that it is larger in dull light and smaller in bright.

Cameras are conveniently classified by the size of the film used. The cheapest ones are the cartridge type, in which the film is in plastic cartridges which are easy to load. The 110 camera produces a negative of 17 × 13 mm (0.6 × 0.5 in), and the 126, a negative of 28 × 28 mm (1.1 × 1.1 in). These cameras are simple to use and suitable for still subjects and views.

Exposure guidelines for ASA 64 film. The higher the ASA rating of a film, the less light it needs to produce a good result. This is a slow film needing a long exposure.

Bright or hazy sun on sand or snow
aperture: *f*16
shutter: 1/125

Bright or hazy sun with distinct shadows
aperture: *f*11
shutter: 1/125

Weak hazy sun with soft shadows
aperture: *f*8
shutter: 1/125

Cloudy but bright with no shadows
aperture: *f*5.6
shutter: 1/125

Cloudy and dull
aperture: *f*4
shutter: 1/125

The 35 mm camera is a little more expensive but is a good all-round camera, producing negatives of 24 × 36 mm (0.9 × 1.4 in). A cheap 35 mm is probably the best for a beginner.

The 120 cameras provide larger negatives of around 6 × 6 cm (2.3 × 2.3 in) and are usually expensive, although a 120 TLR can be reasonably priced.

There are many kinds of instant cameras, most useful if you like to see the result of your work immediately.

Whichever camera you buy, read the instructions carefully and get to know what it will do and how it operates.

Always protect your camera's lens. Never touch it; keep the lens cap on when not in use; and clean it carefully with a lens brush.

The light is the most important element in taking a photograph. With the sun behind you the scene will be well lit with little shadow, but a more solid '3D' effect can be obtained with the light coming from over your shoulder, or even at right angles to the subject. With the sun behind the subject a silhouette effect will be produced.

Think of perspective. Getting low down or high up can alter the impact and interest of a picture. Look for pleasing lines in a street or row of trees, and try the effect of foreground foliage or windows or arches to 'frame' your picture. Interesting patterns, reflections and shadows will make interesting photographs. Look-out for the unusual angle and your photographs will command attention.

Do not think of black and white photographs as 'old-fashioned' and not as good as colour. In some ways it is easier to make a startling black and white photograph. The stark

contrasts of light and shade can be more impressive without the distraction of colours.

Most photographs feature people as their main subjects, and the unthinking ask their subjects to stand in front of the camera face on and smile self-consciously. Better pictures can be obtained by taking subjects in profile or in three-quarter view. Get your subject to do something, like holding a pet, biting an apple, opening a gate. But be careful of making people pose.

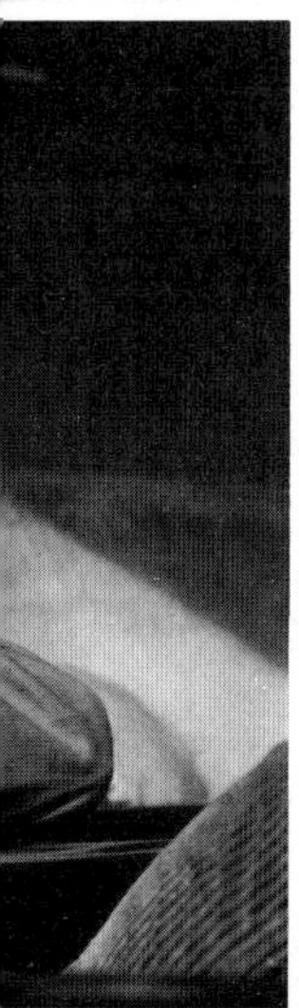

Left: photographs of pets can be more charming when their owners are included. Below left: black and white photographs can produce simple but striking results. Below: the dark background of this informal portrait concentrates attention on the girl.

The best pictures are taken when the subject is unaware, so try to be always ready and unobtrusive for that 'candid' shot – an ordinary typical gesture adds life to a picture.

Make sure the person being photographed is clear. Do not try to get everything in and consequently stand too far from the subject. Move around to eliminate an unattractive background. If the background is important, do not necessarily set your main subject in the centre of the frame – try to compose the background as complementary to the subject.

When photographing a group of people arrange them on different levels. Have some sitting on a wall while others stand, and get them close together. Try the effect of asking them to look at an object to one side of you, or take the picture from one side, so that they are not staring at the camera.

With fast-moving subjects passing in front of you try 'panning' the camera – moving it with the subject so that the subject remains in the viewfinder. Sometimes a blur, either of the subject or the background, adds drama to your picture.

In all your photography, do not be afraid of experiment or mistakes – your increasing successes will amply make up for these.

CYCLING

Cycling can be a sport, a group leisure activity, a hobby, or often just the quickest and cheapest way to get from one place to another. It allows you to see the countryside, it keeps you healthy, and it doesn't pollute the atmosphere with fumes or noise. Small wonder that cycling is enjoying a boom in popularity in many parts of the world.

Bicycles come in a variety of models from fun ones for small children, strange ones with high handlebars for teenagers, small-wheeled ones for compactness and manoeuvrability in towns, folding ones for placing in car boots, streamlined ones for sporting racers and even stationary ones for keeping fit.

Choose the model you buy according to your needs. If you want to tour the land, buy a sturdy touring cycle with a frame designed to carry the weight of the luggage, not a lightweight racing model which will look impressive but not take kindly to bumps and thumps. Don't buy a second-hand bicycle unless you are confident mechanically, or know somebody who will help you. Beware bikes which might have crashed – look for slightly bent forks, wheels which do not run quite true and steering which isn't smooth. And examine the bike for rust, or the tell-tale rough spots under the new paint.

Whether you buy a new or second-hand bike, it is best to go to a reputable dealer who will give you

You should be familiar with the many parts of your bicycle, and check them regularly to make sure they are working properly.

a guarantee with it.

You must make sure the bicycle you buy is the right size for you. A rough way to do this is to measure the seat tube from where the pedals are hung to where the seat enters the frame. This should be 25 cm (10 in) less than your inside leg measurement. Try sitting on the saddle. Both toes should just reach the ground; or, if one foot is on the pedal, the ball of the other foot should rest on the ground. Have a test ride, to see that your heels do not touch the back carrier or lights, and knees and body do not touch the handlebars.

A good basic bike is illustrated on these pages. Things you should watch for when buying or using the

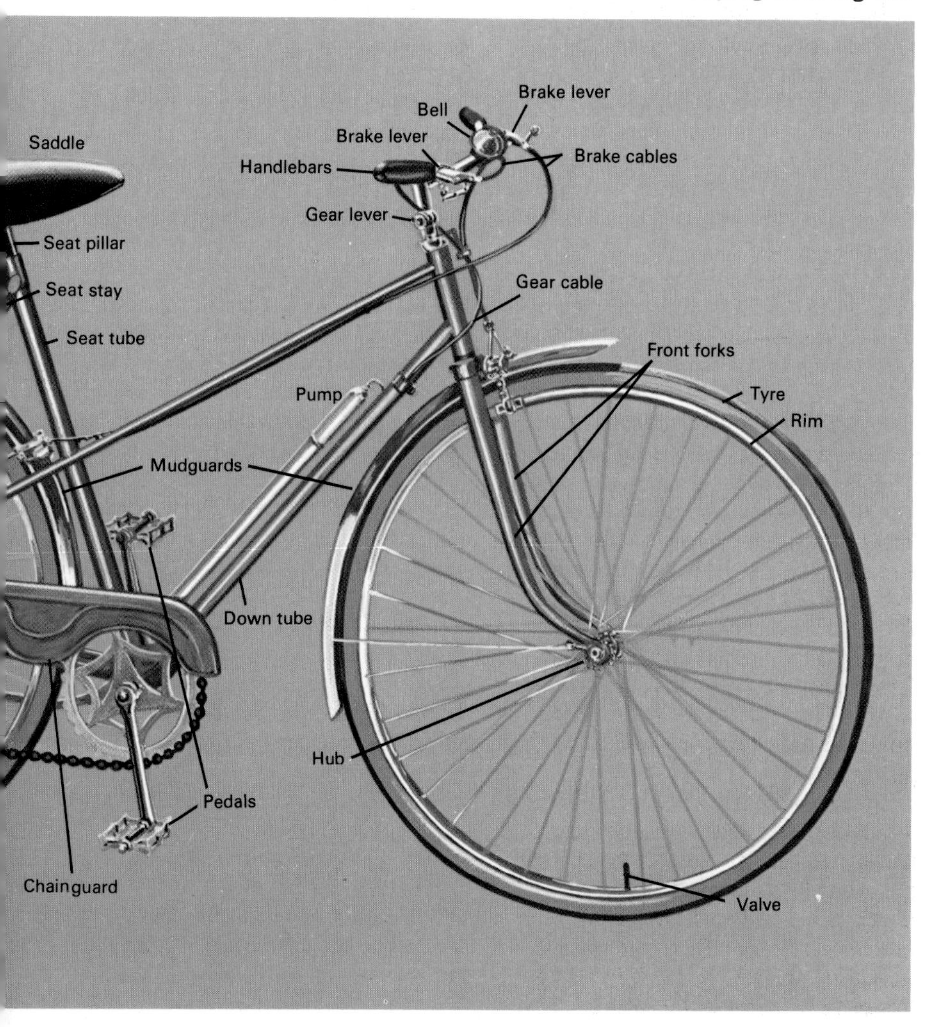

bike are listed here.

Saddle The saddle should be easily adjustable for height and angle. Always make sure that at least 5 cm (2 in) of the seat pillar is within the seat tube.

Handlebars For day-to-day cycling the handlebars should be about level with the saddle. If you do a lot of cycling you might prefer drop handlebars, which give a variety of hand positions while throwing your body further forward.

Brakes Good brakes are essential. Ensure that with your hands on the handlebars you can operate the brakes quickly and easily. Constantly check that the cables are in good condition and tight, and that the blocks at the wheel end connect properly and are not getting worn. Grease the cables where they enter holes and oil the pivot points and brake levers.

Gears A lot of effort is taken out of cycling by gears, which enable the wheels to turn faster than you pedal. Derailleur gears, as shown in the illustration, are common. Make sure the gear lever is tightly fastened, and oil the gear cable at each end.

Chain Oil your chain thoroughly, making sure it is not loose.

Tyres Replace tyres that become worn. Keep the tyres well pumped up and watch out for slow punctures.

The basic rules when maintaining a bicycle are to see that all parts work properly and are clean, that all nuts and bolts are tightened, and that wheels and forks are true (ie not bent). Parts which run on ball bearings, such as pedal spindles and wheel hubs, should be well-greased, and other moving parts oiled, to prevent friction. Oiling can be replaced by the use of a petroleum distillate spray, an easy way to lubricate chains, gears, brakes etc.

Cycling is more fun if you can maintain your bicycle yourself, so watch the mechanic in the shop and learn from friends. A basic tool kit, which will enable you to do the small repair jobs, is set out on the opposite page. Do not attempt anything beyond your scope, however, as a wrongly assembled part could lead to an accident. Should you ever have an accident on your bike, ask a dealer to check the bike over and service it.

If you are a young beginner, you might be able to get on a cycling course. In Great Britain, the Royal Society for the Prevention of Accidents organizes them through schools. Your school or police station will provide details. Before cycling on public roads, you must know the rules of the road, which means learning the highway code, or similar. When you venture out, use common sense and do not ride 'no hands' or two and three abreast in narrow or busy streets.

A keen cyclist will want to spend days out on long trips to see new parts of the countryside. Make sure your gear range is right – you'll need low gears if you're going to climb hills. Your cycle dealer can adjust your gears.

The clothing you wear is important. Even on a hot day you will be glad of something warm when there's a breeze. A sweater can be put on and taken off easily,

(*continued on page 130*)

Basic Tool Kit

Puncture outfit
Small adjustable spanner
'Dumbell' spanner
Screwdriver
Allen keys (if your machine has any allen key fittings).
Tyre levers
Pliers

Choosing your spanners is a matter of common sense. There are several inexpensive multi-purpose spanners which use either British or metric sizes. Pick whichever one suits most of the nuts on your bicycle, and let the adjustable take care of the rest. Similarly, use a medium-sized screwdriver, with a blade thin enough to engage the small screw-heads on, say, your derailleur gear adjusters, yet wide enough to tackle the bigger jobs.

Things to Add

Chain-link rivet-extractor
Spoke key
Large adjustable wrench (useful for headsets)
Phillips screwdriver (if you have any such screws)
Cable cutter

Once you start building up a toolbox, it's quite easy to go on and on, and you'll find yourself building up a stock of useful spares, such as gear and brake cables, spokes and cable casing. It's always worth having an extra toe-strap or two as well. They come in useful for all kinds of purposes, such as holding your cape underneath your saddle, keeping a chain taut if you've removed the rear wheel (strap it to the brake-bridge between the seat stays), or fixing luggage securely to front or rear carriers.

Satisfy yourself that you have the tools to tackle any normal repair job on your bike, and keep them together, in an orderly way. And don't forget you'll also need oil or petroleum distillate spray, plus medium weight grease.

Adjusting brakes

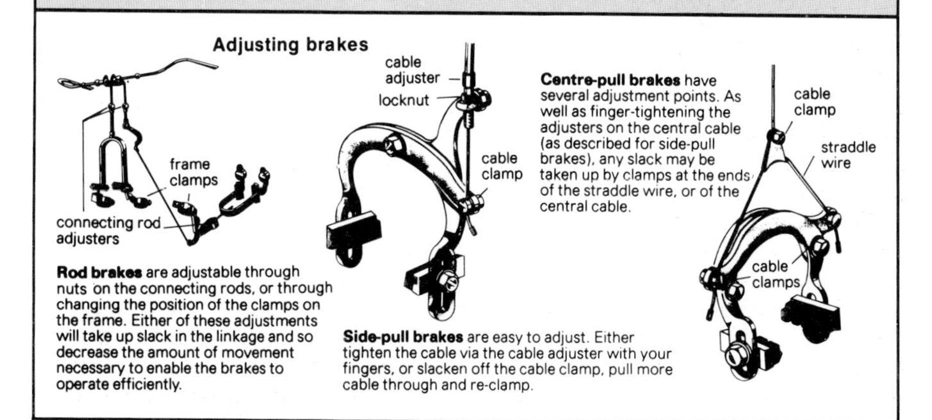

Rod brakes are adjustable through nuts on the connecting rods, or through changing the position of the clamps on the frame. Either of these adjustments will take up slack in the linkage and so decrease the amount of movement necessary to enable the brakes to operate efficiently.

Side-pull brakes are easy to adjust. Either tighten the cable via the cable adjuster with your fingers, or slacken off the cable clamp, pull more cable through and re-clamp.

Centre-pull brakes have several adjustment points. As well as finger-tightening the adjusters on the central cable (as described for side-pull brakes), any slack may be taken up by clamps at the ends of the straddle wire, or of the central cable.

and a light windproof jacket is also useful to carry. Otherwise clothes must be comfortable, especially where you sit down – shorts should be of thick material and not liable to ruck up round the saddle and make your legs sore. Cycling trousers are convenient. Ordinary trousers or slacks must give you the room to pedal comfortably without tightening at the knee, and of course, you must wear cycle clips to keep them from flapping into the chain. You will also need protection against the rain – either a rain suit or a cape.

What you take with you will depend on how long your trip will be. Camping holidays by bicycle are fun, in which case you will need all the gear associated with camping. For a day trip you will need a small tool kit, puncture repair kit, food and drink, spare lamp batteries, pump, cycle lock, small first-aid kit, waterproofs, perhaps a camera, maps, etc. This might seem a lot, but it can all be carried in a saddle-bag on the rear carrier of your bike.

You will probably do much of your cycling with friends. It can be fun to join a cycling club, which will go for 'club runs', in which a group of cyclists go off on a trip. In a well-organized run the group will set off in pairs, taking turns to lead. Riding in a group reduces wind-resistance, and you get 'pulled along'. And of course a cycling club will provide willing helpers and advisers on any problems. You can often learn more about cycling by talking to experienced cyclists than you can from years of cycling yourself.

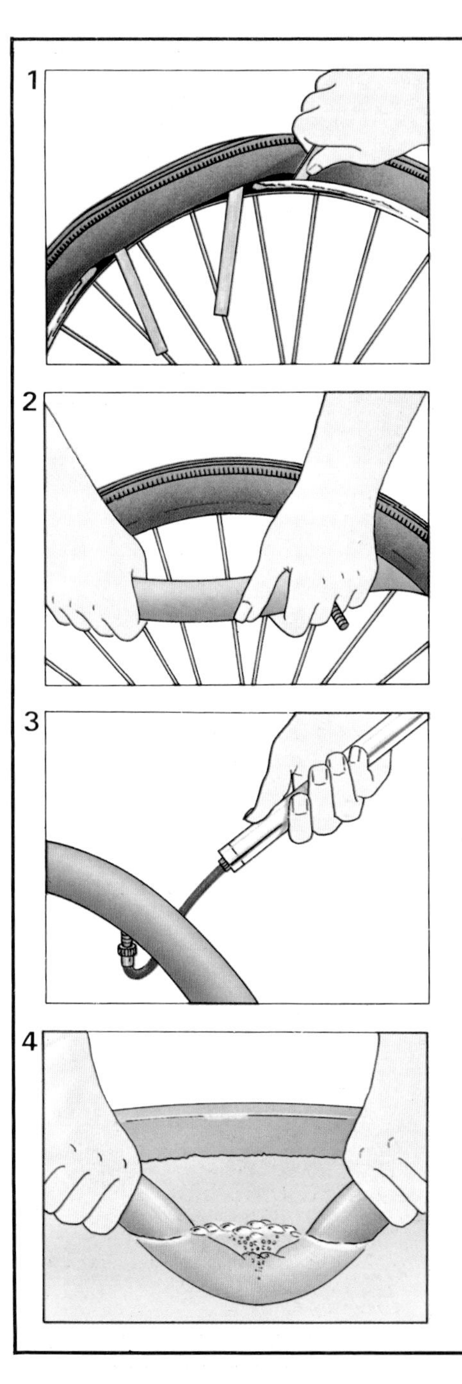

5

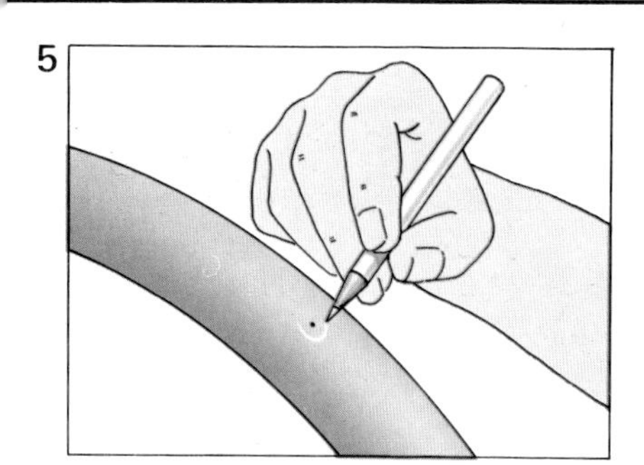

6

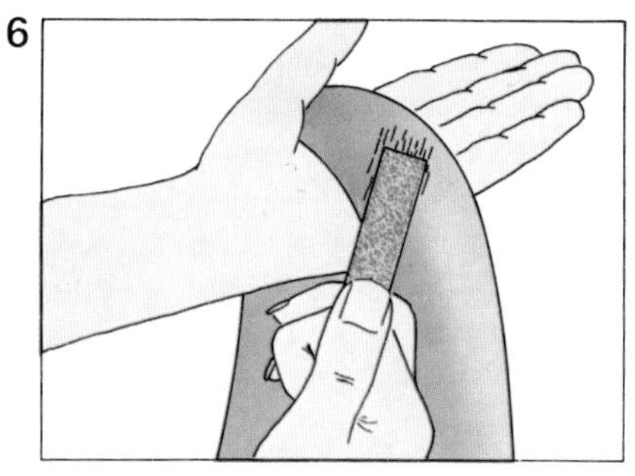

7

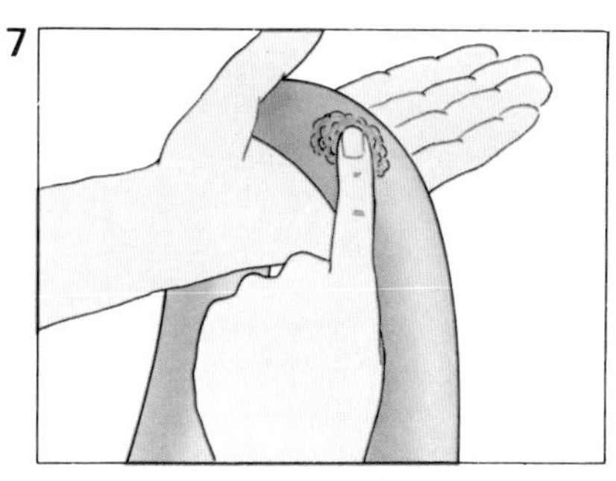

8

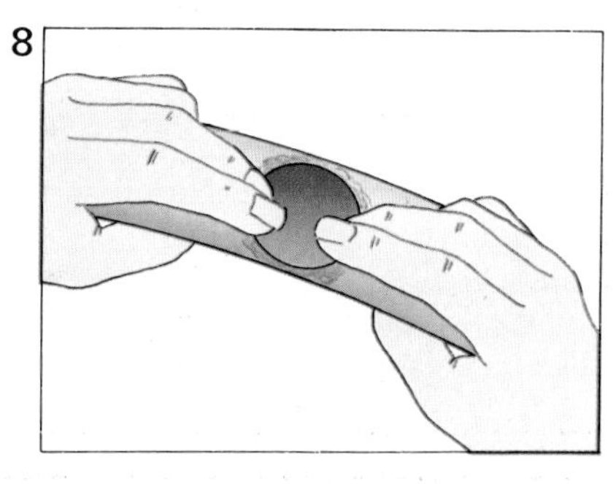

9

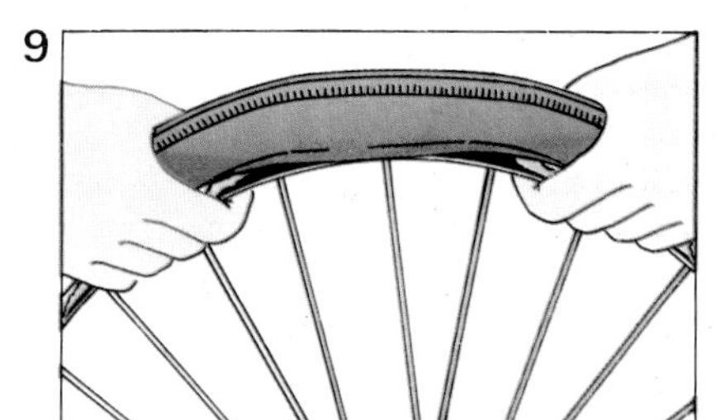

Mending a Puncture

1. Use tyre levers to get the rim of the tyre free of the wheel, being careful not to pinch the inner tube.

2. Remove the section of the tube where the puncture is, and try to find the cause.

3. If you can't find the puncture, remove the tube completely and inflate it.

4. Then put the tube in water – escaping bubbles will soon indicate the puncture.

5. Once the puncture has been found, mark it with biro.

6. Dry the area around the puncture and roughen it with a fine abrasive paper.

7. Spread rubber solution on the tube and wait for it to become 'tacky'.

8. Put the patch on the rubber solution and hold it there firmly for a minute or two. Dust the patched area with chalk to remove any stickiness. Slightly inflate the tube.

9. Push the tube back inside the tyre and replace the tyre inside the rim of the wheel. Don't use tyre levers, but, using a firm grip, roll the tyre back on to the rim. Pump up the tyre.

CAMPING

Camping is adventurous, healthy, inexpensive as a form of holiday and can also be character-building, as it teaches self-reliance and the art of sometimes making the best of difficult circumstances!

In countries with a mild climate, like Great Britain, Australia and New Zealand, it is possible to camp all the year round. However, make your first expedition when the weather forecast is good. If possible, it is best to start by camping with experienced friends, and learning from their experience. Many people acquire their taste for camping, and their skills, through the scout and guide movements.

There are two main types of camping. One involves holiday camping on an established site, controlled by a local authority which provides some facilities including water, toilets, perhaps electricity, a site shop, meal facilities and even forms of entertainment.

Personal camping provides more satisfaction. You might want to combine camping with cycling – otherwise you will have to carry your gear on foot or on public transport (unless a parental car will take you to your site and collect you). Because of this, lightweight kit is essential.

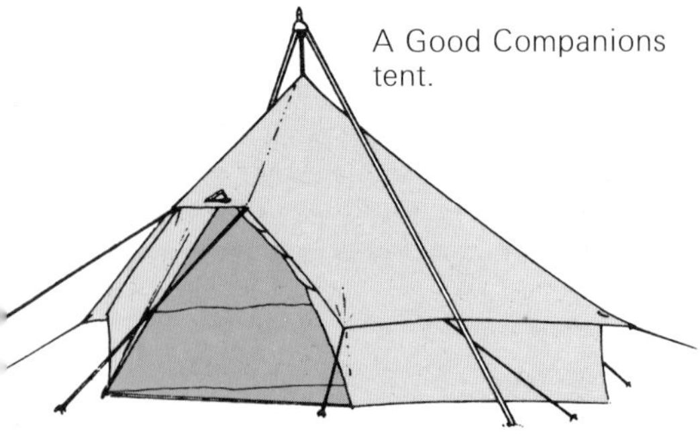

A Good Companions tent.

The tent is the most important basic equipment. Some easily erected, well-tried designs are pictured on these pages, but you will be able to collect some catalogues from shops to help you choose. Buy the best tent you can afford – it will, after all, be your 'home' for a while, and should last you a long time.

You will need a groundsheet, though some tents have them sewn in. Your personal groundsheet should be light, very waterproof, and strong, with taped edges and strong eyelets. The standard junior size is 183 × 76 cm (72 × 30 in), and is made of PVC, oiled cotton or nylon. You will also need a sleeping bag. You can buy convertible bags which zip down one side and can be used as a quilt at other times. A sheet lining bag is essential, and cuts down laundering costs. If you can make do without a pillow you will have less to carry. A mat between sleeping bag and groundsheet provides insulation and comfort.

When you have acquired these items you can test them and your skills on a convenient garden lawn or field. 'Pitch' and 'strike' the tent until you are confident you can handle it easily; spend a night or

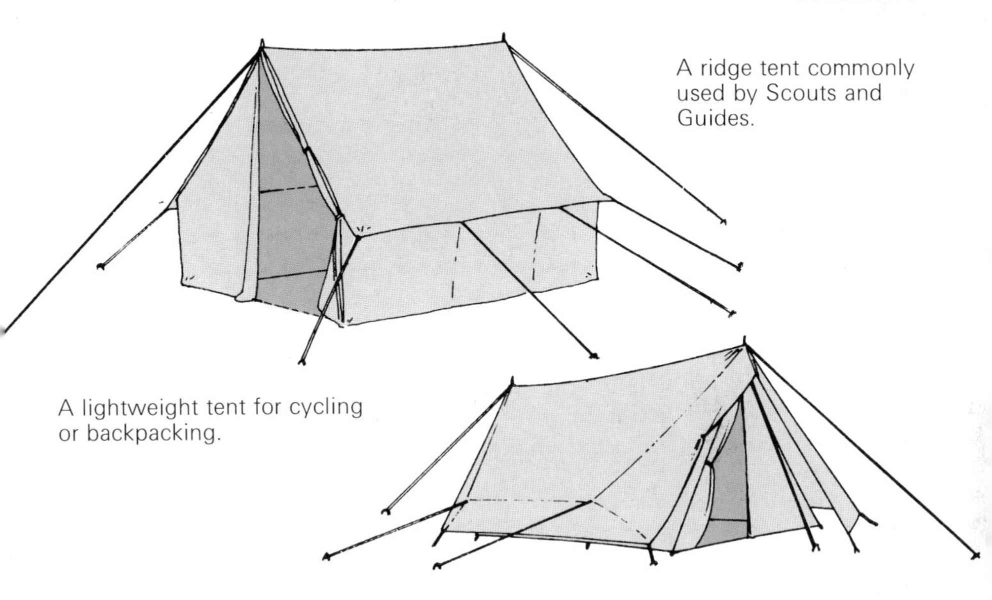

A ridge tent commonly used by Scouts and Guides.

A lightweight tent for cycling or backpacking.

two in the tent; and turn the hose on it to discover any snags which rain might bring.

Your next concern will be with food and drink. Drinking water does not come from taps in the open countryside, and you'll need some containers to collect, carry and store water in. Water containers which collapse and fold are helpful, and these can be obtained in canvas or soft plastic.

For cooking, you will find a conventional primus stove, burning paraffin, or a gas cartridge stove the most convenient method. Make sure you have spares, such as cartridges, meths for priming, a spanner and, of course, matches, preferably in a waterproof box.

You will need a kettle and pots and pans – again lightweight. Food containers are best made of plastic, which is light and washable. Don't forget a mug and plates (plastic or enamel), knife, fork, spoons of varying sizes – and that essential, a tin opener. It is a good idea to carry some basic food such as chocolate, biscuits etc., for emergencies.

A range of sleeping and cooking equipment is shown on pages 134–5. It looks a daunting amount to carry, but don't forget camping is often a communal activity, and the cooking gear can be shared out.

Another thing you will need is a change of clothes: socks, shorts, underwear, tee-shirt, long-sleeved pullover, an anorak or lightweight rainwear, and light footwear such as plimsolls. Then there will be toilet requisites – a towel, soap, toothbrush etc. You might think a map and compass worth taking, and you will need a torch with its spares and your personal gear such as wallet, purse, notebook and pencil, perhaps a camera and spare film.

Assuming you are not going into dangerous terrain, such as mountains, you should not need an emergency survival kit, but you should always carry a first-aid kit. A plastic box or toilet bag containing plasters, lint, cream for cuts and burns, bandages, water-purifying tablets, safety pins and scissors forms a basic kit.

The rucksack in which you carry all this is a vitally important part of your kit, and you should take great care in choosing it.

A rucksack should be large, light and strong, with an aluminium frame. It is carried high on the shoulders at the back, so try different sizes in the shop when buying to ensure it is right for you and is comfortable. It is best to get one made of nylon, divided into compartments for keeping dry and wet articles and clean and dirty clothing separate. It will have plenty of side pockets for things you want to get at quickly, like your map.

When all your kit is assembled, mark each piece of equipment with indelible ink to prevent theft. It is a good idea to insure it against loss, too.

Always look after your camping gear carefully. You will often have to transport wet things, and polythene bags are useful for this. Make sure everything is dried out thoroughly when you get home, particularly the tent, which is dry when the seams are dry, not merely the fabric. Tents folded and stored damp will become ruined by mildew. Brush mud off when dry. Clean all the cooking gear and tent pegs etc, make repairs immediately, and clear dust and grit from your rucksack. It is a good idea to inspect your camping kit every few weeks when not in use, and to use the stove indoors occasionally to keep it in good order.

Mobile camping is becoming popular, in which campers follow a route and move on from place to place each day. It is sometimes called 'backpacking' and is a cross between camping and hiking. It is

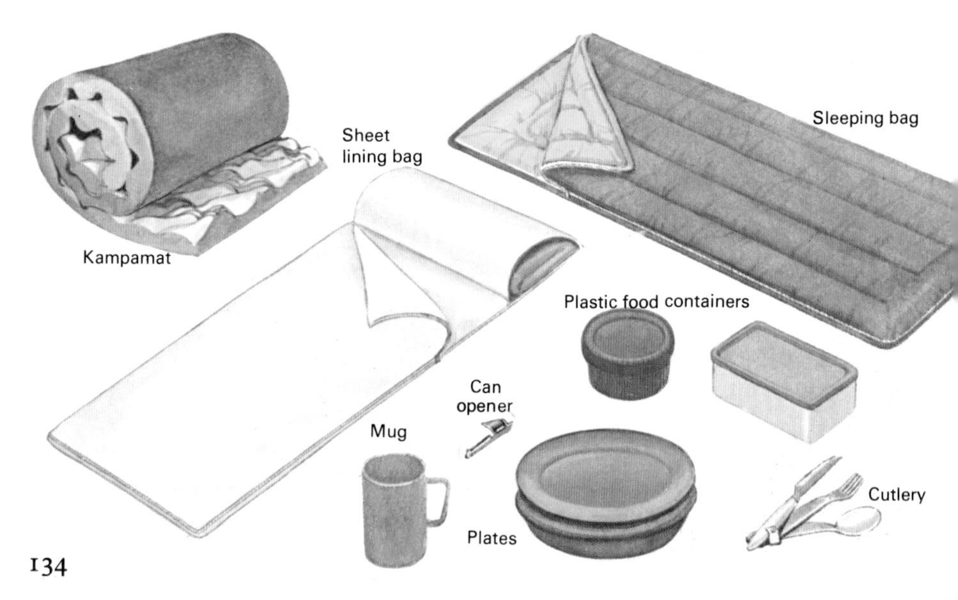

an excellent way to explore a region, and of course the lightness of the equipment becomes even more essential.

Campers soon get to know what to avoid. Do not pitch your tent below trees, where it will get fouled by birds or drips from leaves. Don't wear shoes in the tent. Do not touch the sides in rain, or it will come through (a flysheet will prevent this if you can afford one). Cook near the tent, but not in it. Be careful of fires and burns when cooking. Keep everything clean and tidy.

Lastly, if you are not on an organized site, always obtain the permission of the farmer or landowner to camp. A farmer who will supply milk and eggs is a good friend. And always clear up and respect the land. The aim with all camping and camp cooking should be to see that the site used is disturbed as little as possible and left exactly as nature intended.

FISHING

Angling can provide considerable satisfaction, and in some parts of the world it is the most popular leisure activity. Skill is acquired gradually and even the oldest anglers learn all the time.

There are different forms of angling: sea fishing from shore or boat, fly fishing for salmon and trout, and coarse fishing. Coarse fish are those which live in freshwater, excluding salmon and trout. Wherever you live, there is likely to be freshwater nearby, in a river, stream, canal, pond or gravel pit. Probably the best place for a beginner to start is in a small pond or lake.

Two basic methods are used to catch coarse fish. One is float fishing, with the bait suspended in the water from a float. The other is legering with the bait resting on the river bed, and sometimes trailed. Float fishing is the most popular and convenient for a newcomer.

Rods are either tip action, which allows a rapid strike when the fish takes the bait, or through action (*see* illustration opposite). A glass-fibre through-action rod about 3.5 m long (11 to 12 ft), which can also be used for light legering, makes a good first buy. It will probably be in three pieces which fit together, and is supplied in a rod bag. The typical rod has a cork handle, with rings to carry the line and reel fittings.

Reels to hold the line come in various types (*see* page 139). The fixed spool reel is cheap and the best for the beginner. Closed face reels are similar but the spool is enclosed and has a press button operation. The centre-pin reel gives close contact with the fish when fishing from boats, but is difficult for beginners, and the multiplying reel is for quick retrieval.

Lines are of nylon, and of various breaking strains to suit the strength of the fish being sought. A beginner should use one of about 1 to 2 kg (2 to 5 lb) breaking strain. Fixed spool reels have either a shallow drum, designed for lines up to 1.5 kg (3 lb) breaking strain, or a deep drum. Your line can be wound directly on to a shallow spool, but a deep one will need building up first with circulating tape or string. When correctly filled the line should be about 2 mm (0.3 in) from the rim.

Floats suspend the bait and indicate a bite. They come in many shapes and sizes to suit water and conditions. For a selection of the most popular ones *see* page 138. A beginner should have a small basic set and, at first, use the type of float that other anglers on the water are using. Experience will teach you the characteristics of each. You might need split lead shot between the float and hook, particularly in running water, and this is supplied in various sizes. The line fits into the split and the shot is gently squeezed on.

Hooks, too, come in various numbered sizes, from 1 to 20, 1 being the largest. They have either

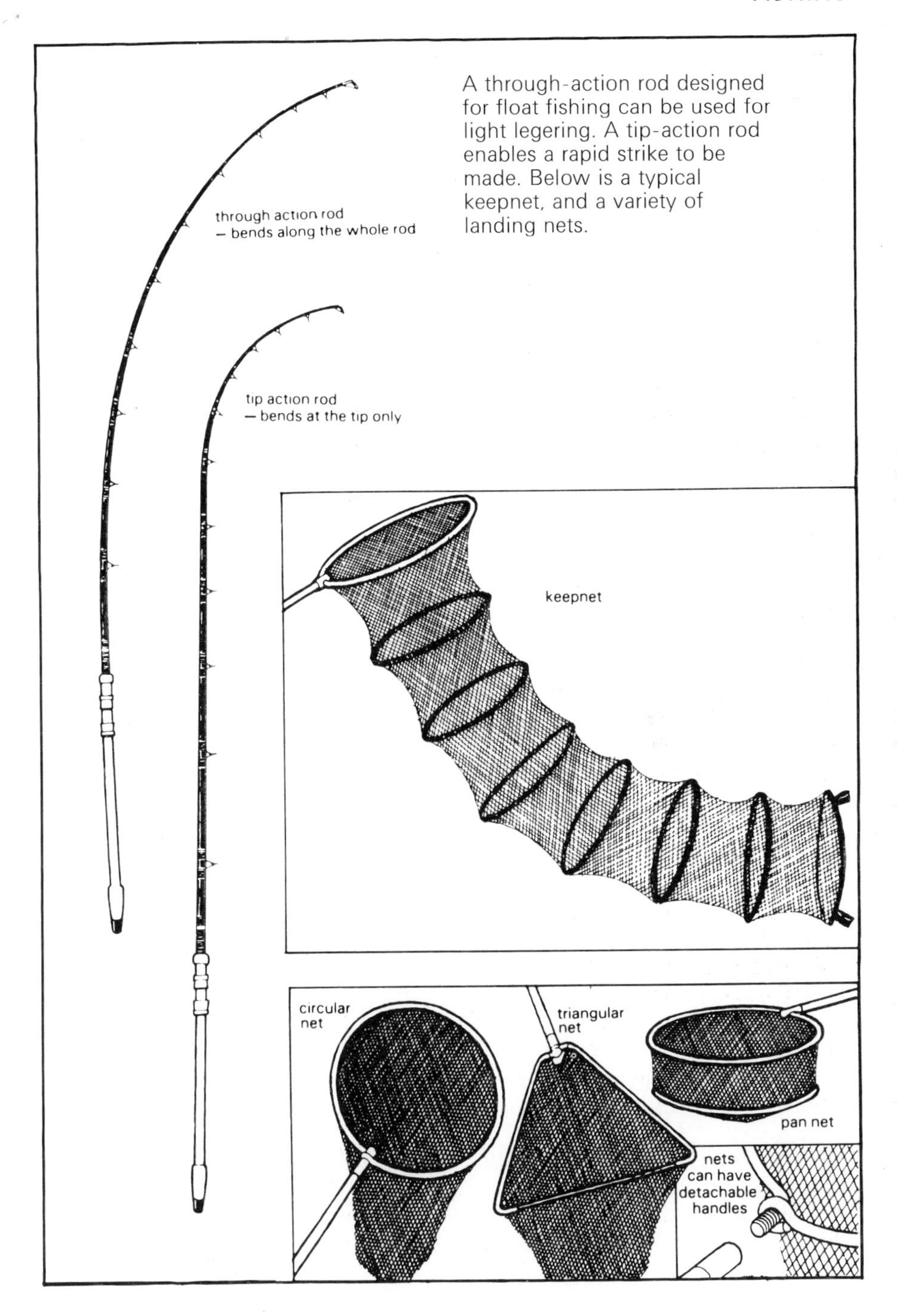
A through-action rod designed for float fishing can be used for light legering. A tip-action rod enables a rapid strike to be made. Below is a typical keepnet, and a variety of landing nets.
through action rod
– bends along the whole rod
tip action rod
– bends at the tip only
keepnet
circular net
triangular net
pan net
nets can have detachable handles

Tying line to a spade-ended hook.

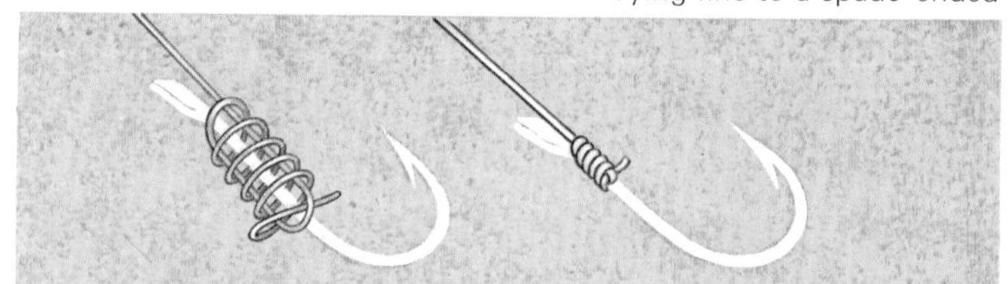

spade or eyed ends to receive the line. The method of tying line to a spade-end is shown above.

Other equipment you will find useful includes a large fishing umbrella, a disgorger or forceps for removing hooks, and, for a long day, a rod rest. You will also want nets to land your larger fish, preferably one without knots because these damage the scales and fins. And if you want to keep your catch to the end of the day you'll need a keepnet. For illustrations of different types of net, *see* page 137. You will also need a chair. Some anglers prefer a folding chair, and carry their equipment in a rucksack. But fishing baskets which carry tackle and double as a seat are very popular. A rod holdall which will carry your umbrella and net handles as well as your rod is also useful.

Now you are equipped, you must learn to cast. Hold the rod handle in your right hand (assuming you are right-handed) just above the reel; pull back the bale arm and trap the

An assortment of floats.

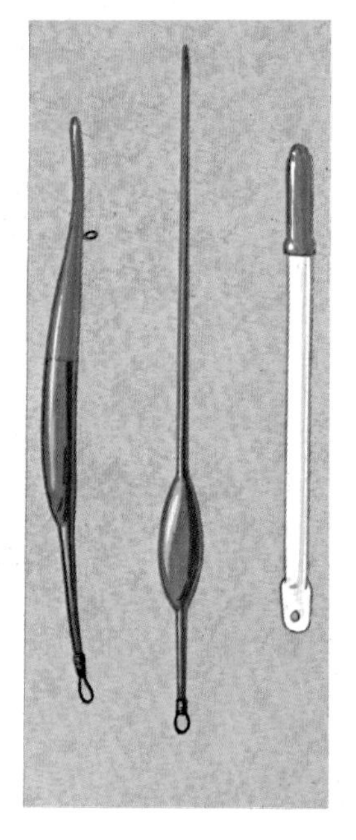

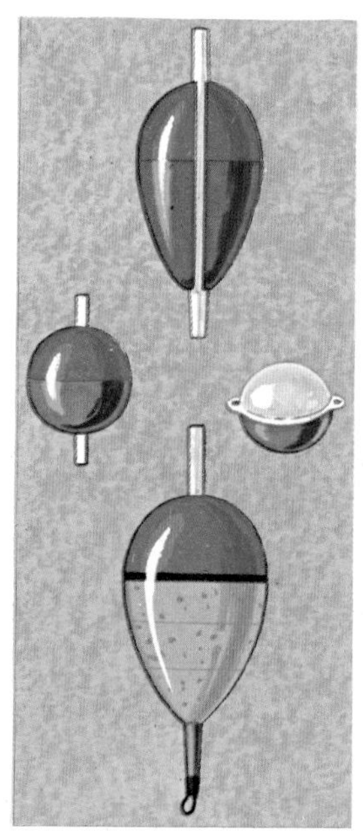

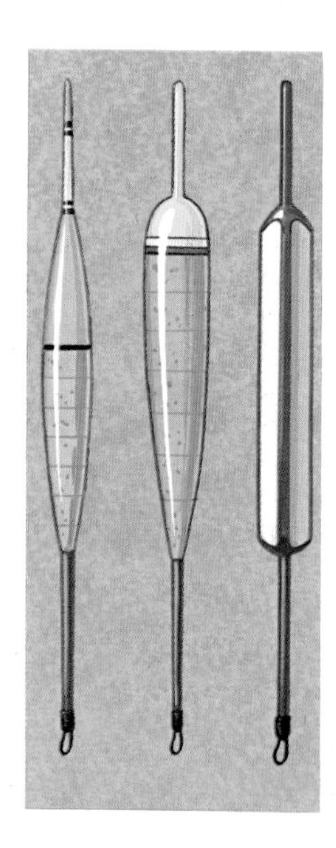

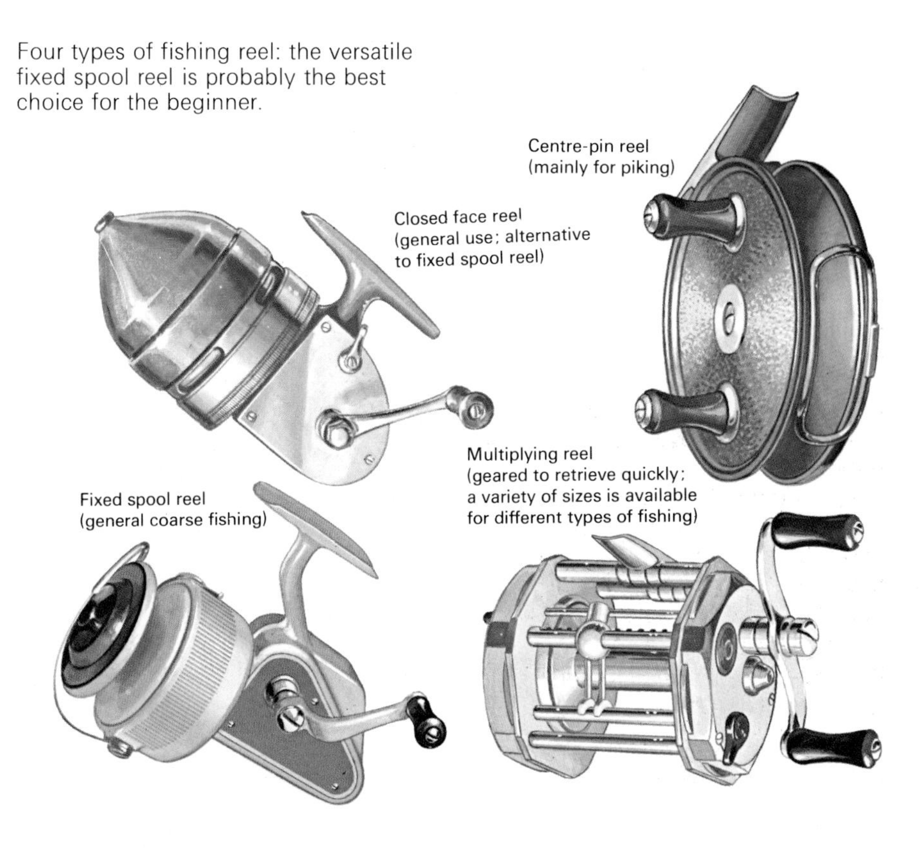

Four types of fishing reel: the versatile fixed spool reel is probably the best choice for the beginner.

line against the spool with your forefinger, holding the end of the rod with your other hand. Take the rod back over your right shoulder and then push forward with your right hand, bringing the rod handle back towards you with your left hand. Release the line from your finger at the moment the rod is vertical. With practice, you will get the line moving smoothly over the water. When the tackle lands, trap the line against the reel spool as before.

Hooks can be baited with maggots, worms, bread, cheese and almost anything edible. See what other anglers who know your patch of water are using. Be careful when unhooking the fish, gently easing the hook from the mouth. Handle larger fish with one hand behind the gill cover and the other just below the tail. Lower them gently into the keepnet and don't place them on the bank. When returning them to the water use care not to damage them.

Lastly, do not leave litter around, particularly line. Anglers are often accused of causing agonizing death to wild life, especially birds, who swallow hooked bait or get tangled in lines. Always leave the bank exactly as you found it.

HORSE-RIDING

Riding well requires a lot of hard work and practice. And looking after a horse or pony is even harder work. You must learn how to make a pony do what you want, keep it clean, well-fed, well-housed, well-groomed and happy. On top of this you must know how to spot when it is not well, and look after its tack. Nevertheless, horse riding can be great fun and very rewarding.

The best way to learn to ride is to take lessons at a good riding school. Before you start, try to become familiar with the points of a horse and get to know all the tack. You will hear the expression 'aids', which are the conventional signals given by the rider to the pony and which young ponies are schooled to obey. The natural aids are the voice, hands, the legs and seat. The legs and seat create impulsion or energy, the hands control the reins and regulate the energy and speed, and guide the pony, and the voice gives commands. Artificial aids are the stick or whip, spurs and so on.

You will need correct clothes for riding. A hard hat is absolutely essential. Even experts fall off sometimes! Your hat should fit well and not fall off when you bend over, and must have a safety strap. A glass fibre hat with a separate moulded peak is best. You will also need proper jodhpur boots in leather or rubber, or strong shoes with a medium high heel.

Tack is the name given to the equipment worn by a horse or pony. It is important that it all fits properly. The saddle is held across the pony's back by a girth, made of leather, webbing or nylon. It is tightened to hold the saddle firmly in place for mounting, and will require further adjustment when the rider is seated. Stirrups are held by leathers slotted into the stirrup bars. The bridle, complete with reins, supports the bit. This fits into the horse's mouth, and will cause pain unless properly fitted.

All tack must be kept clean, which means unbuckling it and cleaning each part separately. Apply saddle soap to clean and preserve all leather parts, and wash all metal parts in warm water.

A pony needs regular grooming to ensure its cleanliness and health, as well as to improve its appearance. For this, you use a grooming kit. A dandy brush will remove dirt, dust and caked mud from the coat, but do not be too vigorous when the coat is thin. A body brush will stimulate the circulation and take dust from the coat. A rubber curry comb is for removing loose hairs and sweat when the winter coat is being shed. A sponge is used to clean eyes, nostrils, sheath and dock. A hay wisp is for massaging and finishing the coat, while a stable rubber is for polishing it. A hoof pick is used for cleaning out the feet, and hoof oil and a brush are used for the final polish. The mane and tail can be brushed out with the

(continued on page 142)

The Points of a Horse

1 Forelock
2 Cheek Bone
3 Nostril
4 Chin Groove
5 Throat
6 Jugular Groove
7 Shoulder
8 Breast
9 Elbow
10 Knee
11 Cannon Bone
12 Coronet
13 Heel
14 Pastern
15 Chestnut
16 Girth
17 Chest
18 Abdomen
19 Sheath
20 Shannon
21 Fetlock
22 Hoof
23 Hollow of Heel
24 Hock
25 Gaskin
26 Stifle
27 Buttock
28 Dock
29 Thigh
30 Croup
31 Haunch
32 Flank
33 Loins
34 Back
35 Ribs
36 Withers
37 Mane
38 Crest
39 Axis
40 Atlas

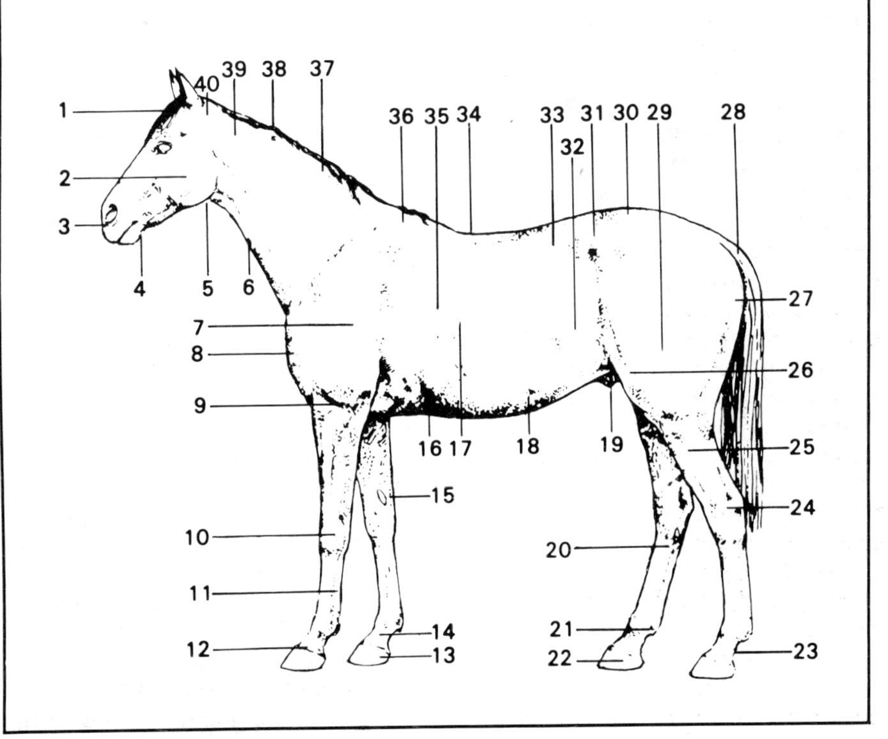

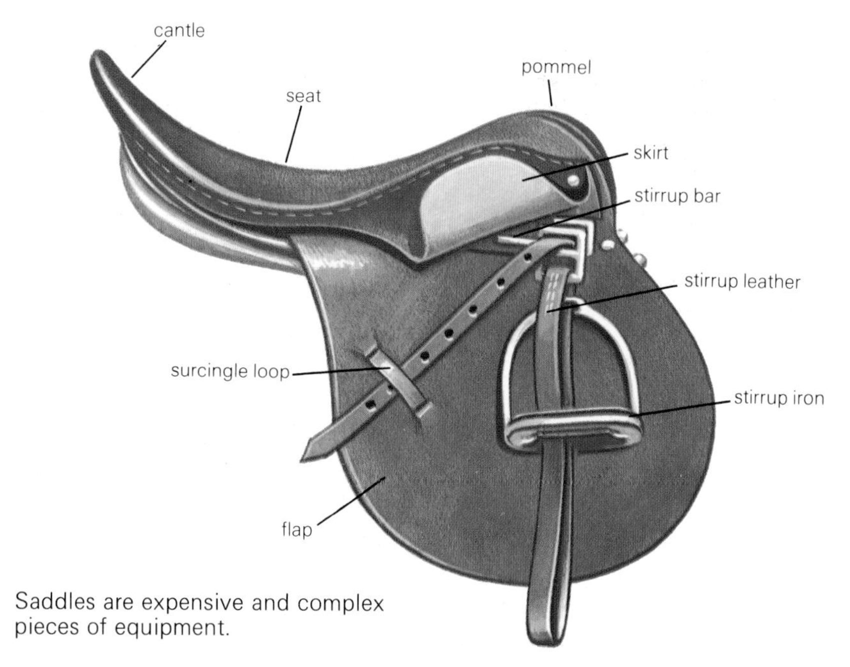

Saddles are expensive and complex pieces of equipment.

body brush. It is best not to use a comb as this breaks the hair.

If you are lucky enough to be allowed your own pony, size is the first consideration when choosing it. When mounted, your feet should hang just above the girth (*see* the points of a horse on page 141). However, you will grow, so a pony slightly too big for you is not a bad buy. On the other hand, it would be foolish to buy one a little too small. It is worth noting that a *horse* is over 14.2 hands high; a *pony*, which is merely a small 'horse', is up to 14.2 hands high.

There are many breeds of pony, some of which, such as Welsh Mountain ponies, are better for all-round riding than others. Most ponies used for general riding purposes are crossbred.

The colour and looks of a pony are of secondary importance to its temperament. It must be even-tempered, sound in body, good in traffic, willing to jump small obstacles, and have no bad habits. If a pony is to be used by the whole family, it must be strong enough for the adults and docile enough for the youngest child.

A pony is best bought from friends or neighbours, who are selling it perhaps because its rider has outgrown it. Otherwise the classified advertisements in specialist horse and riding magazines offer a range for sale. Reputable dealers advertise there too. Avoid markets or horse fairs, and always seek the advice of a knowledgeable friend who can accompany you when looking at a prospective buy.

Once you have your pony, it may

be kept in a stable or kept outside all the year round. A single pony needs about one hectare ($2\frac{1}{2}$ acres) of grazing. Should yours be grass-kept, it will need supplementary feeding in the winter. Good quality hay is necessary with an occasional bran mash in the coldest weather. In the spring it will over-eat, and must be given plenty of exercise.

A pony kept in a field should have a shelter against bad weather. A three-sided shed at the side of the field with its opening protected from the wind is ideal, but the pony should never be tied up or confined in it. The floor should be concrete,

Points to check for a well-fitting bridle.

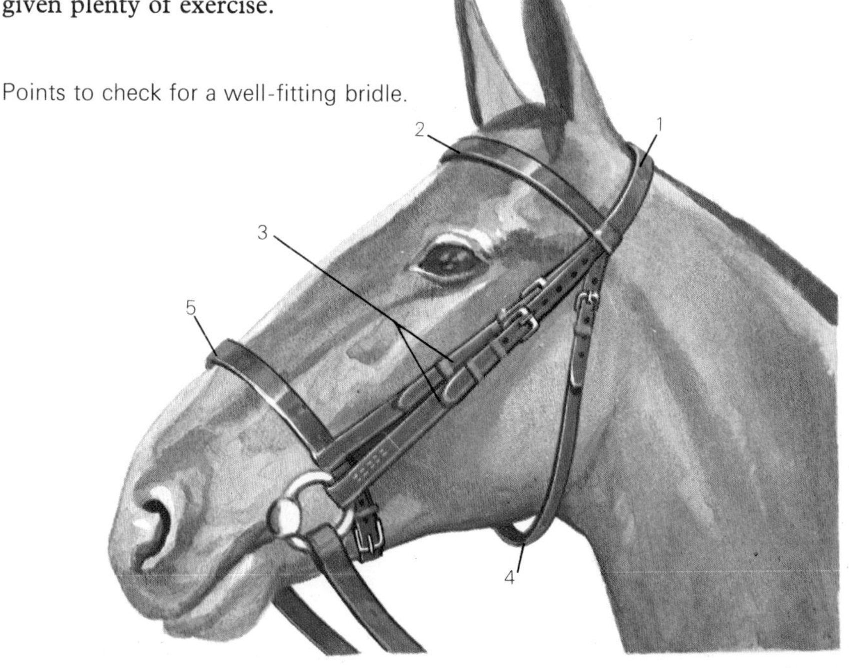

1 The headpiece must not rub the back of the ears.
2 The browband must not fit so tightly that it pulls the headpiece too far forward; on the other hand, neither should it hang too loosely downward.
3 The cheek pieces should hold the bit at the correct height.
4 The throatlatch should buckle up but there should be enough room to allow a clenched fist to be inserted between it and the pony's throat.
5 You should be able to insert two fingers between the pony's nose and the noseband when it is fastened.
6 No buckles when fastened should press on any protruding bones of the pony's head.
7 No buckles should touch.
8 The general appearance of the bridle should be neat and comfortable.

and extend outside the opening to prevent mud getting in. Above all, the shed must not get damp. Ponies like company so do not leave yours alone for too long.

Fresh water must be available all the time. Piped water into a trough or galvanized tank with a ballcock is best, but if you have to take water to the pony's trough you must empty the trough each day and fill it with fresh water. The trough should be thoroughly scrubbed with a stiff brush every three months. Old buckets and baths of water are not a good idea, and stagnant water is very dangerous.

Inspect the pony's field regularly for poisonous plants, and learn to recognize the dangerous ones – including yew, laburnum, ragwort, foxglove, bryony, hemlock, rhododendron, deadly nightshade, privet, laurel, box and lupin. It is no good picking the plants – you must dig up the roots and burn them.

Check the fences. The best types of fencing for fields for ponies are hedges or post-and-rail fences. Posts with tight wire strands are suitable, but barbed wire should be avoided. Remove all rubbish which people have thrown into the field. This applies to grass cuttings, which can be dangerous if a pony eats them.

Many of the points mentioned above can also be applied to horses kept in stables. The ideal stable for a pony is a loosebox, from 3 × 3 m

Grooming

Grooming ensures cleanliness, improves appearance, promotes health, maintains condition and helps prevent disease.

Grooming kit:
Dandy brush – for removing heavy dirt, caked mud and dust from the coat. Should only be used very lightly on clipped ponies, or in summer when their coats are thin.
Body brush – takes out scruff and dust from the coat, mane and tail; stimulates the circulation.
Curry comb – there are two kinds: a metal and a rubber one. The metal one is used only for cleaning the body brush. The rubber curry comb is useful for removing dried mud, loose hairs and sweat, when the pony is shedding his winter coat.
Water brush – used damp on the mane, tail and feet.
Sponge – for cleaning eyes, nostrils, sheath and dock.
Hay wisp – for massage, finishing the coat and toning the muscles.
Stable rubber – for a final polish to the coat.
Hoof pick – to clean out the feet.
Mane comb – for pulling the mane and tail.
Hoof oil and brush – for the final touches to a pony's feet.
Holder – some easily-carried container to hold all the above.

Besides the grooming kit, you will need a bucket for water.

	Healthy pony	Sick pony
Head	Raised	Lowered
Eyes	Clear and bright	Dull and listless
Ears	Pricked, alert	Drooping or back
Breathing	Normal (12–13 breaths a minute at rest)	Irregular, heavy, flanks may heave
Coat	Close-lying, glossy	Staring and dull
Skin	Loose and flexible	Tight and hard
Appetite	Normal	May refuse all food
General appearance	Takes an alert interest in surroundings	Looks dejected, probably resting a leg

Use this list to detect any sign of illness in your pony.

(10 × 10 ft) to 4.5 m × 3.5 m (14 × 12 ft) according to the size of pony or horse.

Bedding should be straw, clean shavings or peat moss. It must be forked over each day, the dirty material removed and fresh bedding added. The whole loosebox must be thoroughly cleaned out in the spring. Cleanliness is important for the pony's health.

The stabled pony must be fed little and often at regular intervals through the day. Hay provides bulk as well as nutrition, and can be bought from farms. If you feed special proprietary cubes, make sure you get the right type for your pony. Fresh water should always be available.

Allow the stabled pony a little grazing each day, but do not work him after a feed. Do not change the pony's diet suddenly, and take advice before offering him any new food.

It will be necessary for you to detect if your pony is unwell. A check list is above. If your pony shows some of the symptoms of being sick, ask a vet to look at him without delay.

When you are a reasonably competent rider, you might like to go on a riding or trekking holiday. These are listed each year in the specialist magazines, and are a good way to learn more about riding and horsemanship.

Whether you ride at a riding school or have your own pony, make friends with it and treat it kindly, and both of you will enjoy the ride more.

SAILING

Sailing is best learned on somebody else's boat. If you have the opportunity to crew for a friend, accept it. If you do not know anybody with a boat, join a sailing club and hope that you will be asked to crew.

The illustration opposite shows a typical dinghy hull (key below). The hull is the basic frame or body of the boat, without its masts, sails, rigging etc. The front is the bow and the back is the stern. Left is port and right is starboard. The width at the widest part is the beam, the depth in the water is the draught. The keel is the backbone of the boat's framework and includes the projection below the hull to keep the boat steady and upright. Spars are the poles supporting or extending the sails, the main upright one being the mast, and that along the bottom of the mainsail being the boom. The rigging is the combination of ropes which support the mast and control the sails. The sails catch the wind and propel the boat.

The number, shape and

1 Burgee (or racing flag): indicates wind directions.
2 Mast: the main spar. Supports the sails.
3 Jib halliard: hoists jib.
4 Forestay: supports the mast (and jib) from forward.
5 Foresail hanks: attach luff of jib to forestay.
6 Jib: the single foresail characteristic of sloop rig.
7 Cleat: fitting for securing rope.
8 Bow plate: metal plate to which forestay is attached.
9 Stem: foremost part of hull.
10 Mast step: takes heel of mast.
11 Centreboard: retractable keel.
12 Centreboard case (or trunk): housing for centreboard.
13 Keel: fore-and-aft centre member.
14 Knee: strengthening member.
15 Rudder: alters direction of boat.
16 Mainsheet horse: metal traveller for mainsheet.
17 Mainsheet: controls angle of mainsail.
18 Outhaul cleat: for securing outhaul.
19 Tiller: lever for steering.
20 Tiller extension: increases length of tiller.
21 Boom: spar along which foot of mainsail is stretched.
22 Kicking strap: keeps the boom from lifting.
23 Jib sheet(s): control(s) angle of jib.
24 Fairlead: alters 'lead' of sheet.
25 Gooseneck: attaches mainsail boom to mast.
26 Shroud(s): lateral support(s) for mast.
27 Outhaul: stretches foot of mainsail.
28 Mainsail: the other sail-component of sloop rig.
29 Battens: support mainsail leech.

The main parts of one of the most popular sailing craft – the sloop-rigged dinghy. (Key opposite)

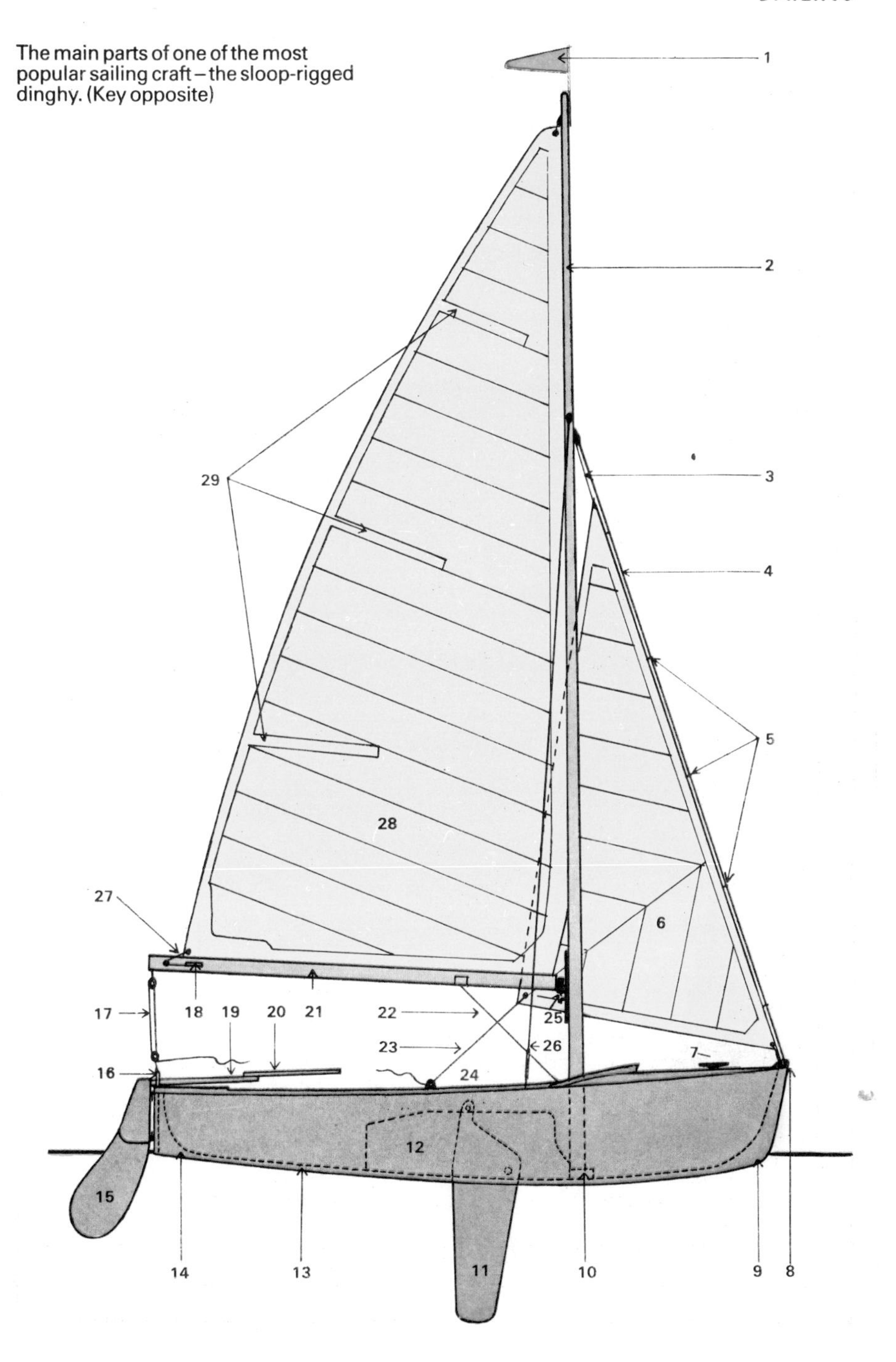

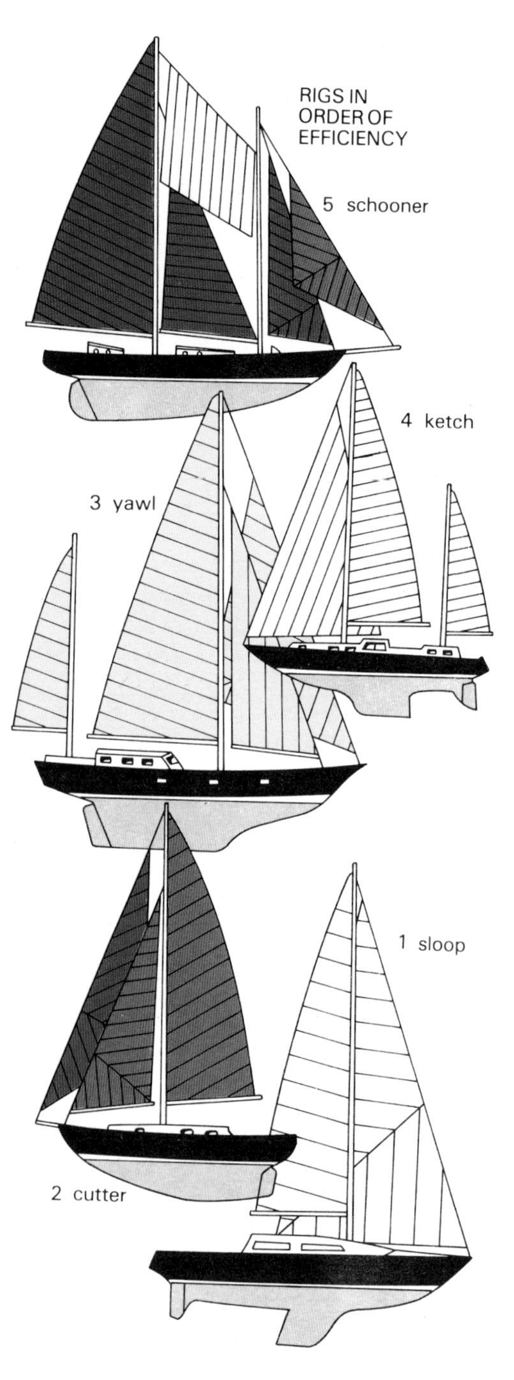

arrangement of the masts and sails is the rig, by which boats are usually described. Dinghies are the cheapest sailing craft, and a sloop rig dinghy has one mast and two sails, the larger mainsail being behind. The sail in front of the mast is called a jib.

The various types of boat differ greatly in performance, and they are shown here in order of all-round efficiency. The sloop is best, and as it is single-masted with only two sails to control, and comes in a wide range of sizes, it is the most popular. When you make your first trip, the first thing you must remember is your life-jacket. Most sailing clubs will not allow anyone aboard a dinghy without a life-jacket, and this is a good rule which should be followed whether it is compulsory or not. Put it on before going aboard and take it off only when back on dry land again.

A vessel rigged like a sloop, with a sail before and after the mast, can travel anywhere it wishes, even if the wind is against it, although in this case it will have to zig-zag.

The direction a boat is moving relative to the wind is called its point of sailing. With the wind behind it the boat is said to be *running*. With the wind coming from the side it is *reaching*. With the wind coming from ahead the boat is travelling against the wind, and it is *beating*.

When *running*, the mainsail is at right angles to the boat, the wind thus pushing the boat straight ahead. The jib will hang limp since it is not getting any wind. You can use both sails by goose-winging, which is to set the sails on opposite sides of the boat, thus catching more wind and travelling faster.

When *reaching* with the wind at right angles to the boat's course, the sails will be at 45° to the fore-and-aft line. If the wind is coming from further ahead, the sails will be sheeted in closer to the fore-and-aft line (a sheet is a rope used for controlling a sail). This is known as a close reach. If the wind is from the side but astern, the sails are let out more (called a broad reach).

It is impossible for a boat to sail directly against the wind. But a sloop can sail closely to that direction, called *beating*, and by changing direction from one side of the wind direction to the other it can make forward progress. This is called *tacking*. When beating, the sails are set closer than for reaching. The air accelerates through the slot between the sails, pushing the boat forward. The correct relationship between the sails is important. With the jib too slack the airflow does not accelerate, and with it too tight the airflow backs the mainsail (i.e. the wind dents the sail from the other side). When tacking, the helmsman gives the order 'ready about', followed by 'lee-oh' when the tiller is pushed over to the lee side of the boat. As the boat alters course and the jib starts to back the crew releases the jib sheet and tightens the slack sheet on the other side. The mainsail will then swing across. When the wind is blowing from the port side, the boat is on a port tack. The opposite tack is a starboard tack.

Sailing is a difficult and dangerous art, and the beginner and expert should always think about safety. Always wear a life-jacket, and make sure the boat is sound. If your dinghy capsizes, stay with it until help comes. Know your limits and never attempt too much.

THE AMERICA'S CUP

The America's Cup takes its name from the yacht *America*, which won a trophy presented by the Royal Yacht Squadron for a race round the Isle of Wight in 1851. The owners gave the trophy to the New York Yacht Club as a perpetual challenge cup, and the Americans successfully defended it until 1983. Since 1958 the results have been (USA unless stated):

Since 1958 the results have been:

1958 *Columbia* beat *Sceptre* (England) 4–0
1962 *Weatherley* beat *Gretel* (Australia) 4–0
1967 *Intrepid* beat *Dame Pattie* (Australia) 4–0
1970 *Intrepid* beat *Gretel II* (Australia) 4–0
1974 *Courageous* beat *Southern Cross* (Australia) 4–0
1977 *Courageous* beat *Australia* (Australia) 4–0
1980 *Freedom* beat *Australia* (Australia) 4–1
1983 *Australia II* (Australia) beat *Liberty* (USA) 4–3
1987 *Stars and Stripes* beat *Kookaburra III* (Australia) 4–0
1988 *Stars and Stripes* beat *New Zealand* (New Zealand) 2–0

FIRST AID

Accidents will happen, particularly to young people performing sports or enjoying outdoor hobbies. A knowledge of first aid is invaluable at such times.

First of all, what is first aid? It is not treatment designed to make the doctor unnecessary. It is *first* aid, performed by a person on the spot to help the patient until such time as proper medical aid arrives. Its purpose is to relieve the patient of unnecessary fear and worry, to reduce their suffering, to prevent, if possible, their injury from worsening, and perhaps to begin their recovery. Speed is usually important, which means that it is no use trying to learn first aid when the accident has happened.

It is possible to learn *some* of the principles of first aid from this section, but the best way to learn is by joining a course. First aid courses are run by the Red Cross and other organizations. Your local telephone directory or perhaps your school teacher will help you to find your nearest branch.

PULSE AND BREATHING RATES

First aiders should know about pulse and breathing rates. The average pulse of a normal adult is between 60 and 80 per minute; a child's is somewhat higher. A shocked patient's pulse rate will be much higher. The best places to take the pulse are just above the wrist or in front of the ear. Find these places on yourself or friends and practise taking pulse rates. The breathing rate can be counted by watching the rise and fall of a person's chest. Normally it will be about 14 per minute at rest. Stress of any kind could increase it a lot.

DROWNING

Serious accidents outdoors are often connected with water, so it is quite possible that first aiders will find themselves coping with cases of drowning. If breathing has stopped, a method of artificial respiration must be practised.

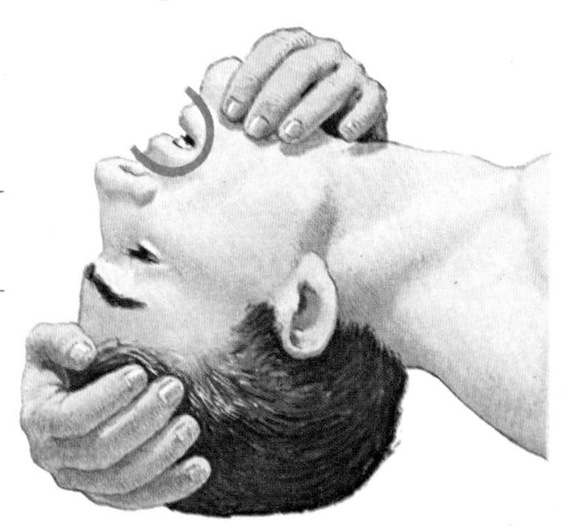

Tilt the patient's head back as far as possible and seal you mouth over the patient's open mouth.

Breathe steadily and firmly into the patient's mouth. If properly performed, the patient's chest will rise.

ARTIFICIAL RESPIRATION

Mouth to Mouth Method
Speed is essential, and the following actions should not be performed deliberately one by one, but should become a smooth routine. On a first aid course, manikins (models) may be provided for practising.

1 Turn the patient on his or her back.

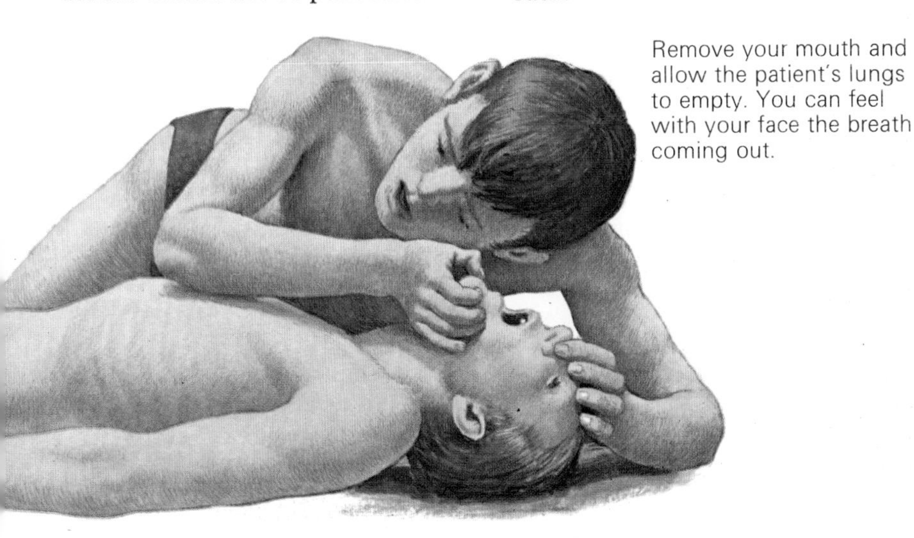

Remove your mouth and allow the patient's lungs to empty. You can feel with your face the breath coming out.

Check list for mouth-to-mouth respiration.

2 Tilt the head back as far as possible, so that the nostrils are pointing upwards.
3 Pinch the nose shut with forefinger and thumb (see illustration on page 151).
4 Make sure the patient's mouth is open. If not, open it by pulling the jaw.
5 Clear the mouth. Stick in your forefinger and quickly run it round the mouth to make sure.
6 Take a deep breath and seal your mouth round the patient's.
7 Breathe steadily and firmly into the patient's mouth. If properly performed, the patient's chest will rise.
8 Remove your mouth and allow the patient's lungs to empty. You can feel with your face the breath coming out (see illustration on page 151).
9 Repeat stages 6, 7 and 8 until the doctor arrives and asks you to stop.

It follows from 9 that you should shout or send for help between breaths. The first five breaths given to the patient should be rapid, to replenish the oxygen in the patient's blood. Afterwards, the breaths should be firm, full and regular rather than fast.

The Holger Nielson Method
This is less effective than the mouth-to-mouth method of respiration, but may be an easier method for the novice to master.
1 As before, make sure that the patient's mouth is absolutely clear.
2 Lay the patient on his or her stomach.
3 Turn the head to lay on the hands.
4 Kneel at the head and place your hands, with thumbs touching and fingers spread, as shown in the first illustration on the next page.
5 Rock forwards until your arms are upright. Do not push

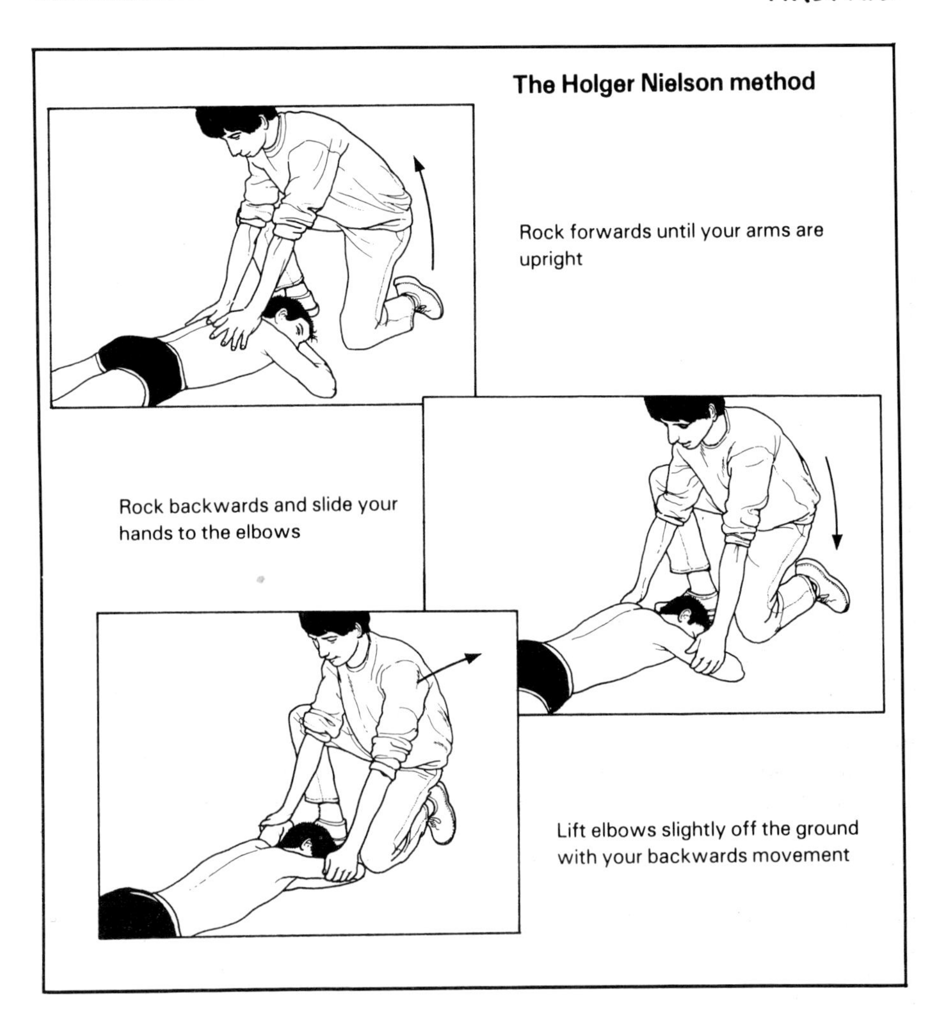

downwards – your weight will be sufficient to drive the air from the patient's lungs (first illustration).

6 Rock backwards, sliding your hands along the patient's upper arm to near the elbows, allowing your backwards movement to lift the elbows slightly off the ground (the second and third illustrations).

7 Return your hands to the position in the first illustration and repeat operations 5 and 6.

Aim at an unhurried, smooth routine.

SHOCK

Severe injury can cause shock – not the bewilderment or fright which an accident might naturally produce in a patient, but a serious condition which, if unchecked, is dangerous. Great loss of blood can cause it, or severe burning or fractures.

Recognition
The shocked patient will be pale or grey, cold yet sweating, probably breathing weakly yet very fast, and with a weak, fast pulse. Mentally he or she might seem distant, slow to understand. The patient might speak slowly and is likely to ask for a drink, but must not be given one.

Prevention
Note the heading – 'prevention'. Patients displaying the above symptoms must be got to hospital at once. They are beyond the first aider, whose job is to *prevent* shock in badly injured patients.

The first task is to stop any bleeding. This is discussed later. Secondly, make patients rest. Insist they lie down on their side, with, if possible, their feet slightly higher than their head. Loosen their clothing. Thirdly, keep them warm. Do not try to increase their temperature, but wrap them with blankets or coats so that they do not lose heat. Put coats beneath them if they are lying on the ground. Lastly, give them comfort and encouragement. Dress their wounds, talk to them quietly and sensibly. Let them know you can look after them. But do not fuss or let any onlookers fuss over them. And remember – allow no drinks. Anything in the mouth could choke them – especially if they become unconscious later.

BLEEDING

Minor cuts and grazes, while benefitting from cleaning and dressing, will frequently heal themselves. This section deals with the action required for a bad wound causing severe bleeding. The first thing to do is to raise the bleeding part. Lay the patient down to raise a

(*continued on page 156*)

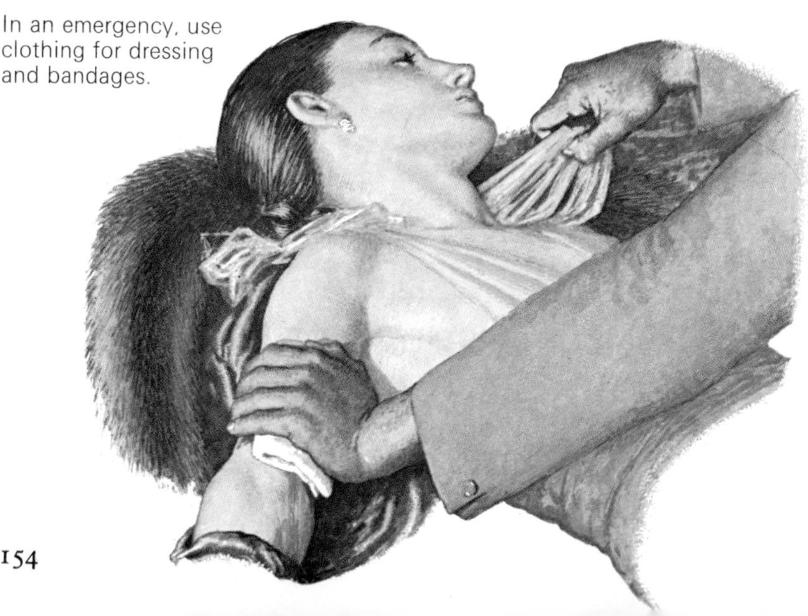
In an emergency, use clothing for dressing and bandages.

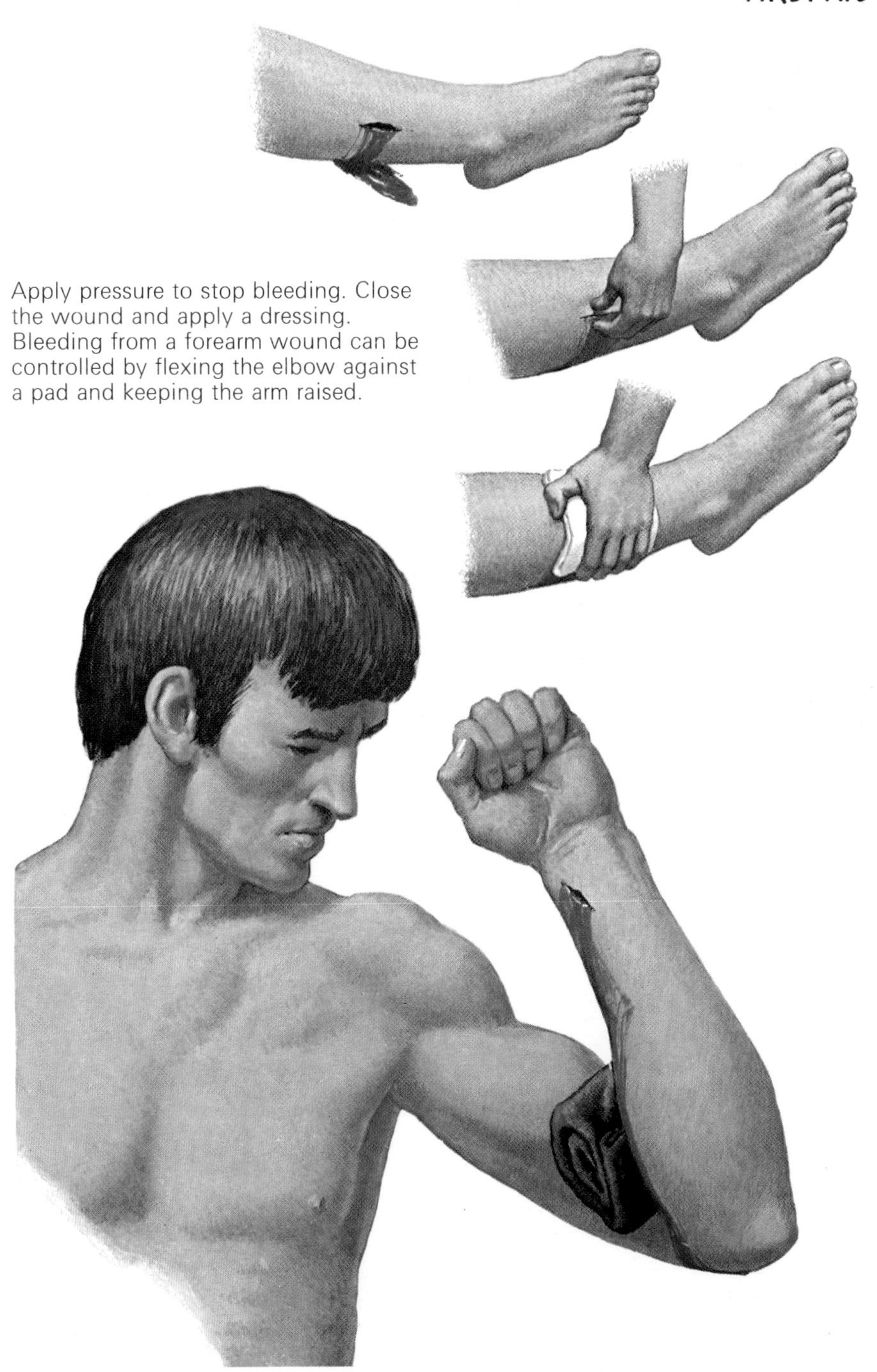

Apply pressure to stop bleeding. Close the wound and apply a dressing. Bleeding from a forearm wound can be controlled by flexing the elbow against a pad and keeping the arm raised.

leg or to raise an arm in the air. However, do not do this if you suspect a fracture. Use your finger and thumb to close the wound and hold the edges together. Apply pressure and maintain it for 10 minutes to allow a clot to form. Press a pad of material over the wound and secure with a bandage. Improvise, if necessary, with handkerchiefs, scarves or material torn from clothing. Press the dressing well on to the wound, into it if necessary. Do not attempt a tourniquet unless you have professional supervision. Keep the injured limb still and raised, and if bleeding persists add further bandages – do not remove the original bandage. Check for shock.

BURNS

If a victim's clothes are flaming, get him or her to the ground at once, and smother the flames by wrapping a blanket or coat round the person. But be sensible – if clothes are only smouldering, rip them off and stamp out the fire.

The burn should be immersed in cold water immediately and kept there until the pain fades, which could take 15 minutes or more. Remember, the patient may suffer shock (see pages 153–4), so take the necessary precautions to prevent it. Remove tight clothing, as swelling may develop. Cover the burn with clean materials to prevent infection. If burnt material is sticking to the burn, do not attempt to remove it. Keep the burn raised, and get the patient to hospital.

FRACTURES AND SPRAINS

Where bones meet at joints, they are kept in position by ligaments. Ligaments may get torn; for example, if a foot is wrenched it may cause tearing of the ankle ligaments. This is known as a sprain. Mild sprains will cause a swelling, which can be treated with a cold compress, that is, a cloth soaked in cold water, wrung out and wrapped round the sprained joint.

When ligaments tear they may displace a bone; this is known as a dislocation. A fracture is when the bone actually breaks. A broken bone nearly always means that ligaments are torn, so you can see that sprains, dislocations and fractures are related, and often occur together.

It is difficult to be sure if a patient has suffered a fracture. If a blow is followed by pain, suspect a fracture. The injured part may look to be bent, or otherwise strangely positioned. The patient may be unable to move it, or it may be swollen.

The first aider's general principles are to prevent movement of the injured part, control severe bleeding, if any, and keep the patient still. Bear in mind, too, that the patient may suffer from shock (see pages 153–4).

An injured limb is secured against the patient's body, for example a broken leg is secured against the good one. Always move the broken limb as little as possible, and put padding between the broken limb and the part to which it is secured. Materials for padding and slings must often be improvised, but it is

Below: a patient with a fractured rib.
Right: arm secured for a broken collar bone.
Bottom: the recovery position (see 'Unconsciousness' on page 158).

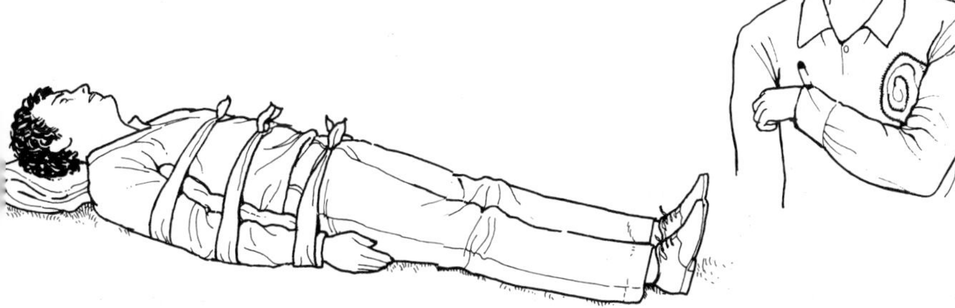

amazing what can be done with socks, scarves, shirts, etc. The illustrations above show treatments for a collar bone fracture and a broken rib. With a collarbone fracture, keep the hand as high as possible; with a broken rib, place padding between the arm and body and bandage round the upper arm, just below the elbow and round the wrist as shown above.

A fractured leg is immobilized by placing padding between the legs and using bandages to tie them together. Tie the feet together, too. Do not put a bandage directly over the fractured part. Treat a fractured hip bone similarly, with the knees and feet bound, and two thick bandages around the hips. If you suspect a fractured spine, you must make the patient lie absolutely still until an ambulance or doctor arrives. Cover him or her with coats. Any movement is dangerous.

Fractures can easily be made worse by rough or clumsy treatment. Try to keep the fracture quite still until medical help arrives.

UNCONSCIOUSNESS

If a patient is unconscious, check first that he or she is breathing. If not, give artificial respiration (see earlier). Always check the mouth, as it is easy for an unconscious person to choke. Clear the mouth (see method earlier) of vomit or loose teeth. Check for fractures. If you suspect a fracture, which makes it unwise to move the patient, concentrate on making sure he or she can breathe. Bend the head back so that the nostrils point upwards and keep the lower jaw open by pulling it down with the thumb. If there seem to be no complications, the patient should be gently placed into the recovery position illustrated on page 157. The patient is on his side, head bent back, with face down. The upper arm and leg are bent; the lower arm and leg are stretched out. Send for help, and watch the patient, particularly the breathing.

SUMMARY

The following is a quick check list on how to behave when in a situation calling for first aid.

If the patient's position is safe, treat him or her there. Check the breathing. Check for choking. Check for bleeding. Reassure the patient. Dress any wounds. Immobilize any fractures. Treat for shock if necessary. Send for help. Look after the patient's property. If you have time, keep notes to help the doctor or police. Stay with the patient until medical help arrives.

This chart indicates what to expect when taking a patient's temperature.

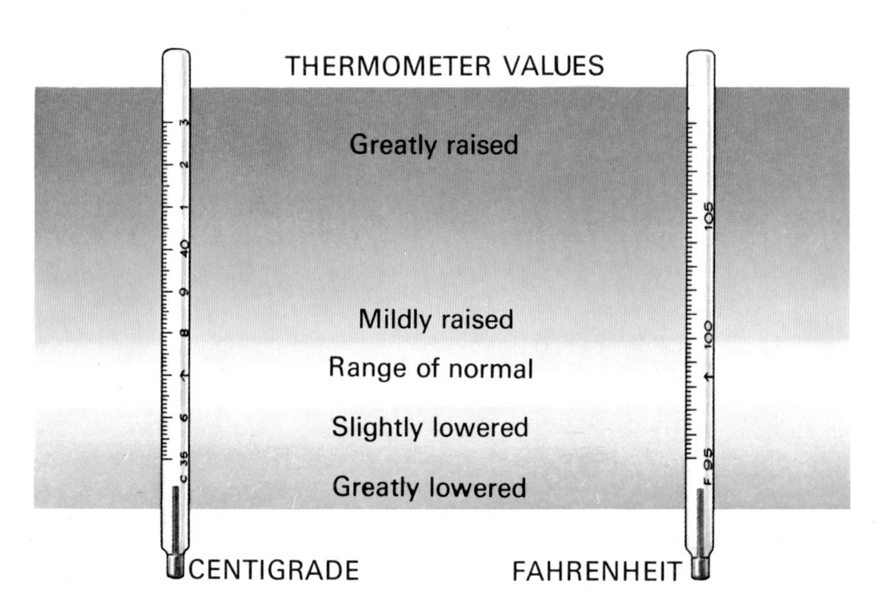

A TO Z OF SCIENCE

AEROPLANE

Powered aeroplanes use engines to give them forward speed, which causes air to flow rapidly over the wings. Each wing is specially shaped so that its top surface is raised: air flows more quickly over the top of the wing than it does underneath, and this creates a low pressure area above the wing, so 'sucking' the aircraft into the sky. Early attempts by human beings to fly by strapping wings to themselves, or turning propellers by pedal, failed because people were not powerful enough to lift the weight of their aircraft.

The five factors which contribute to drag and lift.

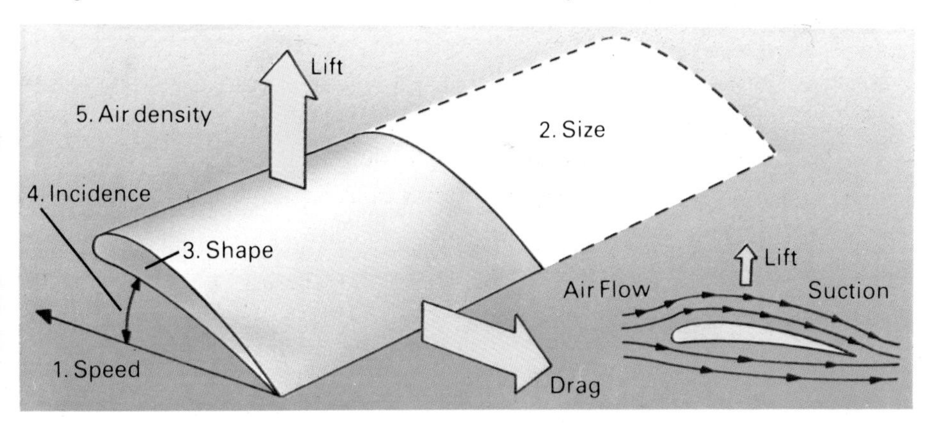

The first true aeroplane to carry a person was built by the Wright brothers in the USA in 1903, but most early development was carried out in Europe, especially in France, where Louis Bleriot made the first air crossing of the English Channel in a single-wing monoplane of his own design on 25 July 1909. Progress was very swift, and by the First World War both armies had fleets of aircraft for reconnaissance. As the war dragged on, fighters and bombers were built, as was the first all-metal aircraft. In 1919 the Atlantic was flown non-stop in a converted bomber.

All these aircraft were powered by internal combustion engines, which continued to dominate both military and civil aviation until well after the Second World War. During that war, however, the jet engine was invented in both Germany and England and this offered far more power with less weight, both desirable in an aeroplane. Once fitted to the first passenger aeroplanes – the British Comet and the American Boeing 707 – jets halved the journey times of propeller-driven aircraft.

Since that time (about 1952) passenger aircraft have become larger (the latest Boeing 747 Jumbo jet carries over 530 people) and fly higher (about 15 000 m/9.32 miles) where the air is thinner and so causes less drag. Because of the high price of fuel, however, modern jets do not fly much faster than those first jets, apart from the very expensive Concorde, the world's only faster-than-sound passenger aeroplane.

CALCULATOR

This is a device which can add, subtract and do other calculations. The abacus was the first calculator. It has coloured beads which can be moved along wires to add and subtract. The ancient Egyptians used it, and it is still sometimes used in the Middle and Far East to teach arithmetic.

The first calculating machine was invented by Blaise Pascal in 1642. This counted using toothed wheels. Today many people use electronic calculators. These can do complicated calculations almost instantly. Many can also store information.

COAL

Coal is the remains of trees which lived millions of years ago. These remains were buried and slowly turned into hard layers of coal. The remains of living things are called fossils, so coal is known as a fossil fuel. It is mainly carbon, and is burned to give heat. Many homes are heated by coal fires, and coal is used in electricity power stations to produce steam which drives turbines.

When coal is heated without air it gives coke, coal gas and coal tar. Coke and coal gas are used as fuels. Coal tar contains many valuable substances which are used to make, for example, soap, medicines, dyes and plastics. See page 162 for a diagram showing the many by-products of coal.

Layers of coal, or coal seams, may be near the surface of the ground. Here, the coal can be removed very easily and the soil replaced afterwards. This is done in open-cast mines. Other seams are deep underground. Mine shafts and tunnels have to be built to reach the coal.

COMPUTER

A computer is like a calculator. However, it can perform much more complicated tasks than a calculator, and can do this very quickly. It can also store large amounts of information, and instructions for using it.

Computers are used in factories, offices and homes. One computer may be able to do many sorts of work and can replace some people in their jobs. In factories, a computer can control a wide variety of machines.

In some schools, computers are used for teaching. Many countries use computers to control electricity, gas and telephone grids.

Scientists can do calculations in minutes on a computer that would otherwise take hundreds of years. Without computers, space travel would not be possible. In these and many other ways, computers are changing the world we live in.

Software is a term used by people who deal with computers. The information stored in a computer is usually called data, and the instructions are known as a program. Together they are called software.

The software has to be written in a language which the computer understands. There are many different computer languages, which are artificial languages, specially made up for computers. The people who prepare software for a computer are called programmers, and they have to learn the computer languages.

Software can be stored in a computer. This store is called the memory.

Hardware is the name given to the machines used in the computer industry. The part of a computer that does the calculations is called the central processing unit (CPU). This also controls all the other parts. Information can be stored on discs or tapes. This store is called the memory.

Machines which are used to put information into the computer and to get answers out are called input and output devices. They may be keyboards on which information is typed. They may be visual display units (VDU), printers or other machines. A visual display unit shows information on a screen, like a television screen. These devices may be a long way away from the computer, connected by telephone.

A microcomputer may have all its parts in one box no bigger than a television, but a large computer may fill several rooms.

ELECTRIC POWER

This is produced by using water power, some form of fuel, or atomic energy. The pressure of water from a dam, or, alternatively, steam created by burning fuel, turns a dynamo. The rotation of this spins a rotor. The rotor is an electro-magnet, which, surrounded by a coil of wire, sets up an electric current in the wire.

There are two sorts of current electricity: direct current (DC) and alternating current (AC). The batteries which power torches and radios produce direct current.

Most of the electricity we use is alternating current. This lights and heats homes and factories and powers most electrical machines. It is produced by generators, usually in power stations. Wind and energy from the sun, called solar energy, are also used to make alternating current.

The alternating current is taken

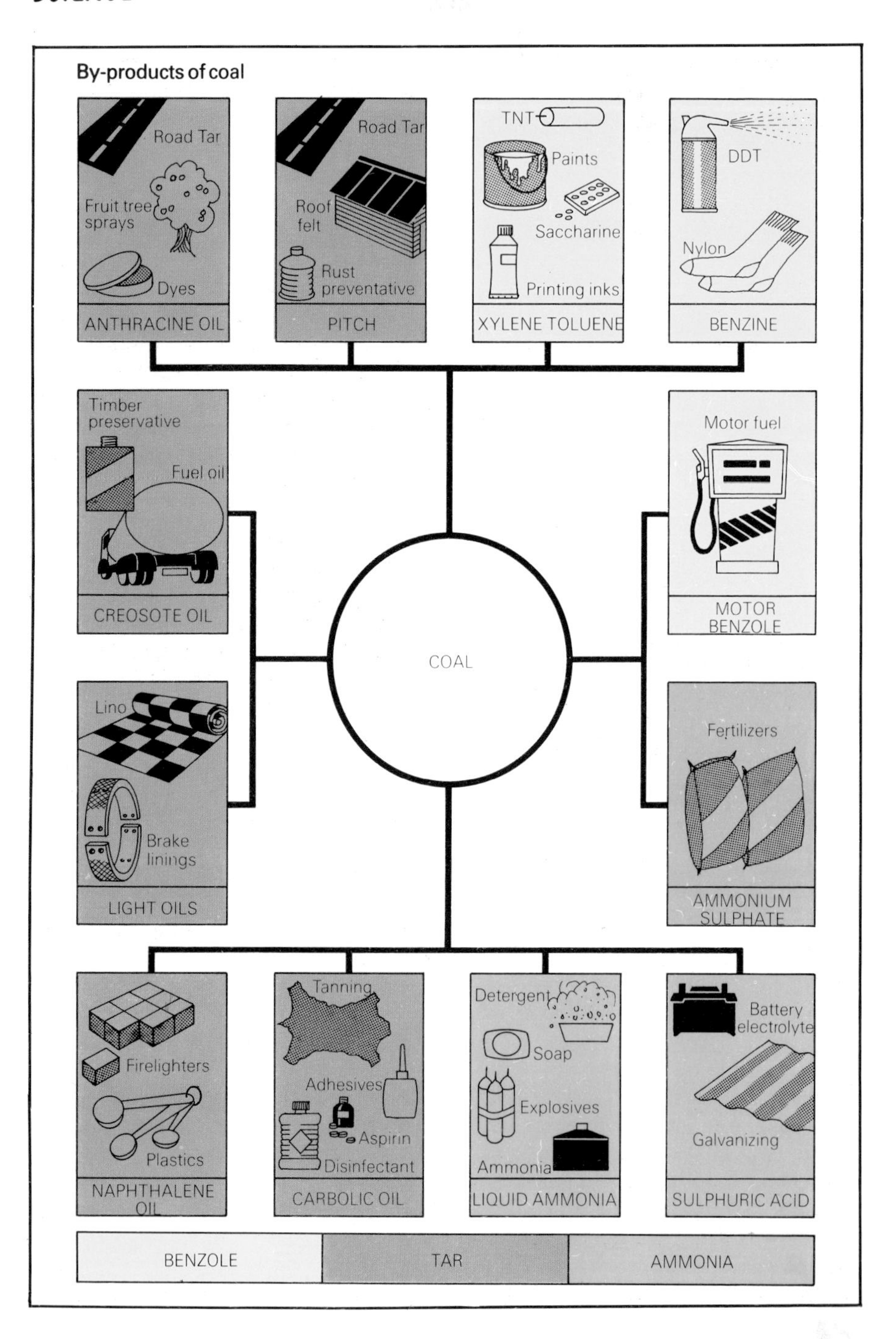
By-products of coal
Road Tar
Fruit tree sprays
Dyes
ANTHRACINE OIL
Road Tar
Roof felt
Rust preventative
PITCH
TNT
Paints
Saccharine
Printing inks
XYLENE TOLUENE
DDT
Nylon
BENZINE
Timber preservative
Fuel oil
CREOSOTE OIL
Motor fuel
MOTOR BENZOLE
COAL
Lino
Brake linings
LIGHT OILS
Fertilizers
AMMONIUM SULPHATE
Firelighters
Plastics
NAPHTHALENE OIL
Tanning
Adhesives
Aspirin
Disinfectant
CARBOLIC OIL
Detergent
Soap
Explosives
Ammonia
LIQUID AMMONIA
Battery electrolyte
Galvanizing
SULPHURIC ACID
BENZOLE
TAR
AMMONIA

by overhead or underground cables to homes and factories. Copper wires carry electricity around the home to sockets and light switches.

Electricity can be very dangerous. For example, touching a metal wire carrying electricity causes an electric shock, which can kill. All electrical equipment, including wires, sockets, switches and plugs, must be kept in good condition and used carefully.

ELECTRONICS

Electronics is a type of science that uses electrons. Moving electrons can produce electricity, radio waves, television waves, X-rays and many other signals. They can be used to make sounds in radios and electronic musical instruments, and can form pictures on television screens. They can also carry information in electronic calculators and computers.

Electronic machines, such as computers, have helped to make many inventions and scientific discoveries. Artists and musicians often use electronics in their work, and some electronic machines can replace people in their jobs.

GAS

Still one of the principal sources of heat for household cooking, gas is made by baking coal in a container or retort. This gives off gas, which is then stored in gasometers until required. By-products of the process include petrol, acids, drugs, perfumes, dyes, tar and coke. Natural gas from the North Sea is being used in Britain for commercial and domestic purposes.

HOVERCRAFT

This is a flat-bottomed vessel which travels on a cushion of air, held in place by a flexible 'skirt' around the base of the vessel. Forward propulsion is by means of propellers mounted on top of the craft. A hovercraft can travel over land and water, but is hard to steer accurately, limiting its use at present to areas where there is ample space. It is especially useful for crossing marshland, where few other vehicles can go. Hovercraft are used in the Arctic regions of Alaska, Canada and the USSR to cross ice in winter and the boggy tundra that replaces it in summer.

The largest hovercraft in regular use carry over 50 cars and over 400 passengers at a time over the English Channel between England and France, a crossing which they can complete in 35 minutes, compared to almost two hours taken by ships.

Hovercraft were invented in 1955 by Englishman Christopher Cockerell (see illustration on page 166).

INTERNAL COMBUSTION ENGINE

This is the name for the petrol engine used in cars, motorcycles and light lorries. A carburettor converts petrol into a fine vapour, and also draws in air which mixes with it. The mixture travels through a valve system into the top of a cylinder and is there exploded under pressure by means of an electric sparking plug. The explosion forces down the piston, from which a connecting rod runs to a crank-shaft. On its return stroke the piston pushes out the burned gases through the valve system; its next journey down draws in a fresh supply of fuel, and its upward journey compresses the fuel in readiness for the next explosion (see illustration on page 167).

JET ENGINE

Jet engines are really heat engines in which a fuel, such as aviation kerosene, is sucked in through the front of the engine, mixed with compressed air, and burned in a combustion chamber where the hot expanding gases provide a thrusting force. A popular misconception is that it is gases streaming out from the tail pipe of a jet which move the plane along, but in fact, the atmosphere only supplies the oxygen needed to make the fuel burn. The actual thrust occurs *inside* the combustion chamber, pushing the engine forward, while the tailpipe serves only to allow the exhaust gases to escape.

The simplest jet is the ramjet, which must be first set in rapid motion through the air by another force. Once travelling through the air, the motion rams air into the front of the engine. Fuel is then added and ignited, and the burning gases leave at the rear.

The intake end of a modern jet engine consists of a huge air compressor, which is operated by the burning gases turning the blades of a turbine which is on the same drive shaft as the compressor. Some engines have two or more compressors driven by two or more turbines to give increased power.

The power of jet engines can be further increased when they are fitted with an 'afterburner', or re-heat system. When pilots require extra power to accelerate the aircraft through the sound barrier, as in Concorde, they open the throttles so that extra fuel is injected into a chamber beyond the main combustion area in the engines. Here, the fuel is ignited in the already intensely hot gases from the main combustion chamber, producing considerable extra thrust.

The principal parts of a jet engine.

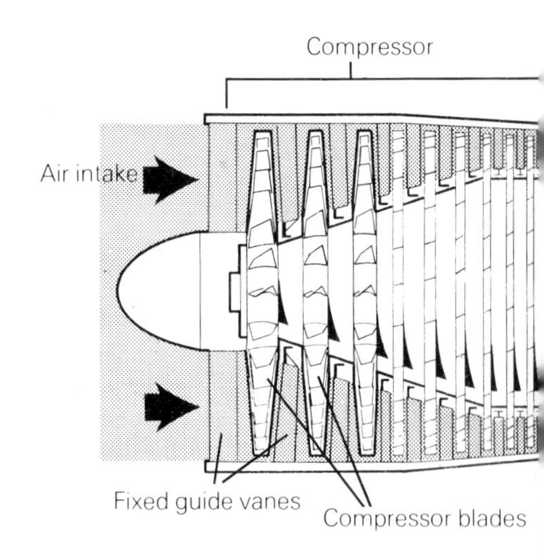

LASER

A laser is an instrument which produces a beam of light. However, laser light is much more powerful than ordinary light. It has such high energy that it can cut through very hard substances such as metal and diamond. Metals are also joined together, or welded, using lasers.

Lasers are used in medicine. Very narrow beams of laser light are used to operate on the eye without cutting it open, or are used in cancer treatment.

Laser beams can measure distances, such as the distance from the earth to the moon, and they are used for photography.

NUCLEAR POWER

Nuclear power is an alternative energy source to coal. Nuclear fuels, such as uranium-235 and plutonium, can be made to undergo an energy release called 'fission', a process that produces heat. Scientists have found a way to control this complicated release of atomic energy so that when a cooling flow of liquid or gas is passed over the hot nuclear fuel, the heat can be used to raise the temperature of water to the level of steam. This can then be used to drive conventional steam turbines connected to dynamos, and electricity is generated.

One great advantage of nuclear fuels is that they are used up very gradually. One tonne (1 ton) of uranium-235 will generate as much heat as 3 000 000 tonnes of coal. There are, however, disadvantages to using nuclear power stations. They are extremely complicated and expensive to build, and there is the problem of disposing of the dangerous radioactive waste which is left behind after most types of nuclear fuel have been used.

Although nuclear reactors have

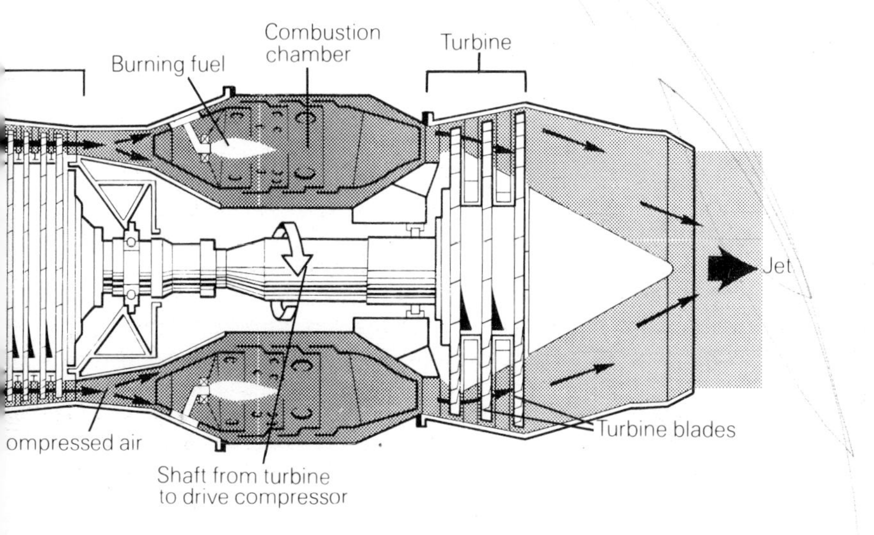

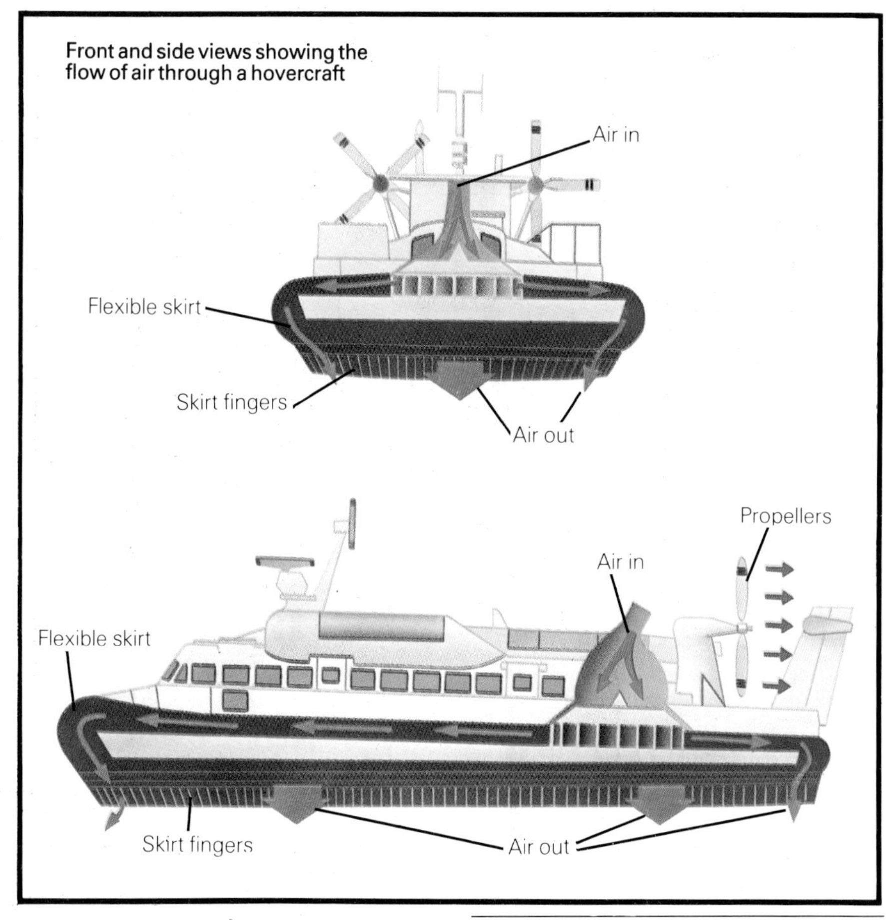

been used successfully in ships and submarines, it is difficult to make them small and light enough to operate small vehicles such as cars and aircraft, which are at present powered by oil-based fuel. There is also the danger of an escape of harmful radioactive material in the event of a crash. Although there will be an increasing amount of electricity generated by nuclear power stations, human beings will have to look elsewhere to satisfy their need for energy.

OIL

The raw product, oil, is found and produced in quantity in only a few countries, but it is made into thousands of products besides petrol or gasoline and used right around the world.

The first commercial oil wells were developed in the USA in the last century. The USSR is now the world's largest producer of crude oil with over 500 million tonnes per year. Saudi Arabia is, however, the

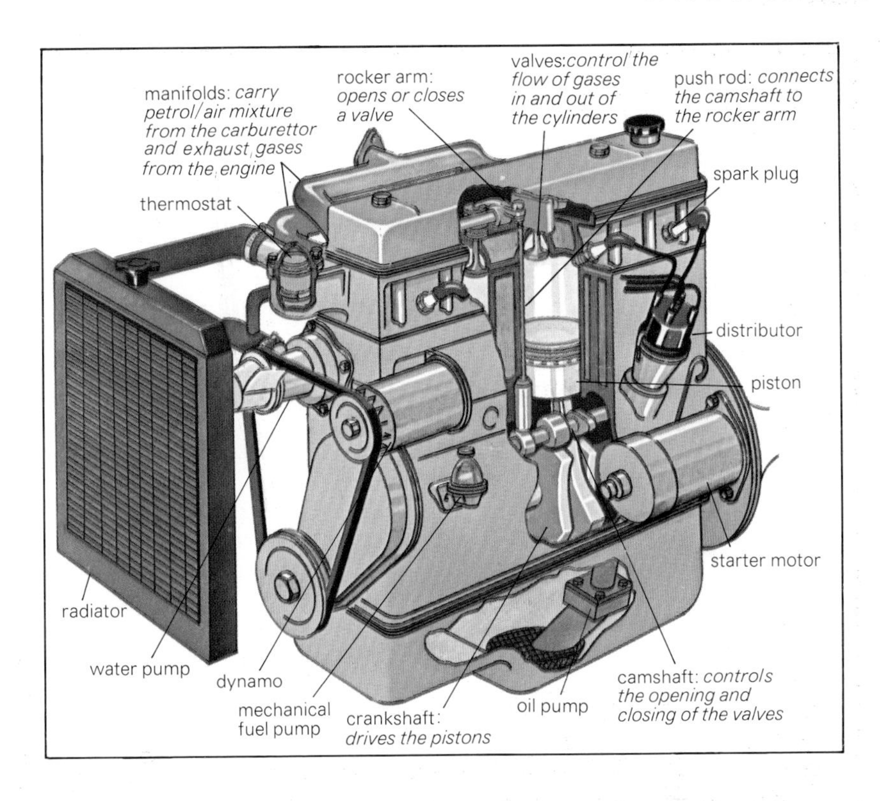

The main parts of a car engine.

most important oil producer in many ways because the Saudis export most of their oil and they produce over 420 million tonnes per annum. The USA is the third largest producer with over 400 million tonnes followed by Iran (300 million tonnes), Venezuela (150 million tonnes) and Kuwait (110 million tonnes).

Production of oil from the major oil fields of the Middle East has been relatively constant but demand for oil has steadily increased. So the oil companies have explored for oil in more remote places. The big successes have been discoveries of large fields under the North Sea and on the northern shores of Alaska.

Oil is the main ingredient in the manufacture of plastics and all kinds of other synthetic materials. The big refineries of the oil companies heat up the thick crude oil and 'crack' it down into different substances. Some become kerosene, gasoline or petrol, and others become ethylenes or 'feed-stocks' for factories which produce polythene for bags, vinyl for floor coverings, and nylon for clothing. The list for oil-based products is enormous and keeps growing.

Oil is the truly indispensable material of the modern world. We rely on it to keep most of our transportation systems going, we burn it to generate power to keep us warm and we modify it to make many products we rely on in everyday life.

PAPER

Paper is used to write and print on, and for packaging. The Ancient Egyptians wrote on a reed called papyrus, and paper is named after the papyrus plant. The Chinese first made paper over 2000 years ago. Many plants have been used to make paper, such as mulberry, cotton and flax.

Today, nearly all paper is made from fast-growing trees such as fir, pine and spruce. Logs from the trees are cut into thin pieces and heated with water and other chemicals. This forms a soft mixture called wood pulp, which is cleaned and whitened. It then flows on to a wire mesh where it is pressed and dried to form paper sheets or rolls.

Waste paper, with the ink or dye removed, is used to make recycled paper.

PLASTIC

There are two types of plastics – thermosetting and thermoplastic. The latter can be reshaped by the application of heat, but the former are subjected to heat during manufacture, and once moulded cannot be altered in shape. Thermoplastics include acrylic, vinyl and polystyrene – all in common use for household purposes and in toy-making. Many plastics are formed by treating coal derivatives such as phenol.

PRINTING

Printing makes copies of words and pictures on cotton, paper or other surfaces. It is said that the Chinese invented printing about 1200 years ago. Carved wooden blocks were inked and pressed down on material to make a copy. Letters raised in metal are still sometimes used to print words. People or machines, called typesetters, put the letters in the right order. They are then inked and paper is pressed on them. This is called letterpress printing and was widely used for all kinds of printing until the 1960s.

Grease and water do not mix. This principle is used in another sort of printing, lithography. The text or picture is marked on a flat plate with a grease. Water is put on the plate. A greasy ink will stick to the greasy parts of the plate and not the wet parts. Paper can then be pressed on to the plate to make a print. Lithography became the most popular printing process with the development of high-speed offset printing presses in the 1950s and 1960s.

Today, much use is made of photographic processes in printing. Also typesetting and printing are often computer-aided and use very fast machines. There are many other methods of printing, such as silk-screen, which are available for special needs.

RADAR

Radar is a system using very short wave radio signals to determine the location of ships, aircraft and other objects. The name is short for Radio Detection and Ranging, and the machinery generates powerful radio waves which are 'bounced off' the object to be detected, the time taken for the signal to return allowing the sender to calculate the object's distance, direction and height.

Crude radar sets were in use during the late 1930s, but radar was very heavily developed in Britain just before the Second World War, and played a major part in the war's outcome. Modern radar can detect enemy missiles over 3000 km (1860 miles) away, and the radar receiver is basically the same as the radio telescope used for long-range astronomy.

RADIO

Radio uses radio waves to carry sound from one place to another. In radio broadcasting, voices, music or other sounds are turned into electromagnetic waves in a microphone. These are transmitted by an aerial, or a tall mast. They are picked up by another aerial on a receiver. The radio sets in homes are receivers. They change the signal back into sound.

The radio was invented by Guglielmo Marconi, in 1895. The first radios sent messages in morse code. Today, messages are sent all over the world by radio, which is called radiotelegraphy. Soldiers, police, doctors and other groups can keep in touch with each other by radio.

The first radio programmes for entertainment were broadcast from radio stations in the 1920s. Now most countries have a number of radio stations.

RAILWAYS

In the first railways, wagons were drawn by horse along wooden tracks, and carried material from mines, probably as early as the 14th century. The first public railway (still for freight only) opened near Croydon, London, in 1803; the first public passenger-carrying railway was at Swansea, South Wales, in 1806 – both these were horse-drawn.

Following the invention of steam engines, railways quickly gained in popularity, as it became clear that they could carry people far faster than existing methods of transport. The first true public railway was George Stevenson's Stockton & Darlington, which opened in County Durham in 1825 and used steam-powered locomotives.

Railways now operate throughout the world, crossing Asia, America and Australia, and even climbing such formidable mountain ranges as the Andes, the Alps and the Rockies. Steam locomotives are still in use, but most railways favour diesel or electric power.

The largest railway station in the world is the Grand Central Terminal in New York, with 77 tracks on two floors, but the longest platform is at Kharpur in India and measures over 830 m (2723 ft). The oldest station is at Liverpool Road, Manchester, England, first opened in 1830.

ROADS

For most of history, roads were rough tracks, usually following the most popular route between any two places. Some of the first permanent roads were built by the Romans during their widespread colonization of Europe (circa 1st century BC) and the straight lines of these roads survive in many places today. The motor car proved too much for many 'roads', the heavy vehicles often sinking through badly prepared surfaces. Roadbuilding was revolutionized by Scottish inventor John McAdam, who developed a system of breaking hard rocks into pieces small enough to form a smooth surface. When tar

Various stages in car production. Robots do many of these tasks in modern factories.

was later added to bind the stones, modern tarmac was born.

To give modern roads strength to withstand heavy traffic, they are made up of several different layers.

SONAR

This is a system for detecting underwater submarines, developed by the British during the First World War to hunt German U-boats, which were sinking large numbers of Allied ships. The name means Sound Navigation and Ranging, and it works rather like radar, except that sound pulses are used instead of radio waves. The sound, which is very high-pitched (well beyond human ears), is transmitted and sensitive microphones pick up its echo, measuring the time taken and the direction.

(*continued on page 172*)

Facts and figures about roads and their use

Country	*kilometres paved road*	*square kilometres land per kilometre road*	*vehicles per 1000 inhabitants*
Australia	238 000	32.28	503
Brazil	1 344 374	6.33	41
Federal Republic of Germany	169 146	1.47	360
Great Britain	331 483	0.69	329
Mali	7 500	160.00	0.3
Norway	36 976	8.75	350
Switzerland	18 515	2.22	340
USA	4 961 126	1.84	654
USSR	689 700	32.47	figures unavailable

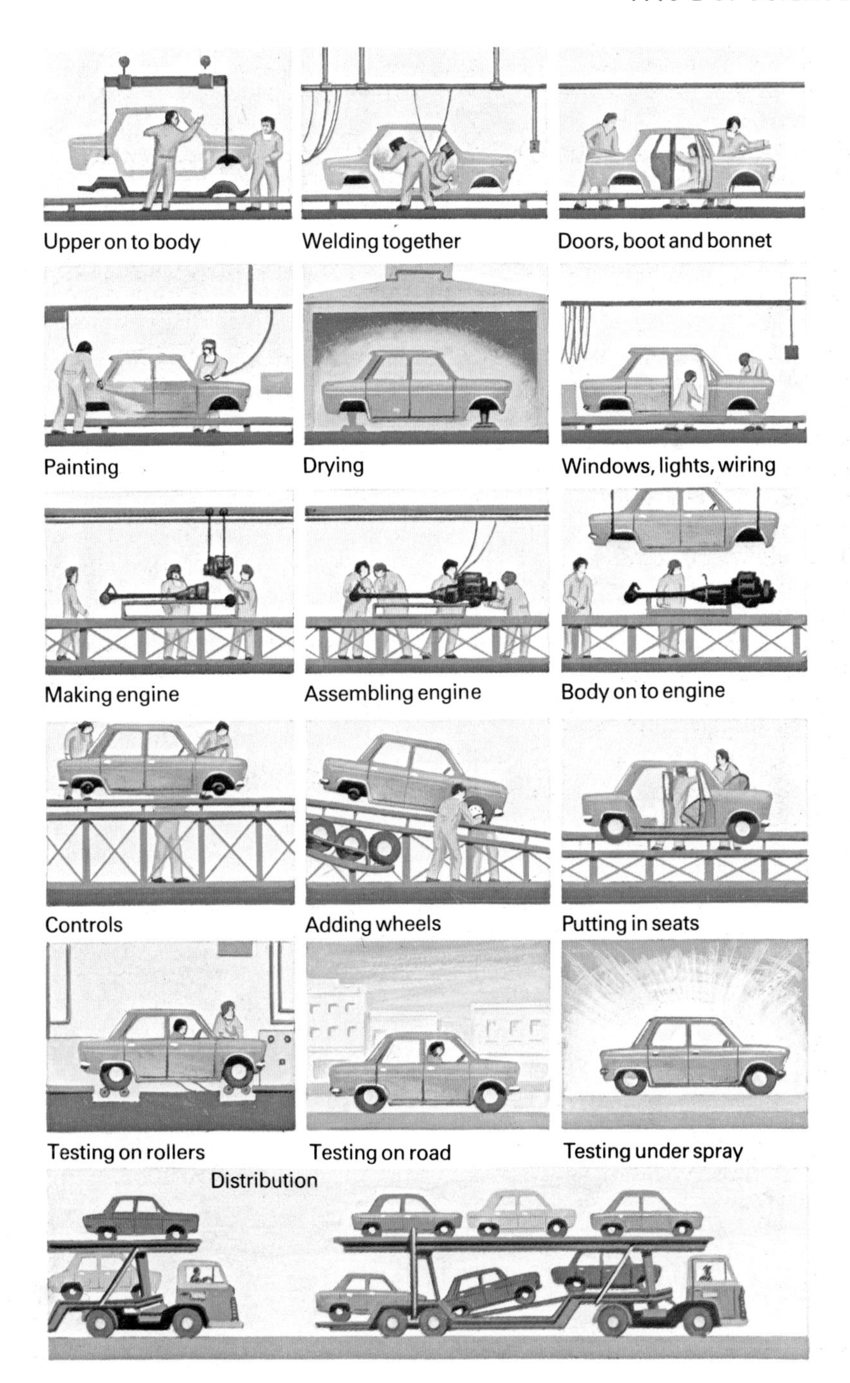
Upper on to body
Welding together
Doors, boot and bonnet
Painting
Drying
Windows, lights, wiring
Making engine
Assembling engine
Body on to engine
Controls
Adding wheels
Putting in seats
Testing on rollers
Testing on road
Testing under spray
Distribution

Sonar equipment is carried on ships, submarines and helicopters and can be fitted to sonar buoys, which work remotely, radioing their findings to aircraft. Apart from military purposes, sonar is used by craft navigating in shallow waters to detect underwater obstacles.

STEEL

Steel is an alloy of iron and carbon. Vast amounts of steel are made each year. Without it, the world would look very different. It is used in buildings, bridges, trains and other sorts of transport. Many of the things we use are made with steel tools and they are held together by steel nuts, bolts and screws.

Iron is found naturally, mixed with many substances, including carbon. All these are taken away from the iron in a refinery. Accurate amounts of carbon are then added to make steel. Other minerals may be added to make special types of steel. Stainless steel contains chromium and nickel. Steel may be hardened by heating it to very high temperatures and then cooling it very quickly. This is known as tempering.

TELEPHONE

A telephone is an instrument used to speak to people over long distances. It has a mouthpiece into which we speak and an earpiece through which we listen.

The mouthpiece contains a microphone. This changes the spoken word into electrical signals. The electrical signals can be sent through telephone cables or transmitted as radio waves where there are no cables. Radiotelephone waves can be sent to all parts of the earth, via satellites.

The telephone earpiece changes the electromagnetic signals back into sound.

The first really usable telephone was invented by Alexander Bell in 1876. Now many countries have millions of telephones and it is possible to speak to somebody on the other side of the earth just by dialling the correct number.

TELEVISION

Television is a system which sends out and receives moving pictures and sound. The first practical television system was invented by John Logie Baird, a Scotsman, in 1926. The pictures are filmed with a television camera and turned into radio signals. These are sent out, or broadcast, from tall masts called transmitters. Television sets or receivers in homes pick up the signals through an aerial.

There are millions of television receivers in the world. Most of

Baird's first television set.

them are used for entertainment. They receive plays, films, sport, news and other programmes. A programme can be seen all over the world at the same time, and television programmes can be recorded as they are being watched.

WATER SUPPLY AND DRAINAGE

Water as it comes from most rivers is not pure enough to drink. Also, we cannot depend on a river for supplies at all times of the year. The solutions to these two problems are purification and the use of reservoirs. River water, pumped into a reservoir, is taken out as required and placed in tanks containing purifying chemicals. From these, it flows to open tanks in which there are layers of gravel that filter away impurities. The final stage involves the addition of still more chemicals, and the water is then kept in covered tanks and reservoirs until pumped through the mains to individual houses.

Hot water is produced in the modern house by one of these methods: gas, electricity or solid fuel. In the first method, water is led over powerful burners, usually by means of a spiral tube, so that while the outlet tap is running the water is receiving heat from the burners. Water is warmed electrically by means of an immersion heater, which is an electric heating element, protected by a tube, placed inside a water tank. Heating water by a solid fuel stove requires an enclosed fire containing a water-jacket or an open fire with a back-boiler device. From the cold-water tank in the loft, water runs down to the hot-water tank (often in a cupboard), and from there down a pipe to the bottom of the water-jacket. As the fire heats the water it rises up a second pipe to the hot-water tank. It is replaced automatically by colder water coming down the first pipe, and the circulation provides a constant supply of hot water in the tank from which yet another pipe leads out, at the top, to supply the hot taps in the kitchen and bathroom.

Our modern drainage system is just as important as our water supply. In the past, refuse was thrown into open drains in the streets. Insects and germs breeding in these drains spread disease. Modern sewers all run below ground. The 'U' tube under the sink, bath and lavatory in which water always remains, prevents gases and unpleasant smells from coming up from the sewers into which the waste pipes lead. When the sewage reaches the sewage farm it is mechanically sieved to remove grit which is later used for concrete and road-works. Then the solids are separated from the liquids in settling tanks. The liquids are agitated by a jet of compressed air, which makes the bacteria multiply rapidly and breaks down any remaining solids into small particles. The final products are a harmless liquid which can be released into a river or the sea, and mud which, when fermented, gives off a gas that supplies the main source of power of the sewage farm.

GREAT INVENTIONS AND DISCOVERIES

Discovery or invention	*Person responsible*	*Country*	*Year*
Aeroplane	Wilbur and Orville Wright	USA	1903
Airship, non-rigid	Henri Giffard	France	1852
rigid	Graf Ferdinand von Zeppelin	Germany	1900
Aspirin	Herman Dreser	Germany	1899
Atomic structure	Lord Rutherford	Britain	1910–11
Balloon	Joseph and Jacques Montgolfier	France	1783
Ballpoint pen	John J. Loud	USA	1888
Barometer	Evangelista Toricelli	Italy	1643
Bathysphere	W. Bebbe	USA	1934
Bicycle	Kirkpatrick MacMillan	Britain	1839
Bicycle tyre, pneumatic	John Boyd Dunlop	Britain	1888
Calculating machine	Charles Babbage	Britain	1823
Carburettor	Gottlieb Daimler	Germany	1876
Clock, pendulum	Christiaan Huygens	Netherlands	1656
Dynamite	Alfred Nobel	Sweden	1867
Dynamo	Michael Faraday	Britain	1831
Electric arc lamp	Sir Humphry Davy	Britain	1809
Electric battery	Alessandro Volta	Italy	1800
Electric generator (DC)	Michael Faraday	Britain	1831
Electric lamp, carbon filament	Thomas Edison	USA	1879
Engine, internal combustion (gas)	Etienne Lenoir	France	1860
Engine, internal combustion (petrol)	Gottlieb Daimler	Germany	1883
Engine, internal combustion (diesel)	Herbert Akroyd Stuart Rudolf Diesel	Britain Germany	1890–2
Engine, jet	Frank Whittle	Britain	1930
Gas lighting	William Murdock	Britain	1792
Gramophone	Thomas A. Edison	USA	1877
Gyroscope	Jean Foncault	France	1852
Helicopter	Louis G. Breguet	France	1909
Hovercraft	C. S. Cockerell	Britain	1955
Lift	Elisha Otis	USA	1852
Lightning conductor	Benjamin Franklin	USA	1752
Locomotive, steam	Richard Trevithick	Britain	1803
Machine gun	Richard Gatling	USA	1862
Match, friction	John Walker	Britain	1827

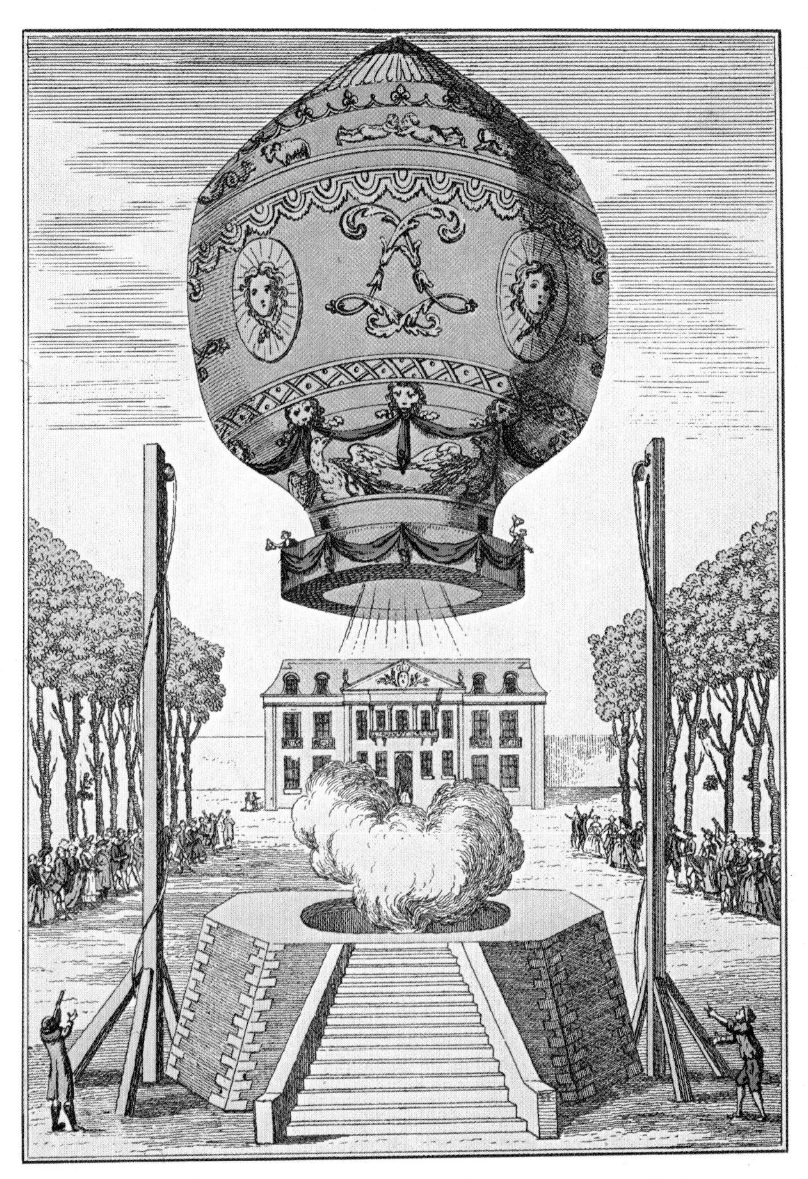

The first true flight made by humans was in a hot-air balloon. It was built in 1783 by two Frenchman, the Montgolfier brothers, and made a flight over Paris. This is a contemporary artist's impression.

Discovery or invention	*Person responsible*	*Country*	*Year*
Match, safety	J. E. Lundstrom	Sweden	1855
Microscope, compound	Zacharias Janssen	Netherlands	1590
Motion-picture camera	William Friese-Greene	Britain	1888
Motor car	Karl Benz	Germany	1885
Motorcycle	Gottlieb Daimler	Germany	1885
Nylon	W. H. Carothers	USA	1938
Parachute	J. P. Blanchard	France	1785
Pen, fountain	Lewis E. Waterman	USA	1884
Penicillin	Sir Alexander Fleming	Britain	1929
Photography	J. Nicéphore Niépce	France	1822
Pianoforte	Bartolommeo Cristofori	Italy	1709
Pneumatic tyre	Robert Thompson	Britain	1845
Postage stamp	Sir Rowland Hill	Britain	1840
Power loom	Edmund Cartwright	Britain	1786
Printing, moveable type	Johann Gutenberg	Germany	*c.* 1440
Radar	Robert Watson-Watt	Britain	1935
Radio telescope	Karl Jansky	USA	1931
Radium	Pierre and Marie Curie	France	1898
Razor, electric	Col. Jacob Shick	USA	1931
Safety lamp, miner's	Sir Humphry Davy	Britain	1816
Safety pin	Walter Hunt	USA	1849
Sewing machine	Walter Hunt	USA	1832
Sextant	John Hadley	Britain	1731
Steam engine	James Watt	Britain	1769
Steam locomotive	Richard Trevithick	Britain	1803
Steam turbine	Sir Charles A. Parsons	Britain	1884
Stethoscope	René Laënnec	France	1816
Submarine	David Bushnell	USA	1776
Tank	Sir Ernest Swinton	Britain	1914
Telephone	Alexander Graham Bell	USA	1876
Telescope, refracting	Hans Lippershey	Netherlands	1608
Telescope, reflecting	Isaac Newton	Britain	1669
Television	James Logie Baird	Britain	1926
Torpedo (modern)	Robert Whitehead	Britain	1868
Transistor	Bardeen, Brattain and Shockley	USA	1948
Typewriter	Christopher Sholes	USA	1868
Umbrella	Samuel Fox	Britain	1852
Vaccination	Edward Jenner	Britain	1796
Wireless telegraphy	Guglielmo Marconi	Italy	1895
X-ray	Wilhelm Roentgen	Germany	1895
Zip fastener	Whitcomb L. Judson	USA	1891

SPACE TRAVEL

The first space probes were the two Russian satellites, *Sputnik I* and *Sputnik II*, in 1957, which were propelled by multiple-stage rockets to a distance of several hundred kilometres above the earth's surface, and then directed into orbit so that they circled the earth on a definite course at a speed of about 29 000 km/h (18 000 mph).

The Americans launched their first satellites in the early part of 1958, and then, in October, fired a multiple-stage rocket, designed to explore the moon. It was equipped with television gear and it was hoped that it would send back a picture of the far side of the moon. This was a failure; at some 24 000 m (80 000 ft) the flight ended and the rocket returned to the earth's atmosphere.

In September 1959, the Russian rocket *Lunik II* reached the moon and photographed its far side.

In August 1960, another Russian rocket was put into orbit containing two dogs. This satellite reached its target back on earth with the dogs unharmed. In the spring of 1961, the Americans made a similar flight with a chimpanzee.

Then on 12 April of that year the first man was launched into space, when the Russians sent up Maj. Yuri Gagarin who made one orbit of the world before landing. This was improved on when fellow Russian Maj. Gherman Titov made 17 orbits on 6 August 1961.

Much of America's space prestige was restored when they sent up their first astronaut on 20 February 1962. Col. John Glenn made three orbits in his *Friendship 7*. This was followed by another three-orbit flight by Maj. Scott Carpenter in his space capsule *Aurora 7*. In 1965, *Mariner IV* (USA) sent back to earth close-up pictures of the surface of Mars, and Maj. Virgil Grissom (the first man to fly twice in space) and Lt. Cdr. John Young completed a two-man American space mission, manoeuvring their craft's height and direction in orbit for the first time.

On 15 December, 1965, America's *Gemini VI* and *VII* effected the first-ever human meeting in space. Meanwhile, also in 1965, Col. Belyaev piloted a two-man Russian spaceship while his companion, Lt. Col. Leonov, became the first man to walk into space, floating at the end of a 4.5 m (15 ft) lifeline for 20 minutes.

In 1967, both American and Russian space probes landed on the moon and sent information back to earth.

The American space programme reached its climax in July 1969 when the huge *Saturn V* rocket blasted off from Cape Kennedy carrying *Apollo XI* and the three-man crew, Neil Armstrong, Edwin Aldrin and Michael Collins. In the early hours of 21 July, Neil Armstrong became the first human being to set foot on the moon. He was followed by Aldrin, while

Collins piloted the command module orbiting above.

America's 1971 *Apollo 15* mission to the moon proved an enormous success. That same year the Russians also made a major breakthrough when *Soyuz II* docked with the *Salyut* space station. In 1972, *Mariner 9*, an unmanned spacecraft went into orbit around Mars and sent photographs back to earth that enabled scientists to map 85 per cent of the planet's surface. *Skylab*, an American experimental space station was also launched in this year. (*Skylab* fell to earth in 1979, scattering debris across western Australia.)

In 1975, Russian cosmonauts and American astronauts completed a successful rendezvous when their *Soyuz* and *Apollo* spacecraft docked in space. Two American spacecraft, *Vikings 1* and *2*, landed on the surface of Mars in July and September 1976. In 1978 Russian (*Venera 11* and *12*) and American (*Pioneer*) space probes landed on Venus. In 1979 the American *Voyager* space probes took a close-up look at Jupiter, and in 1980 *Voyager I* flew on past Saturn. Meanwhile in 1980, Russian cosmonauts set a new record by spending 180 days in space. The first NASA space shuttle launch took place in 1981. The worst space disaster occurred in 1986 when the US space shuttle *Challenger* exploded after take-off with the loss of all seven aboard, including a woman schoolteacher.

GLOSSARY OF SPACE TERMS

Acceleration In space flights accelerations are expressed in terms of g – the acceleration due to gravity.
Aerospace Relating to flight in the earth's atmosphere and in space.
Apogee A satellite orbiting around the earth is at apogee when it is farthest away.
Artificial gravity Gravity which is induced in space by rotating a spacecraft. Objects in the craft are flung outwards by centrifugal force, which imitates gravity.
Attitude The position of a spacecraft relative to something else in space, for example, the horizon.
Back-up A replacement. For example, every team that trains for a space mission has a back-up team ready to take over if needed.
Booster The first stage of a launch vehicle, or a separate rocket attached to the main one.
Burn The period a rocket fires.
Capsule The small craft in which early astronauts ventured in space.
Centrifuge A machine astronauts train in. It whirls them rapidly round and creates strong centrifugal forces similar to those that they encounter in space.
Cosmic rays Rays that strike the Earth from outer space.
Countdown The counting down of time before a space mission, before the rocket takes off. During this period the rocket is prepared and checked. If anything appears wrong, the countdown is held until the trouble is rectified. Then it resumes.
Debug Curing equipment troubles.
Docking Linking two spacecraft in orbit.
Elliptical orbit The usual orbit of a satellite, whose height above the

earth thus varies from time to time.
Escape velocity The speed a probe must reach to escape from the earth's gravity – over 40 000 km/h (25 000 mph).
Exobiology The study of living things that may exist in outer space.
Extraterrestrial intelligence (ETI) Intelligent creatures that may live in outer space.
g The acceleration due to gravity which every object experiences when it is dropped. It is about 10 m (30 ft) per second.
Gantry A servicing tower located next to a rocket on the launch pad.
g-forces The forces astronauts experience during launch and re-entry when they are rapidly accelerated or slowed down, which may be as great as 5g.
Heat shield A plastic coating on a spacecraft, which protects the astronauts inside from the heat of re-entry.
Hold The period when a countdown is temporarily stopped.
Launch pad The platform from which a rocket is launched.
Launch window The period during which a rocket can be launched to reach its required orbit or target.
Life-support system The air-conditioning system which supplies a spacecraft with a fresh, pressurized atmosphere.
Lift-off The moment that a rocket leaves the ground.
Lox Liquid oxygen, used as a rocket propellant.
Mock-up A full-scale model.
Module A section of a spacecraft.
Multistage rocket A rocket made up of several stages linked together one on top of the other.
Nose cone The conical cover at the front of a rocket, which protects the payload during launch.
Orbit The path of a spacecraft as it travels around the earth.
Orbital period The time it takes a spacecraft to make one orbit.
Orbital velocity The speed of a satellite, which varies with the height of its orbit.
Oxidant The rocket propellant which supplies oxygen.
Payload The object a rocket carries into orbit.
Perigee A satellite is at perigee when it is closest to the earth.
Probe A spacecraft launched to seek information about other heavenly bodies.
Propellant The material burned in a rocket motor to produce hot propulsive gases. Typical propellants are kerosene and liquid hydrogen.
Re-entry The return of a spacecraft into the atmosphere.
Regenerative cooling The method of cooling the nozzle of a rocket motor by circulating cold fuel through it.
Retro-rocket A rocket fired in the direction of travel to reduce a spacecraft's speed.
Rocket An engine which carries both fuel and oxygen and burns them to provide a propulsive jet.
Satellite A small body which orbits a planet.
Sputnik The Russian word for a satellite.
Stage One of the rocket sections of a multistage rocket.
Stationary orbit One in which a satellite appears stationary in the sky, which happens at an altitude of about 35 900 kilometres (22 500 miles).
Step-rocket Another term for multistage rocket.
Telemetry Measuring from a distance which is how we obtain information from space.
Trajectory The flight path of a spacecraft.
Umbilical The tube which connects an astronaut's spacesuit to his spacecraft's life-support system.
Weightlessness The condition astronauts experience in space, when they appear to have no weight.
Zero-g No-gravity; weightlessness.

USEFUL FACTS AND FIGURES

ATOMS AND ELEMENTS

The smallest particles of any substance are atoms. Surprisingly, given the great number of substances in the universe, there are only just over 100 different types of atoms. Some things, like gold and oxygen, are made from just one type of atom. These things are called elements. Everything else is made from combinations of two or more types of atoms.

TABLE OF ELEMENTS

Atomic number/ element		*Symbol*	*Atomic weight*
1	Hydrogen	H	1.008
2	Helium	He	4.003
3	Lithium	Li	6.399
4	Beryllium	Be	9
5	Boron	B	10.811
6	Carbon	C	12.011
7	Nitrogen	N	14.007
8	Oxygen	O	15.99
9	Fluorine	F	18.998
10	Neon	Ne	20.183
11	Sodium	Na	22.990
12	Magnesium	Mg	24.312
13	Aluminium	Al	26.982
14	Silicon	Si	28.086
15	Phosphorus	P	30.974
16	Sulphur	S	32.064
17	Chlorine	Cl	35.453
18	Argon	Ar	39.948
19	Potassium	K	39.102
20	Calcium	Ca	40.080
21	Scandium	Sc	44.956
22	Titanium	Ti	47.900
23	Vanadium	V	50.942
24	Chromium	Cr	51.996
25	Manganese	Mn	54.938
26	Iron	Fe	55.847
27	Cobalt	Co	58.933
28	Nickel	Ni	58.710
20	Copper	Cu	63.546
30	Zinc	Zn	65.370
31	Gallium	Ga	69.720
32	Germanium	Ge	72.590
33	Arsenic	As	74.922
34	Selenium	Se	78.960
35	Bromine	Br	79.904
36	Krypton	Kr	83.800
37	Rubidium	Rb	85.470
38	Strontium	Sr	87.620
39	Yttrium	Y	88.905
40	Zirconium	Zr	91.220
41	Niobium	Nb	92.906
42	Molybdenum	Mo	95.940
43	Technetium	Tc	99.000
44	Ruthenium	Ru	101.700
45	Rhodium	Rh	102.905
46	Palladium	Pd	106.400
47	Silver	Ag	107.868
48	Cadmium	Cd	112.400
49	Indium	In	114.820
50	Tin	Sn	118.690
51	Antimony	Sb	121.750
52	Tellurium	Te	127.600
53	Iodine	I	126.904
54	Xenon	Xe	131.300
55	Caesium	Cs	132.905
56	Barium	Ba	137.340
57	Lanthanum	La	138.910
58	Cerium	Ce	140.120
59	Praseodymium	Pr	140.907
60	Neodymium	Nd	144.240
61	Promethium	Pm	145.000
62	Samarium	Sm	150.350

Atomic number/ element		*Symbol*	*Atomic weight*	*Atomic number/ element*		*Symbol*	*Atomic weight*
63	Europium	Eu	151.9	84	Polonium	Po	210.000
64	Gadolinium	Gd	157.250	85	Astatine	At	210.000
65	Terbium	Tb	158.924	86	Radon	Rn	222.000
66	Dysprosium	Dy	162.500	87	Francium	Fr	223.000
67	Holmium	Ho	164.930	88	Radium	Ra	226.000
68	Erbium	Er	167.260	89	Actinium	Ac	227.000
69	Thulium	Tm	168.93	90	Thorium	Th	232.038
70	Ytterbium	Yb	173.040	91	Protoactinium	Pa	231.000
71	Lutetium	Lu	174.970	92	Uranium	U	238.030
72	Hafnium	Hf	178.490	93	Neptunium	Np	237.000
73	Tantalum	Ta	180.948	94	Plutonium	Pu	242.000
74	Tungsten	W	183.850	95	Americium	Am	243.000
75	Rhenium	Re	186.200	96	Curium	Cm	245.000
76	Osmium	Os	190.200	97	Berkelium	Bk	249.000
77	Iridium	Ir	192.20	98	Californium	Cf	249.000
78	Platinum	Pt	195.090	99	Einsteinium	Es	251.000
79	Gold	Au	196.967	100	Fermium	Fm	253.000
80	Mercury	Hg	200.590	101	Mendelevium	Md	256.000
81	Thallium	Tl	204.370	102	Nobelium	No	253.000
82	Lead	Pb	207.190	103	Lawrencium	Lr	257.000
83	Bismuth	Bi	208.98				

THERMOMETER READINGS

The three systems for marking thermometers are Celsius (the Centigrade scale), Fahrenheit and Reáumur. Celsius, which shows 0° for freezing and 100° for boiling water, is used throughout the world for scientific purposes; it is used for general purposes in Europe. Fahrenheit, in which 32° is the freezing temperature and 212° the boiling temperature of water, is the scale previously used in Britain (now transferring to the Centigrade scale) and still employed in the United States. Reáumur, with 0° for freezing and 80° for boiling water, is nearly obsolete, but is occasionally found in old books of European origin on scientific matters and cookery.

Celsius		*Fahrenheit*	*Celsius*		*Fahrenheit*	*Celsius*		*Fahrenheit*
−20	=	−4	10	=	50	45	=	113
−17.8	=	0	15	=	59	50	=	122
−15	=	5	20	=	68	60	=	140
−10	=	14	25	=	77	70	=	158
−5	=	23	30	=	86	80	=	176
0	=	32	35	=	95	90	=	194
5	=	41	40	=	104	100	=	212

To change Celsius to Fahrenheit, multiply by 9, divide by 5 and add 32.
To change Fahrenheit to Celsius, subtract 32, multiply by 5 and divide by 9.
Normal blood temperature in human beings is 36.9°C (98.4°F).

TEMPERATURES

−273°C	Absolute zero, the coldest temperature possible
−230°C	Surface of the planet Pluto
−196°C	Air becomes liquid
−88°C	Coldest temperature recorded on earth (Antarctica)
−39°C	Mercury becomes solid
0°C	Water freezes
37°C	Normal body temperature
58°C	Hottest temperature recorded on earth (Libya)
100°C	Water boils
250°C	Wood catches fire
600°C	Gas cooker flame
1063°C	Gold melts
5500°C	Surface of sun
16 million°C	Centre of sun

COMMON FORMULAE

Circumference of circle	=	$2\pi r$ ($\pi = 3.1416$; r = radius)
Area of circle	=	πr^2
Volume of sphere	=	$\frac{4}{3}\pi r^3$
Surface of sphere	=	$4\pi r^2$
Volume of cylinder	=	$\pi r^2 h$ (h = height)

CHEMICAL NAMES OF EVERYDAY SUBSTANCES

Substance	*Chemical name*	*Substance*	*Chemical name*
acetylene	ethyne	ether	ethoxyethane
alcohol	ethanol	gypsum	calcium sulphate
alum	aluminium potassium sulphate	hypo	sodium thiosulphate
baking powder	sodium bicarbonate	iron pyrites	iron(II) disulphide
borax	sodium borate	limestone	calcium carbonate
calamine	zinc carbonate	magnesia	magnesium oxide
caustic soda	sodium hydroxide	marble	calcium carbonate
chalk	calcium carbonate	natural gas	methane
common salt	sodium chloride	plaster of Paris	calcium sulphate
common sugar	sucrose	PVC	polyvinyl chloride
Epsom salts	magnesium sulphate	TCP	trichlorophenol
		vinegar	ethanoic acid
		washing soda	hydrated sodium carbonate

CHEMICAL INDICATORS

Indicators show whether a substance is alkaline, acid or neutral. The following list gives the effect of adding an indicator.

Indicator	*Alkaline*	*Acid*	*Neutral*
Litmus	turns blue	turns red	turns purple
Methyl orange	turns yellow	turns pink	remains orange

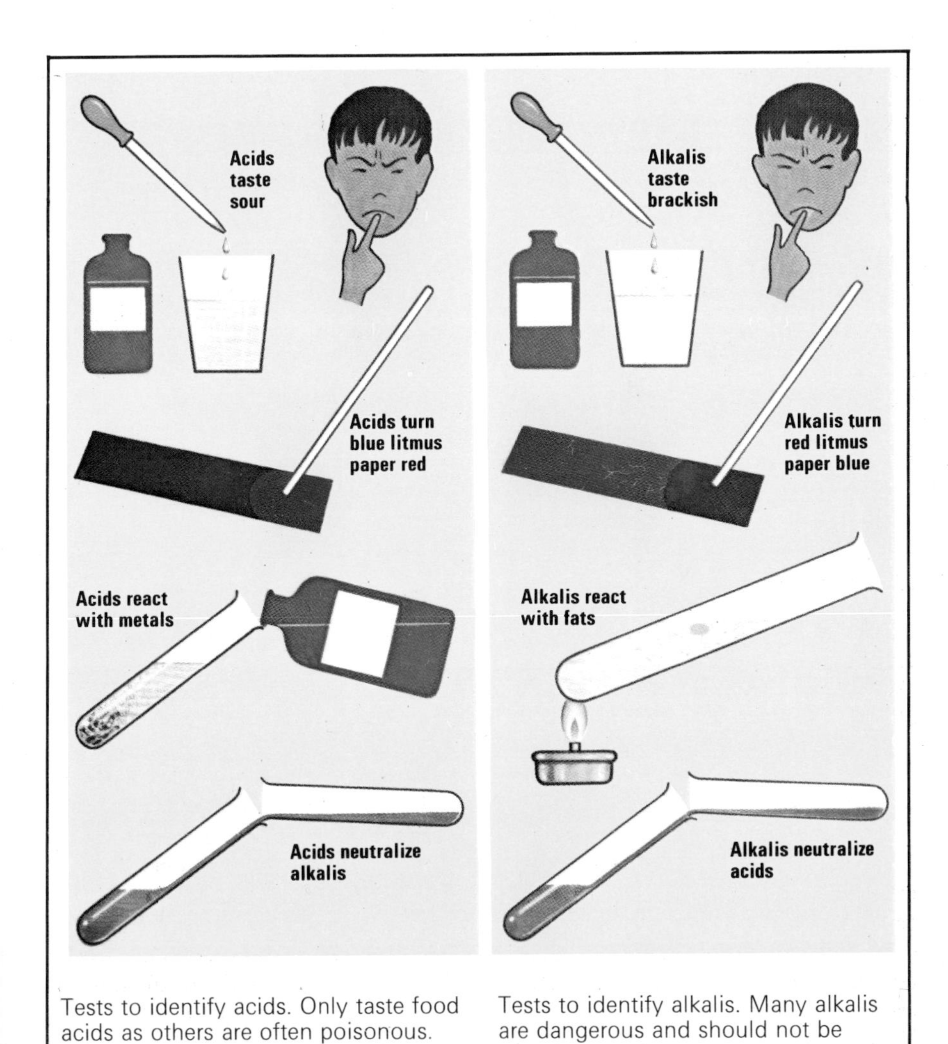

Tests to identify acids. Only taste food acids as others are often poisonous.

Tests to identify alkalis. Many alkalis are dangerous and should not be tasted.

FACTS AND FIGURES

THE ANIMAL KINGDOM

Largest: the largest living animal is the Blue Whale (*Balaenoptera musculus*). This marine mammal can grow to a length of over 33 m (100 ft), and to a weight of more than 170 tonnes. Minute, shrimp-like creatures known as krill make up its entire diet. The largest living land animal is the African Elephant (*Loxodonta africanus*); This mammal has been recorded at a height of almost 4 m (13 ft), and with a weight of nearly 11 tonnes.

Smallest: the smallest mammal in the world is Kitti's Hog-nosed Bat or Bumblebee Bat, which has a wingspan of 160 mm (6.29 in). The smallest bird is Helena's hummingbird, which is 58 mm (2.28 in) long. The smallest reptile is the Gecko *Sphaerodactylus parthenopion*, which is 18 mm (0.71 in) long, and the smallest fish is the Dwarf Pygmy Goby, which is 7.5 mm (0.28 in) long.

Longest: the ribbon or bootlace worm (*Lineus longissimus*) which lives in shallow waters on the North Sea coast, is the longest animal ever recorded at 54 m (170 ft) (a specimen washed ashore at St Andrews, Fife, Scotland, in 1864).

Tallest: The Giraffe (*Giraffa camelopardalis*), found in parts of Africa, may measure 6 m (19 ft) from the ground to the tips of its horns.

Fastest: the fastest animal is the spine-tailed Swift (*Chaetura caudacuta*). This bird can fly at well over 170 km/h (100 mph). On land, the Cheetah (*Acinonyx jubata*), and the Prong-horned Antelope (*Antilocarpa americana*) of North America, can both reach speeds of 100 km/h (60 mph).

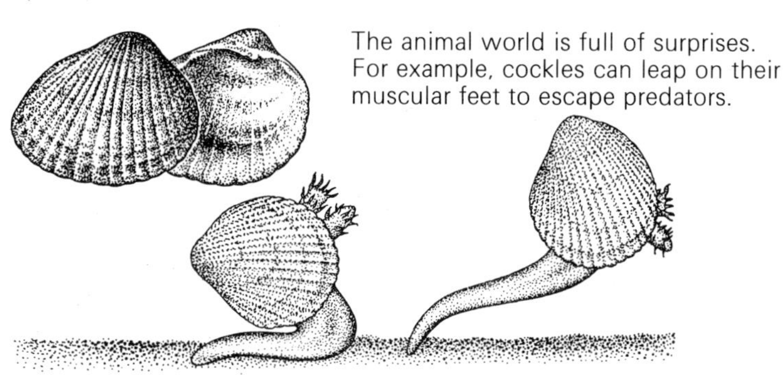

The animal world is full of surprises. For example, cockles can leap on their muscular feet to escape predators.

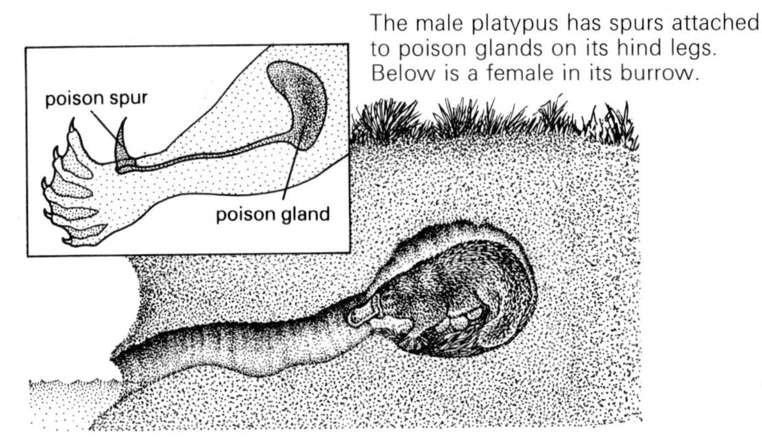

The male platypus has spurs attached to poison glands on its hind legs. Below is a female in its burrow.

Rarest: the shrew-like Tenrec *Dasogale fantoyanti* from Madagascar is probably the claimant to this title. Only one specimen has ever been found. (The commonest organisms are bacteria. They make up three-quarters of all living things.)

Strangest: the animal kingdom is full of strange and exotic creatures. One of the most curious classes of animals belongs to a group of mammals called monotremes. They are the primitive egg-laying mammals, and they share features in common with both the reptiles and the mammals. The Platypus (*Ornithorhynchus anatinus*) inhabits the fresh waters of Australia and Tasmania. The soft, duck-billed snout is used for finding worms. It swims with the aid of its webbed feet and flattened tail. The Spiny Anteaters (*Tachyglossus* from Australia, and *Zaglossus* from Papua New Guinea) have a long snout and a sticky tongue for feeding on worms and ants which they extract from burrows. Unlike other mammals, all monotremes have spurs on their hind legs armed with venom.

Most poisonous: the most poisonous, or venomous, animal is a north Australian jellyfish known as the sea wasp (*Chironex fleckeri*). It has been estimated that its poison is more than 350 times more potent that that of the Portuguese Man o'War. The poison acts so quickly – death usually occurs only a few minutes after being stung – that there is usually no chance to attempt treatment.

The most venomous land animal is the Funnelweb Spider (*Atrax robustus*), a large south Australian species. No really effective treatment has been found for its venom, which is far more potent than that of the most deadly snake.

THE PLANT KINGDOM

Largest: the 'General Sherman' tree (*Sequoiadendron giganteum*), an evergreen tree in the Sequoia National Park, has grown to a height of 83 m (272 ft). At one place

its girth is over 24 m (78 ft). Its weight is estimated to be over 2000 tonnes.
Tallest: The Coast Redwood (*Sequoia sempervirens*) of Oregon and California can grow to a height of 112 m (360 ft). Britain's tallest tree is the Grand Fir (*Abies grandis*), which is 57 m (187 ft) high.
Rarest: it is difficult to estimate the world's rarest plant, since many species are only known from one location, and some plants may not yet have been discovered. Among Britain's rarest are the Adder's Tongue Spearwort (*Ranunculus ophiglossifolius*), and the Coral Orchid *Epipogium aphyllum*.
Commonest: the world's commonest (in other words most widely distributed) plant is a grass known by its scientific name of *Cynodon dactylon*. It is found in South Africa, South America, Canada, New Zealand and Japan.
Deepest roots: the roots of a fig tree in South Africa are reputed to have penetrated the soil to a depth of 120 m (390 ft).
Oldest living: the oldest living tree is a Bristlecone Pine (*Pinus longaeva*) growing high up in the White Mountains, California. It was found to be 4600 years old.
Strangest: the most bizarre group of plants must surely be the carnivorous, insectivorous plants. Of these, the Venus Fly Trap (*Dionaea musciplua*) of North America is considered by many to be the most unusual. The Venus Fly Trap lives in soil lacking in nitrogen, so it obtains nitrogen from the bodies of flies and other small insects. The leaves have special traps on their ends and, when an insect lands on a trap, it snaps shut. The plant then digests the insect.

THE WORLD OF THE PAST

Largest animal: *Brachiosaurus*, the Arm Lizard, is the largest land creature ever known to have lived. Bones have been found which indicate a specimen with a weight of over 100 tonnes. This reptilian dinosaur lived in the swamplands of the Mesozoic Era, over 150 million years ago. From the ground to its head it measured over 13 m (42 ft), and was 26 m (85 ft) long from head to tail. Despite its enormous size, *Brachiosaurus* was a vegetarian, feeding on the plant growth it found around its swampland home. The largest carnivore (meat eater) ever known is *Tyrannosaurus*, the Tyrant Lizard, a fearsome dinosaur with massive jaws armed with rows of pointed teeth. *Tyrannosaurus* was over 10 m (32 ft) long and stood over 5 m (16 ft) tall.
Longest animal: the longest known land animal was the dinosaur *Diplodocus*, which attained a length of 27 m (33 ft). It is possible that some extinct marine animals, such as the early forms of whale, exceeded this, however.
Earliest forms of plant life: fossil evidence shows that simple forms of plant life existed over 3000 million years ago.
Earliest flowering plant: the earliest fossil flower is a palm-like plant over 65 million years old, found in North America.

FOOD CHAIN

This is a term used to describe how the animals and plants in a habitat feed, and how many of them are food for other creatures, and also how they vary their food requirements according to the seasons.

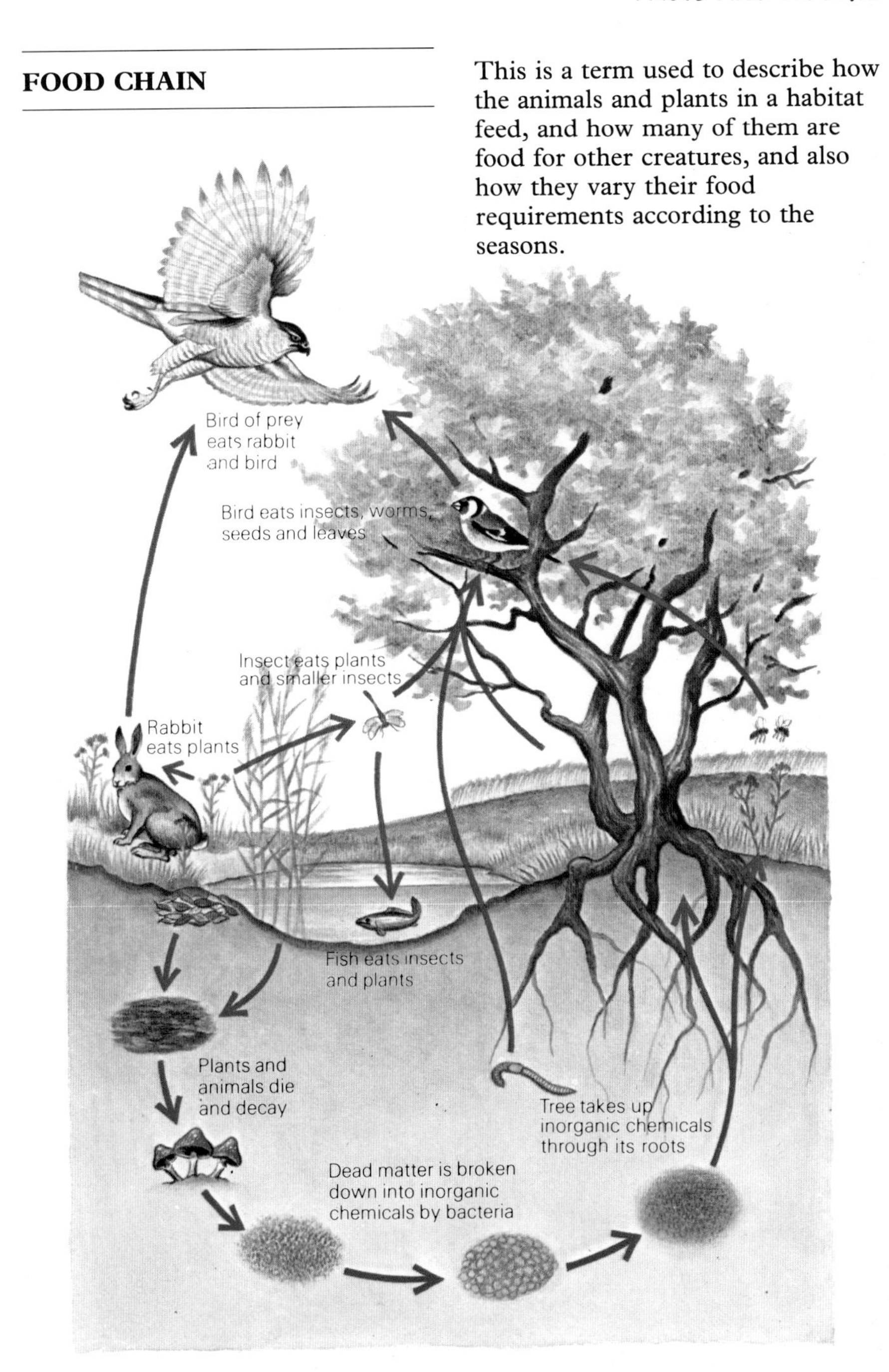

Suppose a small creature such as an aphid eats a leaf, and a ladybird eats the aphid, which in turn is eaten by a bird, and then the bird is eaten by a fox.

This sequence is called a food chain, for food has passed, in a chain-like fashion, from the leaf to the fox. In nature, many such chains exist, but normally the chains are linked, invisibly of course, to other food chains. For instance, the aphid in our example may be eaten directly by a bird which is already part of another food chain. This complicated series of connecting food chains is called the food web.

CLASSIFICATION

Classification is the method of grouping together organisms which have features in common. It also allows us to study the relationships that exist between one group and another. Within large groups of organisms with some common features, smaller groups are arranged with more features in common with each other (see page 190). Usually systems of classification are arranged with the most primitive, or lowly, groups of animals or plants placed first, leading up to the most advanced. A few minor groups, and most extinct groups, have been excluded from the lists which follow.

Species	The smallest unit of classification. Members can breed among themselves to produce offspring which can themselves breed. The species of an animal or plant is always written in Latin, beginning with a small letter.
Genus (plural genera)	A group containing similar species of animals or plants having common structural characteristics distinct from those of other groups. The genus of an animal or plant is always written in Latin, beginning with a capital letter.
Family	A group consisting of similar genera of animals or plants with certain characteristics in common. The Latin name ends in -idae for zoological families and -aceae for plant families.
Order	A group consisting of a number of families of animals or plants with certain characteristics in common.
Class	A group consisting of a number of orders of animals or plants with certain characteristics in common.
Phylum	One of the major classificatory divisions of the plant and animal kingdoms, comprising organisms with many features in common.

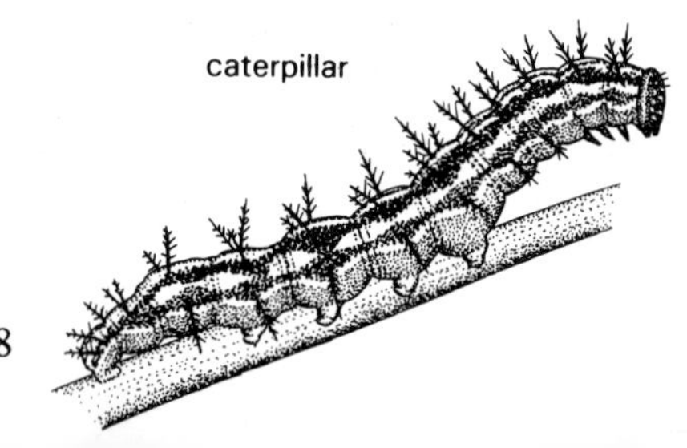

CLASSIFICATION OF THE ANIMAL KINGDOM

Subkingdom Protozoa: single-celled animals.
Phylum Protozoa: Microscopic, single-celled animals. *Subphylum Sarcomastigophora*: amoebas and flagellates. *Subphylum Sporozoa*: parasitic protozoans. *Subphylum Cnidospora*: parasitic protozoans with filamentous capsules on their spores (spores are resting stages in the life cycle). *Subphylum Ciliophora*: forms with hair-like cilia used for locomotion or feeding.
Subkingdom Metazoa: many-celled animals.
Phylum Porifera: sponges; the most lowly of the many celled animals; all are aquatic.
Phylum Cnidaria: mainly flower-like animals with bodies composed of two cell layers separated by a jelly-like layer called the mesoglea; food is usually captured by means of stinging tentacles. *Class Hydrozoa*: sea firs; also includes the Portuguese Man-o'War. *Class Scyphozoa*: the jellyfishes; mainly free-swimming, bell-shaped creatures. *Class Anthozoa*: sea-anemones and corals (corals secrete a stony covering in which the anemone-like creature lives).
Phylum Ctenophora: comb jellies; variously shaped animals with cilia which beat to drive the animal along.
Phylum Platyhelminthes: flatworms; leaf-like worms. *Class Turbellaria*: free-living worms found in water. *Class Trematoda*: the flukes; parasitic animals with complex life-cycles. *Class Cestoda*: tapeworms.
Phylum Nemertina: ribbon worms; often extremely long worms, usually found on the seashore.
Phylum Nemertoda: roundworms; free-living and parasitic types (e.g. hookworms) are found.
Phylum Brachiopoda: lamp shells; small animals attached to seabed by a stalk, and enclosed in a two-valved shell.
Phylum Annelida: segmented worms; a large phylum consisting of worms with a true body cavity (the coelom). *Class Polychaeta*: bristle worms; marine worms with well-defined heads; including ragworms, lugworms and tube-dwelling worms. *Class Oligochaeta*: earthworms; mainly terrestrial or freshwater worms with a reduced head. *Class Hirudinea*: leeches; blood-sucking parasitic worms that attach themselves to their victim by suckers.
Phylum Mollusca: snails, slugs, bivalves and octopuses; many forms are covered in a hard shell, secreted by an outer body layer called the mantle; many fossils are known. *Class Monoplacophora*: simplest shelled molluscs. *Class Amphineura*: chitons; shell usually in eight parts. *Class Gastropoda*: slugs, snails and limpets; the shell is in one piece or, as in slugs, absent. *Class Bivalvia*: mussels, oysters; the shell is in two parts, hinged together. *Class Scaphopoda*: the tusk shells. *Class Cephalopoda*: squids and octopuses; most highly developed molluscs with powerful eyes, large 'brains' and tentacles for food capture.
Phylum Arthropoda: joint-legged animals; a huge phylum containing over 80 per cent of the entire animal kingdom; the body organs are contained within a hard exoskeleton. *Class Onychophora*: possible links between the worms and the arthropods. *Class Trilobita*: extinct clawed marine animals. *Class Merostomata*: king crabs. *Class Pycnogonida*: sea-spiders. *Class Arachnida*: spiders, scorpions, ticks and mites; 8-legged animals with the body divided into 2 parts. *Class Crustacea*: crabs, shrimps, lobsters, barnacles and woodlice. *Class Insecta*: insects; 3 pairs of legs and 2

Classification of an Arabian Camel

pairs of wings are usually present; body divided into 3 parts; three-quarters of all animals are insects.

Phylum Ectoprocta: moss animals; tiny aquatic animals living in tubes, the whole mass together resembling seaweed.

Phylum Echinodermata: marine animals having bodies built on a 5-rayed plan; movement is by means of the water vascular system, a curious arrangement of water-filled canals which operate the tube feet. *Class Crinoidea*: feather-stars and sea-lilies; 5 pairs of arms; usually attached to the bottom. *Class Asteroidea*: starfishes. *Class Ophiuroidea*: brittle-stars; possess long, spiny arms. *Class Echinoidea*: sea-urchins, heart-urchins and sand-dollars; spherical creatures with long spines extending from the skin. *Class Holothuroidea*: sea-cucumbers; cucumber or worm-shaped creatures with a ring of tentacles surrounding the mouth.

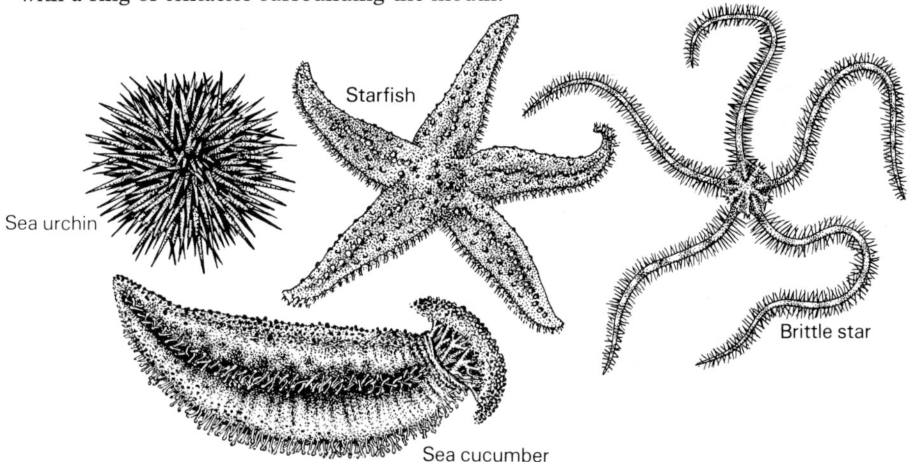

Phylum Chaetognatha: arrow-worms; tiny, dart-like animals.

Phylum Hemichordata: worm-like animals whose body is divided into proboscis, collar and trunk.

Phylum Chordata: important phylum which includes the vertebrates, such as man; all chordates possess a hollow dorsal nerve cord.

Subphylum Urochordata: salps; barrel-shaped animals.

Subphylum Cephalochordata: lancelets; small, burrowing, fish-like creatures.

Subphylum Vertebrata: vertebrates; the most advanced of all animals; vertebrates possess a brain-case, well-developed sense organs, a backbone of many separate bones (vertebrae) and usually paired limbs.

Class Agnatha: jawless fishes (hagfishes and lampreys).

Class Chondrichthyes: fishes with cartilaginous skeletons (sharks, skates and rays).

Class Osteichthyes: fishes with bony skeletons.

Class Amphibia: air-breathing land vertebrates which return to water to lay and fertilize their eggs. *Order Apoda*: limbless, burrowing forms. *Order Urodela*: newts and salamanders. *Order Anura*: frogs and toads.

Class Reptilia: cold-blooded vertebrates whose skin is usually covered in scales; eggs are fertilized inside the female and are usually laid within a protective shell. *Order Chelonia*: turtles and tortoises. *Order Rhynchocephalia*: tuatara lizard. *Order Crocodilia*: crocodiles, caimans and alligators. *Order Squamata*: lizards and snakes.

The class Reptilia also includes some very important groups of extinct animals. Among these are the marine Ichthyosaurs, the flying pterosaurs, the mammal-like reptiles and the Saurischians and Ornithischians – these last two groups comprised the Dinosaurs.
Class Aves: birds; warm-blooded vertebrates with bodies covered with feathers; most birds can fly – all have the front limbs modified for wings. *Order Impennes*: penguins. *Order Struthioniformes*: ostriches. *Order Casuariiformes*: emus and cassowaries. *Order Apterygiformes*: moas and kiwis. *Order Rheiformes*: rheas. *Order Tinamiformes*: tinamous. *Order Gaviformes*: loons and divers. *Order Procellariformes*: albatrosses, petrels and shearwaters. *Order Pelecaniformes*: pelicans and cormorants. *Order Ciconiiformes*: herons and bitterns. *Order Anseriformes*: ducks, geese and swans. *Order Falconiformes*: vultures, hawks, eagles, ospreys and falcons. *Order Columbiformes*: pigeons and doves. *Order Caprimulgiformes*: nightjars. *Order Coraciiformes*: kingfishers, toucans and woodpeckers. *Order Colymbiformes*: grebes. *Order Galliformes*: grouse and pheasants. *Order Gruiformes:* coots, rails and cranes. *Order Charadriiformes*: waders and gulls. *Order Psittaciformes*: parrots and macaws. *Order Cuculiformes*: cuckoos and road-runners. *Order Strigiformes*: owls. *Order Apodiformes*: swifts and hummingbirds. *Order Trogoniformes*: trogons. *Order Passeriformes*: perching birds; the largest order of birds containing many species such as larks, swallows, crows, tits, wrens, thrushes, robins, warblers, flycatchers, starlings, finches and buntings.
Class Mammalia: mammals; warm-blooded creatures whose bodies are usually covered with hair; young develop inside the mother, except in primitive forms; young are suckled. *Subclass Prototheria, Order Monotremata*: egg-laying mammals; platypus and spiny anteaters. *Subclass Metatheria, Order Marsupalia*: primitive mammals in which the young develop in a pouch called the marsupium; marsupials are found in Australasia and parts of America; wombats, wallabies, kangaroos, bandicoots and phalangers. *Subclass Eutheria*: the most advanced mammals; the young develop inside a special internal structure called the placenta. *Order Insectivora*: moles, flying

Tree shrew

lemurs, hedgehogs and shrews. *Order Chiroptera*: bats. *Order Primata*: monkeys, apes, lemurs, lorises and man. *Order Edentata*: sloths, armadillos and anteaters. *Order Pholidota*: pangolins. *Order Rodenta*: rats, mice, hamsters, squirrels, beavers, guinea pigs and porcupines. *Order Lagomorpha*: hares and rabbits. *Order Carnivora*: includes the Feloidea (mongoose, hyena, lynx, bobcats, tigers, lion and cheetah); the Canoidea (stoats, weasels, wolves, foxes, jackals, pandas, racoons and bears); the Phocoidea (seals) and the Otaroidea (walrus, furseals and sealions). *Order Cetacea*: whales, dolphins and porpoises. *Order Tubulidentata*; aardvark *Order Proboscidea*: elephants and hyraxes. *Order Sirenia*: dugongs and manatees. *Order Perissodactyla*: horses, tapirs and rhinoceroses. *Order Artiodactyla*: pigs, camels, llamas, cattle, deer, giraffes, hippopotamuses and sheep.

CLASSIFICATION OF THE PLANT KINGDOM

Phylum Fungi: non-flowering plants lacking the green pigment chlorophyll, and which therefore do not make their own food; they obtain their food by absorbing the juices of dead matter (as saprophytes) or living matter (as parasites); plant body is a mass of threads called a mycelium. *Class Mycetozoa*: slime moulds; primitive jelly-like fungi. *Class Phycomycetes*: simple mycelium, free-living and parasitic forms. *Class Ascomycetes*: largest group of fungi; spores produced in a club-shaped ascus; includes the yeasts and truffles. *Class Basidiomycetes*: includes the familiar mushrooms and toadstools as well as the earthstars, puffballs and rusts.
Phylum Lichenes: lichens; plants formed by the close association of a fungus (usually an Ascomycete) with an alga (usually a green, or blue-green variety); the fungus provides anchorage and absorbs minerals and water, the alga makes food and passes some to the fungus; lichens often appear as black, green or yellow growths on rocks and trees.
Phylum Algae: non-flowering plants ranging from single-celled forms to large, multicellular seaweeds; algae can be classified according to the colour of the pigments they contain. *Class Cyanophyta*: blue-green algae; single-celled or filamentous forms. *Class Chlorophyta*: green algae; ranging from single-celled to branched and lettuce-like forms; includes green seaweeds. *Class Xanthophyta*: forms possessing unequal whiplash flagella. *Class Chrysophyta*: very large class, includes members of the plankton. *Class Bacillariophyta*: diatoms; part of the plankton. *Class Rhodophyta*: red algae; includes the red seaweeds – mainly deep water varieties. *Class Phaeophyta*: brown algae; commonest seaweeds on most rocky shores; includes the kelps and wracks.
Phylum Bryophyta: small, non-flowering plants often found in damp places. *Class Hepaticae*: liverworts; prostrate plants attached to the ground by root-like rhizoids. *Class Anthocerotae*: hornworts. *Class Musci*: mosses, usually erect plants with spiral leaves.
Phylum Pteridophyta: non-flowering plants with true stems, leaves and tissues, mainly terrestrial. *Class Psilopsida*: similar to earliest land plants; creeping stems and poorly developed leaves. *Class Lycopsida*: clubmosses. *Class Sphenopsida*: horsetails; ribbed, jointed stems bear whorls of leaves. *Class Pteropsida*: ferns; usually feathery plants; some aquatic forms.

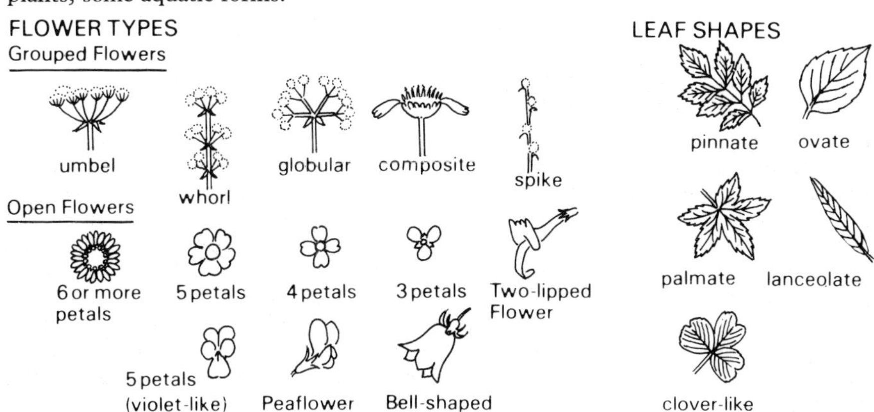

Phylum Gymnospermae: primitive seed plants; unprotected ovules are borne in cones; commonly evergreen trees. *Class Cycadopsida*: cycads; common trees in the tropics. *Class Coniferopsida*: conifers; trees with needle-like leaves; common trees in cool places. *Class Gnetopsida*: ovules are borne in flower-like structures, not cones; includes bizarre desert forms.
Phylum Angiospermae: higher, or flowering, plants; ovules are enclosed inside the protective ovary; most abundant plants on land, ranging from the familiar flowers, to bushes and trees. *Class Monocotyledoneae*: plants with one seed leaf (cotyledon) in the embryo; includes cereals, grasses, palms, lilies, daffodils, irises and orchids. *Class Dicotyledoneae*: plants with two seed leaves (cotyledons) in the embryo; includes deciduous trees (such as oak, beech, walnut and birch), fruit trees, food plants (such as potatoes, beans, cabbages and carrots), and an enormous variety of bushes, shrubs and flowers (such as roses, tulips, ivy, nettles, honeysuckles, daisies, heathers, rhododendrons and geraniums).

EVOLUTION

The earth has been in existence for over 4500 million years, and for much of that time no life existed. To begin with, harsh winds and violent rain storms lashed the earth, and a vast sea covered much of its surface.

The first scant signs of life have been discovered in rocks about 2000 million years old, and were primitive kinds of bacteria. Although we do not know exactly how life began, we imagine that certain chemicals were present at the dawn of life, and that somehow the chemicals from this 'primaeval soup' combined together, perhaps as a result of fierce electrical storms, to form protein molecules which could reproduce themselves.

Eventually, as conditions on earth slowly changed, the protein molecules became more complicated and organized into cells. Some cells became plants, some bacteria and others animals. Some life forms were able to live on almost unchanged because conditions changed only very little. This is true of the sharks, which have lived in the sea for hundreds of millions of years.

On land, the story was different. The wet, warm climate of the Carboniferous and Permian became drier, and so the many types of amphibians which had flourished had to meet this change. Some types died out forever, but from other types, the reptiles evolved. Later still, conditions suited the rise of the mammals – active, warm-blooded creatures with the ability to control their own body temperature.

Evolution is a continuing process, and although the present conditions on earth have allowed mammals (and especially man) to dominate the animal kingdom, and angiosperms to dominate the plant kingdom, perhaps in millions of years to come, their place will have been taken by new forms.

Stages in the Earth's History

age in millions of years	period	era
2	Pleistocene	Caenozoic
10	Pliocene	
25	Miocene	
40	Oligocene	
60	Eocene	
70	Palaeocene	
	Cretaceous	Mesozoic
135	Jurassic	
180	Triassic	
225	Permian	Palaeozoic
270	Carboniferous	
350	Devonian	
400	Silurian	
440	Ordovician	
500	Cambrian	
600	Precambrian	

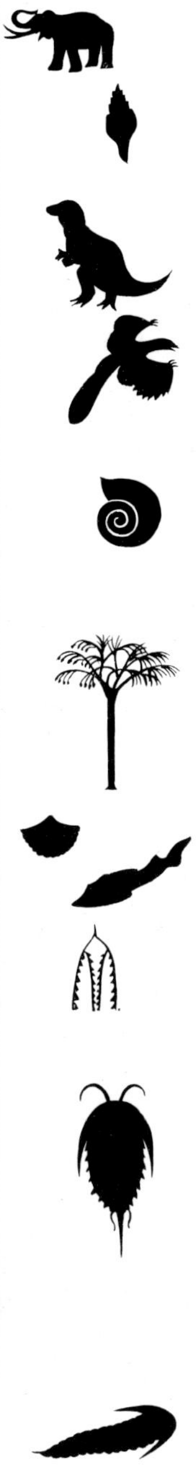

ARTS, HISTORY AND THE MODERN WORLD

WRITERS AND THEIR BOOKS

One of the earliest writers we know about was the Greek poet Homer, who lived about 700 BC. He wrote two epic poems, the *Iliad* and the *Odyssey*. The *Iliad* tells of the siege of Troy and the story of Achilles. In the *Odyssey* Homer tells of the return of Odysseus after twenty years away from his home. Other famous Greek writers were Plato and Aristotle.

Among Roman writers around the 1st century BC were Cicero, who was a famous public speaker and wrote books on oratory, and Julius Caesar, one of the greatest generals in history, whose best-known work is his history of the Roman wars in Gaul. Three Latin poets were Virgil, Horace and Ovid. The hero of Virgil's *Aeneid* is Aeneas, a Trojan prince who tried to found a new Trojan empire in Italy. Virgil did not finish this book before he died and left instructions for it to be destroyed, but this fortunately did not happen.

The *Fables* of Aesop are a collection of Greek fables which were first brought together in the 2nd century AD and made into a book by a monk in the 14th century. Aesop is said to have been a slave on the island of Samos in the 6th century BC.

The stories in the *Arabian Nights* – stories of Aladdin, Ali Baba and others – in fact come from India, but they were put into Arabic in the 11th century. The names of the characters are Persian and it is thought that the stories travelled from India to Persia and then to Arabia. The stories are the work of several writers.

The Latin language was used in Europe until the Middle Ages. One of the first great works in Italian was Dante's long poem, *The Divine Comedy*, written in the 14th century. In the same century in England Geoffrey Chaucer wrote *The Canterbury Tales*. This is a story of pilgrims travelling to Canterbury. Each pilgrim tells a story on the way. Chaucer had intended to have 120 tales in all, but the work was not finished.

In France in the 16th century lived the writer François Rabelais. His book, *Gargantua*, tells the story of a giant and is full of humorous satire.

It was in Spain in 1605 that the first adventure novel, *Don Quixote*, was written. Miguel de Cervantes is said to have started it when he was in prison. It describes the adventures of Don Quixote, who leaves his home with a servant, Sancho Panza.

The greatest poem of John Milton, who was born in 1608, was *Paradise Lost*. This tells of the rebellion of Satan and the fall of man. When the poem was published it was a great success. *Pilgrim's Progress*, written by another Englishman, John Bunyan, is called a moral fable. It was written in two parts, the first in 1674 and the second in 1684.

Daniel Defoe was a government agent, a traveller and journalist. He was nearly sixty when he wrote *Robinson Crusoe*, but he went on to write many more books. *Robinson Crusoe* became popular at once and has remained so. Jonathan Swift's most famous book is *Gulliver's Travels*, published in 1726. On the surface this is a charming fable, but underneath is a sharp attack on society. Man is shown as a small creature, with his many faults magnified.

One of the first great English novelists was Henry Fielding. His masterpiece was *Tom Jones*, written in 1759. Also in the 18th century, Samuel Johnson spent eight years compiling his *Dictionary of the English Language*. Boswell, a friend of Johnson, wrote a famous biography of him, and Edward Gibbon wrote a great history, *The Decline and Fall of the Roman Empire*, during the same period. Two French writers at this time were Voltaire and Rousseau. Both of them were philosophers, but they also wrote novels.

At the beginning of the 19th century in England Jane Austen wrote her six novels, the best known being *Pride and Prejudice*. Sir Walter Scott was a romantic writer, who often wrote about Scotland, as in *Rob Roy*.

One of the major novelists of the 19th century was Charles Dickens. After an unhappy childhood he became a journalist. The *Pickwick Papers* were published in 1836 and were a great success. Dickens's books include *David Copperfield* and *Oliver Twist*. There were many other novelists in England. Thackeray's books include *Vanity Fair* and Trollope wrote *Barchester Towers*. Charlotte Brontë wrote *Jane Eyre* and her sister Emily, *Wuthering Heights*. George Eliot was a pen name for Mary Ann Evans, who wrote *Middlemarch*. Thomas Hardy wrote novels set in Dorset, such as *Tess of the D'Urbervilles*.

Minor novelists included Captain Marryat, who wrote *The Children of the New Forest* and many sea stories; and Charles Kingsley, who wrote a fairy tale, *The Water Babies* and historical novels like *Westward Ho!* Robert Louis Stevenson was a highly successful writer. He wrote *Treasure Island* and *Kidnapped* and many other books. Rudyard Kipling was born in India and wrote about that country in books like *Kim* and his two *Jungle Books*.

There were many great writers in Europe in the 19th century. The first major Russian novelist was Nikolai Gogol who wrote an amusing book, *Dead Souls*. Another

The Brontë sisters, (left to right) Charlotte, Emily and Anne, were the daughters of an eccentric Irish-born Yorkshire curate.

Russian was the short story writer, Ivan Turgenev. Leo Tolstoy's great work was *War and Peace*, a novel which tells the history of Russia's part in the Napoleonic Wars. Dostoevsky, one of the most brilliant Russian writers, wrote *Crime and Punishment*.

In France in the 19th century Honoré de Balzac wrote 90 works in 20 years. *The Human Comedy* is a series of novels giving a complete picture of life at that time. Three other French writers were Stendhal, who wrote *The Red and the Black*, Zola, who wrote *Thérèse Raquin*, and Gustave Flaubert, whose best-known book is *Madame Bovary*.

The first truly American writers appeared in the 19th century. One was Fenimore Cooper who wrote *The Last of the Mohicans*. Another, Herman Melville, wrote tales of the sea, such as *Moby Dick*. Samuel Clemens, writing under the name of Mark Twain, wrote *Tom Sawyer*. *Uncle Tom's Cabin*, the famous anti-slavery novel, was written by Harriet Beecher Stowe. Henry James's many books include *Portrait of a Lady*.

American 20th-century writers include Ernest Hemingway, who wrote *For Whom the Bell Tolls*, and John Steinbeck, one of whose best-known books is *The Grapes of Wrath*. In Europe, among the vast number of famous writers we find James Joyce, D. H. Lawrence, Franz Kafka, Thomas Mann, Marcel Proust and André Gide.

FAMOUS WRITERS

AESOP (629–560 BC). Greek slave who compiled a large collection of moral fables, many of which are as applicable today as they were when first told.
AUSTEN, Jane (1775–1817). English novelist. Wrote six books, *Sense and Sensibility, Pride and Prejudice, Northanger Abbey, Mansfield Park, Emma* and *Persuasion,* which are among the greatest novels in the English language.
BALZAC, Honoré de (1779–1850). French novelist, famous for his penetrating studies of the society of his time. Among his best-known novels are *Le Père Goriot* and *La Cousine Bette.*
BLAKE, William (1757–1827). British poet and artist; author of many religious works, among them the *Prophetic Books* from which the hymn 'Jerusalem' is taken.
BRONTË, Sisters; Charlotte (1816–1855), Emily (1818–1848) and Anne (1820–1849). English novelists. Charlotte's books include *Jane Eyre, Shirley* and *Villette*; Emily wrote *Wuthering Heights*; Anne's two books are *Agnes Grey* and *The Tenant of Wildfell Hall.*
BROWNING, Robert (1812–1889). English poet. Some of his best-known works are *Paracelsus, Sordello* and *The Ring and the Book.*
BURNS, Robert (1759–1796). Scottish poet, famous for such poems as *Tam o'Shanter* and *The Cotter's Saturday Night* and for such songs as *Auld Lang Syne.*
BYRON, George Gordon, Lord (1788–1824). English poet, whose work has remained constantly 'in print' for a century and a half. He died in Greece, to which he had gone to aid the Greeks in their struggle for independence.
CHAUCER, Geoffrey (1340?–1400). One of the greatest English poets. His *Canterbury Tales* are widely read and enjoyed today.
CHEKHOV, Anton (1860–1904). Russian writer of short stories and plays. Among his works are the plays *The Cherry Orchard, The Three Sisters* and *Uncle Vanya.*
COLERIDGE, Samuel Taylor (1772–1834). Poet, philosopher and critic. In the first rank of English poets. Some of his best-known works are *Kubla Khan, The Ancient Mariner* and *Christabel.*
DANTE ALIGHIERI (1265–1321). Italy's greatest poet. He was also a soldier and politician and at one time was sentenced to be burned at the stake for his political allegiance, but was exiled instead. His greatest work is the *Divinia Commedia.*
DICKENS, Charles (1812–1870). Leading English novelist, who is still widely read. His best-known works include *David Copperfield, Oliver Twist, The Pickwick Papers, Great Expectations* and *A Christmas Carol.*
DOSTOEVSKY, Fyodor (1821–1881). Russian novelist, whose work has had much influence on subsequent writing. Among his best-known novels are *Crime and Punishment, The Idiot* and *The Brothers Karamazov.*
DUMAS, Alexandre (1802–1870). French novelist and dramatist. His best-remembered novels are *The Three Musketeers* and *Twenty Years After.*
ELIOT, Thomas Stearns (1888–1964). American-born but British-domiciled poet and playwright, whose poems have greatly influenced modern poetry. As well as his serious works he also wrote the amusing *Old Possum's Book of Practical Cats.*
FAULKNER, William (1897–1962). An American novelist who used new techniques in his novels, which include *The Sound and the Fury* and *As I Lay Dying.*
FLAUBERT, Gustave (1821–1880). French author. His novel *Madame Bovary,* brought a new realism to novel writing.
GOETHE, Johann Wolfgang von (1749–1832). German poet; the most famous of

his works is his play *Faust*. In German writing he takes much the same position as Shakespeare does in the history of English literature and drama. He was also a scientist of considerable importance.
GOGOL, Nikolai Vasilievich (1809–1852). Russian novelist and dramatist. His best-known works are his novel *Dead Souls* and his play *The Government Inspector*.
HARDY, Thomas (1840–1928). English poet and novelist. Among his best-known novels are *Tess of the d'Ubervilles, Far from the Madding Crowd, The Mayor of Casterbridge, The Return of the Native* and *Jude the Obscure*.
HOMER (*c.*850BC?) Probably born in Greece, he wrote two great works, *The Iliad* and *The Odyssey*.
JOHNSON, Samuel (1709–1784). English poet, essayist and lexicographer. Much information regarding him comes to us from his biographer, James Boswell.
JOYCE, James (1882–1941). Irish author; spent most of his life in Italy, Switzerland and France. His best-known works are *A Portrait of the Artist as a Young Man, Ulysses* and *Finnegan's Wake*.
KEATS, John (1795–1821). English poet; wrote for only about five years, but his outstanding work had a tremendous influence on later poets. His poems include *Endymion, The Eve of St Agnes, Ode on a Grecian Urn* and *Ode to a Nightingale*.
LAWRENCE, David Herbert (1885–1930). English novelist and poet; also wrote a number of penetrating travel essays. His leading novels include *Sons and Lovers, Aaron's Rod, The Rainbow* and *Women in Love*.
MAUPASSANT, Guy de (1850–1893). French writer, famous for his short stories.
MELVILLE, Herman (1819–1891). American novelist, many of whose writings dealt with the sea. His best-known books are *Moby Dick, Billy Budd* and *Typee*.
MILTON, John (1608–1674). One of the greatest English poets. Among his best-known works are *Paradise Lost, Samson Agonistes* and *Areopagitica*.
MOLIÈRE, Jean Baptiste Poquelin (1622–1673). Leading French dramatist. His most popular plays include *Tartuffe, Le Bourgeois Gentilhomme* and *L'École des Maris*.
PUSHKIN, Alexander (1799–1837). Russian poet and writer of stories. One of his most famous short stories is *The Queen of Spades*.
SCOTT, Sir Walter (1771–1832). Scottish novelist and poet; wrote novels based on Scottish history and legend, such as *Ivanhoe, Kenilworth, The Heart of Midlothian*.
SHAKESPEARE, William (1564–1616). English dramatist and poet, generally regarded as the world's greatest playright. His wide range of tragedies, historical dramas and comedies has been performed more than the work of any other dramatist.
SHAW, George Bernard (1856–1950). Irish playwright and critic. Among his plays are *Pygmalion, Caesar and Cleopatra, Man and Superman* and *Saint Joan*.
SHELLEY, Percy Bysshe (1792–1822). English poet. In his day he was considered revolutionary; today he is regarded as a poetic genius. Among his best-known writings are *Adonais, Prometheus Unbound* and *To a Skylark*.
STEVENSON, Robert Louis (1850–1894). Scottish novelist and poet, author of *Treasure Island, Kidnapped, The Strange Case of Dr Jekyll and Mr Hyde* and many other novels.
SWIFT, Jonathan (1667–1745). Irish satirist, author of *Gulliver's Travels*.
TENNYSON, Alfred, Lord (1809–1892). English poet. He was made Poet Laureate for his consistently high standard of work over many years. Some of his greatest verses, such as *The Idylls of the King*, had medieval England as their subject.
TOLSTOY, Leo Nikolayevich, Count (1828–1910). Russian novelist, two of whose

works, *War and Peace* and *Anna Karenina*, are considered among the greatest novels of all time.

TWAIN, Mark, Samuel Langhorne Clemens (1835–1910). American novelist; author of *Tom Sawyer, Huckleberry Finn, The Prince and the Pauper* and others.

VERNE, Jules (1828–1905). French novelist; pioneer of science fiction, who wrote *Journey to the Centre of the Earth, Around the World in Eighty Days* and others.

VIRGIL (70–19 BC). Considered the greatest of all the Roman poets. His major work is the unfinished *Aeneid*, based on the story of the settlement of Aeneas in Italy after the destruction of Troy.

VOLTAIRE, François Marie Arouet (1694–1778). French writer and satirist. Among his leading works are *Candide* and the *Dictionnaire Philosophique*.

WOOLF, Virginia (1882–1941). English novelist and critic. Among her best-known novels are *Mrs Dalloway, To the Lighthouse* and *The Waves*.

WORDSWORTH, William (1770–1850). English poet, noted for his supreme mastery of language. Was made Poet Laureate in 1843.

YEATS, William Butler (1865–1939). Irish poet. One of the great poets of recent times, he was awarded the Nobel Prize for Literature in 1923.

ZOLA, Emile (1840–1902). French novelist, whose most famous work is *Germinal*. He wrote about poor people struggling to survive in an unjust world.

BOOKS TO READ

The Adventures of Huckleberry Finn; *The Adventures of Tom Sawyer*, Mark Twain
Alice's Adventures in Wonderland, Lewis Carroll
Ballet Shoes, Noel Streatfeild
Black Beauty, Anna Sewell
Born Free, Joy Adamson
The Borrowers, Mary Norton
The Call of the Wild; White Fang, Jack London
Coral Island, R.M. Ballantyne
David Copperfield; *Great Expectations*, Charles Dickens
The Family from One End Street, Eve Garnett
Gulliver's Travels, Jonathan Swift
Heidi, Johanna Spyri
The Hobbit, J.R.R. Tolkien
The Jungle Book; *Just So Stories*, Rudyard Kipling
Kidnapped; *Treasure Island*, Robert Louis Stevenson
The Little Grey Men, 'BB'
The Lost World, Sir Arthur Conan Doyle
National Velvet, Enid Bagnold
101 Dalmations, Dodie Smith
The Railway Children, E. Nesbit
Robinson Crusoe, Daniel Defoe
The Scarlet Pimpernel, Baroness Orczy
The Secret Garden, Frances Hodgson Burnett
The Snow Goose, Paul Gallico
Strangers in the House, Joan Lingard
Swallows and Amazons, Arthur Ransome
Swiss Family Robinson, W.H.G. Kingston
Tarka the Otter, Henry Williamson
Three Men in a Boat, Jerome K. Jerome
A Town Like Alice, Neville Shute
Twenty Thousand Leagues Under the Sea, Jules Verne
Watership Down, Richard Adams
The Wind in the Willows, Kenneth Grahame

THE THEATRE

Drama grew out of religious festivals and dances. The Greeks of nearly 3000 years ago were the first to make these dramatic and the first to write plays and build theatres in which to act them. At first dances were performed on a dance floor on a hillside, so people could see. Then the Greeks built amphitheatres with seats cut into the hill in a semicircle. Gradually theatres developed from this.

Eventually Sophocles, one of the three great Greek writers of tragedies, that is, moving plays with unhappy endings, introduced stage scenery. He wrote at least 120 plays but we have only seven of them today. His three plays about Oedipus are probably the best known. The other two tragic writers were Aeschylus and Euripides. Another Greek playwright, Aristophanes, is famous for writing comedies – plays with happy endings. These four playwrights lived around the 4th and 5th centuries BC.

When the Romans built their theatres they did not use open hillsides but arranged the seats in tiers inside buildings. They built the first covered theatres. The

The theatre at Epidaurus in Greece was built 2300 years ago and seated 14 000 people.

English medieval mystery plays were performed in the street by members of guilds.

Romans liked plays of action, farces and pantomimes. Roman actors wore masks, and classical actors wore shoes with very high heels.

After the fall of Rome, during the period of the Dark Ages in Europe, which lasted from about the 5th to the 11th centuries AD, theatres were pulled down and the stones used for building. The only drama was provided by troupes of minstrels, jugglers and acrobats who travelled to castles giving performances to the feudal lords. In France troubadours travelled round the country singing love songs and telling legends.

In the East, however, drama was growing. In China during the 13th and 14th centuries plays telling a simple story were popular. In India there was the Indian Classical Theatre which consisted mainly of dancing. Between the 13th and 17th centuries in Japan the Noh theatre developed. The plays had no scenery and very little action, and actors had to perform in a certain way.

The theatre grew again in Europe from the ceremonies of the church, which became more and more dramatic. The story of Easter, for instance, was acted out in the Easter celebrations. By the 14th century religious plays were allowed in England and this was the start of the mystery, miracle and morality plays.

The mystery plays dealt with the creation of the world, the day of judgement and the story of Adam and Eve. The miracle plays were about the miracles of Jesus Christ and the early saints, and the morality plays were about vices, or evil actions.

The best-known morality play is called *Everyman*, and it was written about the end of the 15th century. Stages were erected in market places in towns and villages and the plays were performed by guild members.

The first theatres to be built in Europe after Roman times were in Italy in the 15th century. At this time in Italy there was a form of drama called *Commedia dell' arte*, which later became popular all over Europe. The actors played characters like Harlequin and Columbine, who in turn played the parts in a story.

In 1564 England's greatest playwright, William Shakespeare, was born in Stratford-upon-Avon. The first English theatre was built around 1576 and about 10 years after this Shakespeare went to London where he joined a company of actors. With them he not only acted but directed and wrote the series of over 30 great plays, most of which are still acted regularly all over the world.

Henrik Ibsen

Another famous English dramatist of the period was Ben Jonson, a great scholar whose plays did not enjoy the popular success of those of his friend Shakespeare. One of the most famous writers in France in the 17th century was Molière. He wrote comedies and usually acted the main part in them, amazing the audience with his realistic and forceful acting.

Theatres now had a proscenium arch separating the audience from the stage, and curtains, which could be drawn across the proscenium opening, were introduced. For the first time, performances took place at night. Theatres began to look as they do today: the auditorium was horseshoe shaped and the stage platform was generally built out into the audience. The first 'modern' theatre of which there are complete plans is the famous Schouwburg Theatre in Amsterdam, built in 1637.

The 18th century in England was a period of famous actors and, usually, rather bad plays. One of the most popular actors was David Garrick, who was also a theatre manager and dramatist. The only major playwrights at the time were Richard Sheridan and Oliver Goldsmith, who wrote witty comedies.

In Germany two famous writers of plays were Lessing, who introduced melodrama, and Schiller. The greatest German writer, Goethe, was also a playwright. He was concerned with the practical side of the theatre for he ran the Court Theatre in Weimar for over 40 years.

Throughout the 19th century the theatre in Europe was very popular with ordinary people. They demanded great spectacles and strong melodramas. It was also an age of great 'star' actors and actresses. These included the Englishmen, Edmund Kean and Henry Irving, and the celebrated women actresses, Sarah Bernhardt from France and Eleonora Duse from Italy.

The outstanding playwright towards the end of the 19th century was the Norwegian, Henrik Ibsen. His plays changed the whole course of dramatic writing in Europe.

Two important companies founded at this time were the Abbey Theatre in Dublin, which produced the plays of J.M. Synge and Sean O'Casey. Another was Stanislavsky's Moscow Arts Theatre, where the plays of the great Russian writer Chekhov were first seen.

The modern 'revolution' in the theatre was begun in the 1950s with John Osborne's *Look Back in Anger*, and was continued by Harold Pinter in the 1960s.

Styles of theatre now vary enormously. Most countries have national companies which continue to explore their country's classical heritage in traditional theatres, but new and experimental work also takes place all over the world. In parts of Africa and Asia, Western directors, writers and actors have sought new forms of drama and new forms of language. Politics has been important in drama since before Shakespeare's day and the theatre in many countries continues to be politically involved, with authors using drama to express their views about society. Many small groups band together and travel about using rented halls and rooms to perform new and exciting plays. These groups are sometimes known as *Fringe* or *Off-Broadway* theatre. They are used by writers and performers to introduce unconventional, and sometimes controversial, works which traditional, commercial theatres cannot risk staging for financial reasons.

MUSICIANS AND THEIR MUSIC

Music was one of the first things in human life. Every primitive people possessed a form of music-making, however simple or crude. The human voice was the first musical instrument and people have always expressed their feelings with their voices as a matter of instinct.

It is not possible to say when music became an art, that is the moment when a conscious effort was first made to reproduce sounds which had previously come naturally. We know from the pictures drawn by artists in the ancient worlds of Egypt and Assyria that music played an important part in their lives. For the Egyptians in particular music performed a religious function and had a very serious purpose.

The Greeks used music in their drama, and in fact the plays of the early Greek dramatists, such as Aeschylus and Sophocles, were more like operas. The voice was used as an instrument, particularly in chorus, for declaiming the lines of a play.

In the Middle Ages, music, in common with most forms of art and knowledge, developed within the church, particularly the form of chanting known as Gregorian, which is still used in services today.

The first secular music, that is music which was not composed for religious ceremonies, grew up in the Middle Ages with the minstrels. These wandering vagabonds earned their living by singing and playing for the amusement of anyone who would give them a supper in return for a song. After the minstrels came the troubadours, who were often men of noble birth and were treated with honour and respect.

Opera, which combines acting and singing, began in the 16th century. Some Italian poets and musicians had the idea of setting certain Greek stories to music and performing them on a stage. At first, the dramatic action was much more important than the singing. Monteverdi's operas, composed in the first half of the 17th century, in which the music came first, were the first true operas. Monteverdi was also one of the first composers to employ an orchestra.

The man who did more than any other to establish the shape of the modern orchestra and to develop the symphony as the chief form of musical expression was Haydn. He lived in Vienna in the 18th century when that city was the centre of the musical world. Mozart, Beethoven and Schubert all lived in Vienna during a period when the greatest classical music was written. The 19th century romantic music of Brahms, Schumann and Chopin, and the grand operas of Wagner and Verdi, led to the new musical sounds of the 20th century.

Although modern musical instruments have become complex and often difficult to play, each of the three great classes into which they fall – percussion, wind and

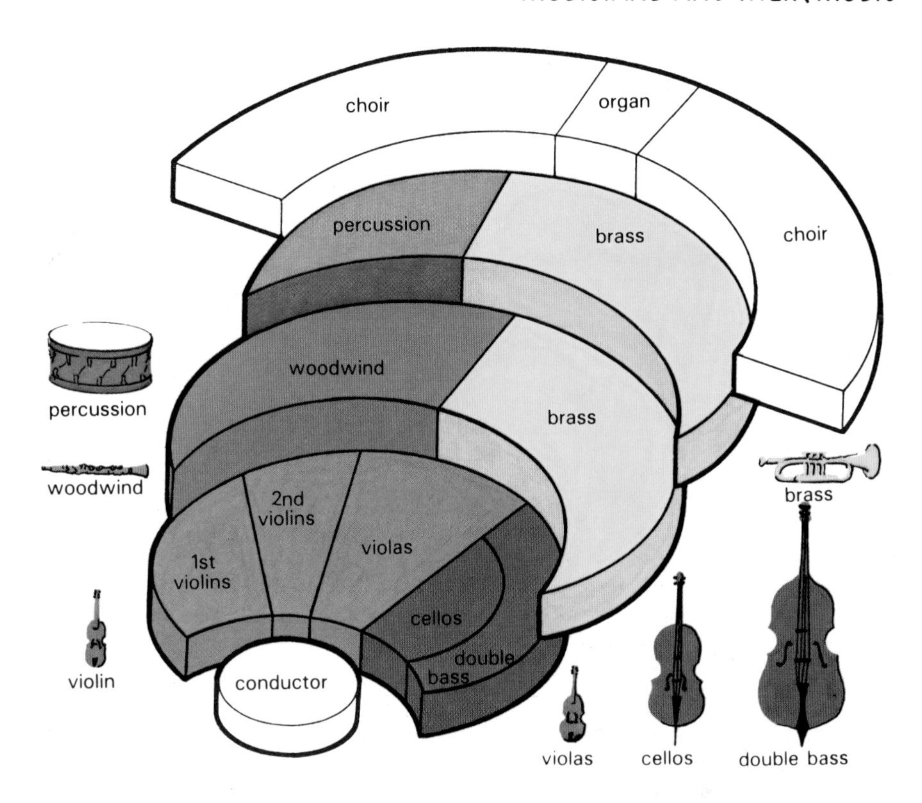

Modern orchestras vary greatly in size, from under 20 members to over 100. Concert halls are usually designed to accomodate a large choir and an organ as well as the orchestra, although these are only called for in major works. The different families of instruments, strings, brass, woodwind and percussion, are grouped together. This basic configuration for the orchestra has been recognized since the 19th century.

stringed – could be found readily to hand by primitive man.

Percussion instruments, such as the drum or triangle, produce sounds by being struck, and almost any hard substance will make some kind of sound if struck with a stone or stick. Wind instruments, such as the trumpet or clarinet, are, basically, hollow tubes through which the player blows. Reed pipes or animals' horns, even without keys and mouthpieces, will produce a 'wind' sound. Stringed instruments work on the principle that any tightly stretched cord can be made to produce sound if it is vibrated; in the case of a violin, for instance, by a bow being drawn across it. The bow and arrow, one of man's first mechanical weapons, would have introduced him to such a sound.

The piano and the guitar are examples of instruments which make use of the principles of both percussion and strings.

FAMOUS COMPOSERS

BACH, Johann Sebastian (1685–1750). German composer and organist; was one of the founders of his country's tradition of orchestral music. Among his works are the *Mass in B Minor*, the *St. Matthew Passion* and many cantatas and works for the organ.

BEETHOVEN, Ludwig van (1770–1827). German composer, famous in particular for his symphonies. By the age of 30 he was nearly deaf, though much of his great music was written after this time.

BERLIOZ, Hector (1803–1869). French composer of symphonies, operas and songs. His best known symphonic work is *Romeo and Juliet*.

BIZET, Georges (1838–1875). French composer of operas, including *The Pearl-Fishers* and *Carmen*, one of the world's most popular operas.

BRAHMS, Johannes (1833–1897). German composer, whose works include several major symphonies, sonatas and much piano music. His finest works are a blend of the Classical style and expressive Romantic music.

BRITTEN, Benjamin (1913–1976). One of Britain's finest composers, his most famous work is the opera *Peter Grimes*. He had a particular interest in working with children, and was closely associated with the Aldeburgh Festival.

CHOPIN, Frédéric (1810–1849). Polish composer and musician, famed for his piano compositions. It was a phrase of his music, broadcast over and over again by Warsaw Radio in 1939, which signalled to the world that the Polish Army was still holding out against the invading Germans.

COPLAND, Aaron (born 1900). American composer whose works, such as the ballets *Rodeo*, *Billy the Kid*, and *Appalachian Spring*, have made him very popular.

DEBUSSY, Claude Achille (1862–1918). French composer; wrote many well-known piano pieces, including *Clair de Lune*. He was a major influence on 20th century music.

DVORAK, Antonin (1841–1904). Bohemian-Czech composer. Wrote concertos, symphonies and instrumental pieces expressing his aspirations for the freedom of his country. His best-loved work, the Ninth Symphony, entitled 'From the New World', was written in the United States.

ELGAR, Sir Edward (1857–1934). English composer; wrote 'Land of Hope and Glory' as part of the *Pomp and Circumstance* march. His *Enigma Variations* is a popular concert work; he also wrote the oratorio, *The Dream of Gerontius*, and the symphonic study *Falstaff*.

GRIEG, Edvard Hagerup (1843–1907). Norwegian composer. A leading nationalist composer of the 19th century, his music growing out of the folk songs and dances of Norway. His most famous works are the Piano Concerto in A minor, and the *Peer Gynt* suite for orchestra.

HANDEL, George Frederick (1685–1759). Composer; German-born, but became a British subject. He wrote nearly 50 operas and many oratorios, including *The Messiah*.

HAYDN, Franz Joseph (1732–1809). Austrian composer of many symphonies, operas, oratorios and anthems. His oratorios *The Creation* and *The Seasons* are performed frequently.

LISZT, Franz (1811–1886). Hungarian pianist and composer. His piano music includes the *Hungarian Rhapsodies*.

MENDELSSOHN-BARTHOLDY, Jakob Ludwig Felix (1809–1847). German

composer, whose best-loved compositions are the oratorio *Elijah*, the *'Scotch' Symphony*, the *'Italian' Symphony* and the overture *Fingal's Cave*.
MONTEVERDI, Claudio (1567–1643). Italian composer who was for many years director of music at St. Mark's basilica in Venice. He was the first important composer of operas, his most famous being *L'Orfeo* and *L'Incoronazione di Poppea*.
MOZART, Wolfgang Amadeus (1756–1791). Austrian composer. His most popular works include the operas *The Magic Flute* and *The Marriage of Figaro*, and many symphonies, concerti and string quartets. The greatest classical composer, he produced an enormous amount of music in his short life but died in poverty.
PUCCINI, Giacomo (1858–1924). Italian composer of many popular operas, including *La Bohème* and *Madame Butterfly*.
PURCELL, Henry (1658–1695). English composer. He wrote much fine church music, including chants for psalms, while organist at London's Westminster Abbey.
RACHMANINOV,Sergei Vassilievich (1873–1943). Russian composer and pianist; wrote many popular concert works and also several operas.
RAVEL, Maurice (1875–1937). French composer who wrote brilliant music for piano and orchestra, including *Jeux d'eau (Fountains)* for piano, the ballet *Daphnis et Chloe*, and *Bolero* for orchestra.
ROSSINI, Gioacchino Antonio (1793–1868). Italian operatic composer, best known for *The Barber of Seville* and *William Tell*.
SCHUBERT, Franz Peter (1797–1828). Austrian composer who wrote over 600 songs, as well as symphonies, string quartets, piano sonatas and other music. One of his most loved works is his *Unfinished Symphony*.
SCHUMANN, Robert (1810–1856). German composer, renowned for his symphonies, chamber music and many major piano works.
SIBELIUS, Jean (1865–1957). Finnish composer, renowned for his tone-poems, particularly *Finlandia*.
STRAVINSKY, Igor (1882–1971). Russian composer who lived for many years in France and finally settled in the USA. For over 50 years he was a central figure in 20th-century music. The ballet scores *The Firebird*, *Petrushka*, and *The Rite of Spring* are among his best-known works.
STRAUSS, Johann, the Younger (1825–1899). Austrian composer. His best-known works include the *Blue Danube Waltz*, *Tales from the Vienna Woods* and the opera *Die Fledermaus*.
STRAUSS, Richard (1864–1949). German composer, best known for such operas as *Der Rosenkavalier* and *Elektra* and such compositions as *Till Eulenspiegal*.
TCHAIKOVSKY, Peter Ilyich (1840–1893). Russian composer of symphonic, operatic and ballet music, including *Swan Lake*, *Nutcracker Suite* and *The Sleeping Beauty*. Among his most popular works are the *1812 Overture* and the Fifth and Sixth symphonies.
VERDI, Giuseppe (1813–1901). Italian composer of church and operatic music. He wrote a number of operas which are widely performed, such as *Aida*, *Rigoletto* and *La Traviata*.
VIVALDI, Antonio (1678–1741). Italian composer, who trained to be a priest as a young man. He wrote operas, chamber music and hundreds of concertos for solo instruments and orchestra, such as *The Four Seasons*.
WAGNER, Richard (1813–1883). German composer, whose operas, revolutionary in style in their day, include *Die Walküre*, *Lohengrin*, *Die Meistersinger* and *Tristan und Isolde*.

HISTORICAL DATES

B.C.	
c.3400	First Egyptian Dynastic Period
2900	The Great Pyramid of Egypt built by Cheops
1300	Phoenicians open up Mediterreanean trade
1230	Exodus of the Israelites from Egypt
1190	Fall of Troy
961	Building of the Temple at Jerusalem begun
776	First Olympic Games held in Greece
753	Founding of Rome
490	Greeks defeat Persians at Marathon
488	Death of Buddha
335–23	The campaigns of Alexander the Great
146	Carthage destroyed by Scipio
55	Julius Caesar invades Britain
4	Actual date of the birth of Christ
A.D.	
30	Crucifixion
43	Conquest of Britain by Rome begun
70	Destruction of Jerusalem
79	Vesuvius erupts, destroying Pompeii and Herculaneum
122	Building of Hadrian's Wall

The pyramids of Giza. The pyramid of Cheops is in the background, and that of Cephren in the centre.

Christopher Columbus with Martin Behaim's globe of 1492.

407 Romans leave Britain
476 Fall of the Roman Empire in the West
569 Birth of Mohammed in Mecca
711 Moors overrun Spain
732 Moors driven from France
1000 Norsemen reach Labrador
1066 Normans conquer Britain
1095 Crusades begin
1215 The Magna Carta sealed by King John
1216 First Parliament in England
1271 Beginning of Marco Polo's travels
1338 Hundred Years War begins
1348 The Black Death sweeps Europe
1440 Printing with moveable type begun in Germany
1453 Eastern Roman Empire falls to Turks
1455–85 Wars of the Roses
1476 First printing press in England
1492 Columbus discovers America
1492 Moors driven from Spain
1500 Portuguese discover Brazil
1519–22 First voyage round the world, by Magellan
1534 Reformation in England
1536 Dissolution of the monasteries in England
1572 St. Bartholomew's day massacre in France
1577–80 Drake's voyage round the world
1588 Drake defeats Spanish Armada
1605 Gunpowder Plot to blow up English Parliament
1607 First permanent colony established in Virginia
1618–48 Thirty Years War

1620	*Mayflower* colonists land in New England
1642	New Zealand and Tasmania discovered
1665	Great Plague of London
1666	Great Fire of London
1707	Act of Union unites England and Scotland
1715	First Jacobite Rebellion
1745	Second Jacobite Rebellion, 'The Forty-five'
1756	Beginning of Seven Years War
1760	British defeat French in Canada
1760	Beginning of Industrial Revolution
1770	Captain Cook discovers New South Wales
1775–83	American War of Independence
1776	American Declaration of Independence
1789	French Revolution begins
1796	Napoleonic Wars begin
1804	Napoleon becomes Emperor of France
1805	Battle of Trafalgar
1815	Battle of Waterloo
1832	First Reform Act in British Parliament
1833	Britain abolishes slavery
1840	Introduction of penny post in Britain
1848	Gold discovered in California
1854–56	Crimean War
1857	Indian Mutiny
1861–65	American Civil War
1863	United States abolishes slavery
1867	Dominion of Canada established
1869	Suez Canal opens
1870–71	Franco-Prussian War
1877–78	Russo-Turkish War breaks power of Turkey in Europe
1899–1902	Boer War
1903	First successful aeroplane flight, by Wright brothers
1904–05	Russo-Japanese War
1909	Blériot makes first cross-Channel flight
1909	Peary reaches North Pole
1911	Amundsen reaches South Pole
1912	Ocean liner *Titanic* sinks, 1513 lost
1914	World War I begins
1915	Ocean liner *Lusitania* torpedoed, 1500 lost
1917	United States enters First World War
1917	Russian Revolution
1918	End of First World War
1919	Alcock and Brown make first non-stop trans-Atlantic flight
1920	First meeting of League of Nations
1922	Mussolini marches on Rome
1924	Death of Lenin
1927	Lindbergh makes first solo flight across Atlantic
1929	Start of the Great Slump
1931	Japan occupies Manchuria
1933	Hitler attains power in Germany

1936–39	Civil War in Spain
1937	Japan begins war on China
1938	Germany annexes Austria, Munich Agreement
1939	Outbreak of Second World War
1940	Germany invades Denmark, Norway, Netherlands, Belgium, France and Luxembourg
1940	Dunkirk evacuation. Paris taken by Germans
1940	Battle of Britain
1941	Russia and United States enter Second World War
1942	All of France occupied by Germans
1943	Russians halt German advance at Stalingrad
1943	Allies invade Italy
1944	Allies invade France
1945	Germany surrenders. Hitler dies
1945	First atomic bomb dropped on Japan
1945	Japan surrenders
1945	End of Second World War
1945	United Nations established
1947	India attains independence
1948	State of Israel proclaimed
1950–53	Korean War
1953	Conquest of Mount Everest
1956	Suez Canal dispute
1957	Russians launch first space satellites
1959	Russians launch first rocket to reach moon and photograph its far side
1960	Piccard descends 7 miles (11 km) under the Pacific
1961	First space flight, by Yuri Gagarin
1963	Assassination of President Kennedy
1966	River Arno overflows and floods two-thirds of the City of Florence, Italy
1967	China explodes complete H-bomb
1969	Neil Armstrong is first man on the moon
1971	Indo-Pakistan conflict. East Pakistan becomes Bangladesh
1971	China admitted to the United Nations
1973	Britain, Ireland, Denmark join EEC
1974	President Nixon resigns
1975	US withdraws from Vietnam War
1976	Death of Mao-tse-tung. Power struggle in China
1978	Peace treaty signed by Egypt and Israel
1978	Cardinal Wojtyla becomes Pope John Paul II
1979	Ayatollah Khomeini comes to power in Iran
1979	Rhodesia renamed Zimbabwe. Black majority government elected
1982	Yuri Andropov becomes President of USSR
1982	Falkland Islands Crisis
1984	Indira Gandhi is assassinated and succeeded by her son Rajiv Gandhi as Prime Minister of India
1985	Mikhail Gorbachev becomes Premier of USSR. Andre Gromyko becomes President
1986	The world's worst nuclear accident at Chernobyl, USSR.
1988	The world's worst earthquake disaster in Armenia, USSR
1989	George Bush inaugurated President of USA

The *Mayflower* which brought Pilgrims to New England in 1620.

EXPLORATION AND DISCOVERIES

1497	East coast of Canada, by John Cabot
1498	Cape route to India, by Vasco da Gama
1498	South America, by Christopher Columbus
1513	Pacific Ocean, by Vasco Nunẽz de Balboa
1519	Magellan Strait, by Ferdinand Magellan
1534	St. Lawrence River, by Jacques Cartier
1605–06	Australia, by Willem Jansz
1610	Hudson Bay (Canada), by Henry Hudson
1616	Baffin Bay (Canada), by William Baffin
1642	New Zealand and Tasmania, by Abel Janszoon Tasman
1778	Hawaii, by James Cook
1820	Antarctic mainland, by Edward Bransfield
1855	Victoria Falls, by David Livingstone
1858	Source of the Nile, by John Hanning Speke
1865	Matterhorn summit first reached, by Edward Whymper
1909	North Pole first reached, by Robert E. Peary
1911	South Pole first reached, by Roald Amundsen
1958	American atomic-powered submarine *Nautilus* makes first undersea crossing beneath the North Pole ice cap in 96 hours
1965	Alexei Leonov becomes the first man to walk in space
1969	Neil Armstrong and Edwin Aldrin become the first men to land on the moon
1972	USA launch *Skylab* – experimental space station
1975	Russian *Soyuz* and American *Apollo* spacecraft successfully dock in space
1976	American spacecraft *Vikings I* and *II* land on Mars
1979	American *Voyager* probes reach Jupiter
1980	*Voyager I* flies past Saturn
1981	American space shuttle launch

PRIME MINISTERS OF GREAT BRITAIN

Sir Robert Walpole	1721–1742
Earl of Wilmington	1742–1743
Henry Pelham	1743–1754
Duke of Newcastle	1754–1756
Duke of Devonshire	1756–1757
Duke of Newcastle	1757–1762
Earl of Bute	1762–1763
George Grenville	1763–1765
Marquis of Rockingham	1765–1766
Earl of Chatham	1766–1767
Duke of Grafton	1767–1770
Lord North	1770–1782
Marquis of Rockingham	1782
Earl of Shelbourne	1782–1783
Duke of Portland	1783
William Pitt the Younger	1783–1801
Henry Addington	1801–1804
William Pitt the Younger	1804–1806
Lord Grenville	1806–1807
Duke of Portland	1807–1809
Spencer Perceval	1809–1812
Earl of Liverpool	1812–1827
George Canning	1827
Viscount Goderich	1827–1828
Duke of Wellington	1828–1830
Earl Gray	1830–1834
Viscount Melbourne	1834
Sir Robert Peel	1834–1835
Viscount Melbourne	1835–1841
Sir Robert Peel	1841–1846
Lord John Russell	1846–1852
Earl of Derby	1852
Earl of Aberdeen	1852–1855
Viscount Palmerston	1855–1858
Earl of Derby	1858–1859
Viscount Palmerston	1859–1865
Earl Russell	1865–1866
Earl of Derby	1866–1868
Benjamin Disraeli	1868
William Gladstone	1868–1874
Benjamin Disraeli	1874–1880
William Gladstone	1880–1885
Marquis of Salisbury	1885–1886
William Gladstone	1886
Marquis of Salisbury	1886–1892
William Gladstone	1892–1894
Earl of Rosebery	1894–1895
Marquis of Salisbury	1895–1902
Arthur Balfour	1902–1905
Sir Henry Campbell-Bannerman	1905–1908
Herbert Asquith	1908–1916
David Lloyd George	1916–1922
Andrew Bonar Law	1922–1923
Stanley Baldwin	1923–1924
Ramsay MacDonald	1924
Stanley Baldwin	1924–1929
Ramsey MacDonald	1929–1935
Stanley Baldwin	1935–1937
Neville Chamberlain	1937–1940
Winston Churchill	1940–1945
Clement Atlee	1945–1951
Winston Churchill	1951–1955
Sir Anthony Eden	1955–1957
Harold Macmillan	1957–1963
Sir Alec Douglas-Home	1963–1964
Harold Wilson	1964–1970
Edward Heath	1970–1974
Harold Wilson	1974–1976
James Callaghan	1976–1979
Margaret Thatcher	1979–

Arthur Wellesley, 1st Duke of Wellington, was Prime Minister of Great Britain 1828–30.

RULERS OF ENGLAND

Saxons	
Egbert	827–839
Ethelwulf	839–858
Ethelbald	858–860
Ethelbert	860–866
Ethelred I	866–871
Alfred the Great	871–899
Edward the Elder	899–924
Athelstan	924–939
Edmund	939–946
Edred	946–955
Edwy	955–959
Edgar	959–975
Edward the Martyr	975–978
Ethelred II the Unready	978–1016
Edmund Ironside	1016
Danes	
Canute	1016–1035
Harold I Harefoot	1035–1040
Hardicanute	1040–1042
Saxons	
Edward the Confessor	1042–1066
Harold II	1066
House of Normandy	
William I the Conqueror	1066–1087
William II	1087–1100
Henry I	1100–1135
Stephen	1135–1154
House of Plantagenet	
Henry II	1154–1189
Richard I	1189–1199
John	1199–1216
Henry III	1216–1272
Edward I	1272–1307
Edward II	1307–1327
Edward III	1327–1377
Richard II	1377–1399
House of Lancaster	
Henry IV	1399–1413
Henry V	1413–1422
Henry VI	1422–1461
House of York	
Edward IV	1461–1483
Edward V	1483
Richard III	1483–1485
House of Tudor	
Henry VII	1485–1509
Henry VIII	1509–1547
Edward VI	1547–1553
Mary I	1553–1558
Elizabeth I	1558–1603

RULERS OF SCOTLAND

Malcolm II	1005–1034
Duncan I	1034–1040
Macbeth (usurper)	1040–1057
Malcolm III Canmore	1057–1093
Donald Bane	1093–1094
Duncan II	1094
Donald Bane (restored)	1094–1097
Edgar	1097–1107
Alexander I	1107–1124
David I	1124–1153
Malcolm IV	1153–1165
William the Lion	1165–1214
Alexander II	1214–1249
Alexander III	1249–1286
Margaret of Norway	1286–1290
(*Interregnum* 1290–1292)	
John Balliol	1292–1296
(*Interregnum* 1296–1306)	
Robert I (Bruce)	1306–1329
David II	1329–1371
House of Stuart	
Robert II	1371–1390
Robert III	1390–1406
James I	1406–1437
James II	1437–1460
James III	1460–1488
James IV	1488–1513
James V	1513–1542
Mary	1542–1567
James VI*	1567–1625

*Became James I of Great Britain in 1603

RULERS OF GREAT BRITAIN

Stuart	
James I	1603–1625
Charles I	1625–1649

Commonwealth	1649–1660
Charles II	1660–1685
James II	1685–1688
William III & Mary	1689–1702
Anne	1702–1714
Hanover	
George I	1714–1727
George II	1727–1760
George III	1760–1820
George IV	1820–1830
William IV	1830–1837
Victoria	1837–1901
Saxe-Coburg	
Edward VII	1901–1910
Windsor	
George V	1910–1936
Edward VIII	1936
George VI	1936–1952
Elizabeth II	1952–

PRESIDENTS OF THE USA

George Washington	1789–1797
John Adams	1797–1801
Thomas Jefferson	1801–1809
James Madison	1809–1817
James Monroe	1817–1825
John Quincy Adams	1825–1829
Andrew Jackson	1829–1837
Martin Van Buren	1837–1841
William H. Harrison	1841
John Tyler	1841–1845
James K. Polk	1845–1849
Zachary Taylor	1849–1850
Millard Fillmore	1850–1853
Franklin Pierce	1853–1857
James Buchanan	1857–1861
Abraham Lincoln	1861–1865
Andrew Johnson	1865–1869
Ulysses S. Grant	1869–1877
Rutherford B. Hayes	1877–1881
James A. Garfield	1881
Chester A. Arthur	1881–1885
Grover Cleveland	1885–1889
Benjamin Harrison	1889–1893
Grover Cleveland	1893–1897
William McKinley	1897–1901
Theodore Roosevelt	1901–1909
William H. Taft	1909–1913
Woodrow Wilson	1913–1921
Warren Gamaliel Harding	1921–1923
Calvin Coolidge	1923–1929
Herbert C. Hoover	1929–1933
Franklin D. Roosevelt	1933–1945
Harry S. Truman	1945–1953
Dwight D. Eisenhower	1953–1961
John F. Kennedy	1961–1963
Lyndon B. Johnson	1963–1969
Richard M. Nixon	1969–1974
Gerald R. Ford	1974–1977
James Earl Carter	1977–1981
Ronald Reagan	1981–1989
George Bush	1989–

PRIME MINISTERS OF CANADA

Sir John A. Macdonald	1867–1873
Alexander Mackenzie	1873–1878
Sir John A. Macdonald	1878–1891
Sir John J.C. Abbott	1891–1892
Sir John S.D. Thompson	1892–1894
Sir Mackenzie Bowell	1894–1896
Sir Charles Tupper	1896
Sir Wilfrid Laurier	1896–1911
Sir Robert L. Borden	1911–1920
Aurther Meighen	1920–1921
W.L. Mackenzie King	1921–1926
Aurther Meighen	1926
W.L. Mackenzie King	1926–1930
Richard B. Bennett	1930–1935
W.L. Mackenzie King	1935–1948
Louis S. St. Laurent	1948–1957
John Diefenbaker	1957–1963
Lester B. Pearson	1963–1968
Pierre Elliott Trudeau	1968–1979
Joe Clarke	1979
Pierre Elliott Trudeau	1980–1984
John Turner	1984
Brian Mulroney	1984

PRIME MINISTERS OF AUSTRALIA

Edmund Barton	1901–1903
Alfred Deakin	1903–1904
John Watson	1904

George Reid	1904–1905
Alfred Deakin	1905–1908
Andrew Fisher	1908–1909
Alfred Deakin	1909–1910
Andrew Fisher	1910–1913
Joseph Cook	1913–1914
Andrew Fisher	1914–1915
William Hughes	1915–1923
Stanley Bruce	1923–1929
James Scullin	1929–1931
Joseph Lyons	1931–1939
Sir Earle Grafton Page	1939
Robert Menzies	1939–1941
Arthur Fadden	1941
John Curtin	1941–1945
Francis Forde	1945
Joseph Chifley	1945–1949
Robert Menzies	1949–1965
Harold Holt	1965–1967
John McEwen	1967–1968
John Gorton	1968–1971
William McMahon	1971–1972
Gough Whitlam	1972–1975
Malcolm Fraser	1975–1983
Bob Hawke	1983

PRIME MINISTERS OF INDIA

Jawãharlãl Nehru	1947–1964
Lal Bahadur Shastri	1964–1966
Indira Gandhi	1966–1977
Morarji Desai	1977–1979
Charan Singh	1979–1980
Indira Gandhi	1980–1984
Rajiv Gandhi	1984

PRESIDENTS OF INDIA

Dr Radendra Prasad	1950–1962
Dr S. Radhakrishnan	1962–1967
Dr Zakir Hussain	1967 1969
Shri V.V. Giri	1969–1974
Fakruddin Ali Ahmed	1974–1977
Sanjiva Reddy	1977–1982
Zail Singh	1982–1987
R. Venkataraman	1987–

THE MODERN WORLD

THE UNITED NATIONS

The 159 members of the United Nations are:

Afghanistan
Albania
Algeria
Angola
Antigua and Barbuda
Argentina
Australia
Austria
Bahamas
Bahrain
Bangladesh
Barbados
Belgium
Belize
Benin
Bhutan
Bolivia
Botswana
Brazil
Brunei Darussalam
Bulgaria
Burkina Faso
Burma
Burundi
Byelorussia
Cambodia
Cameroon
Canada
Cape Verde
Central African Republic
Chad
Chile
China
Colombia
Comoros
Congo
Costa Rica
Côte d'Ivoire
Cuba
Cyprus
Czechoslovakia
Denmark
Djibouti
Dominica
Dominican Republic
Ecuador
Egypt
El Salvador
Equatorial Guinea
Ethiopia
Fiji
Finland

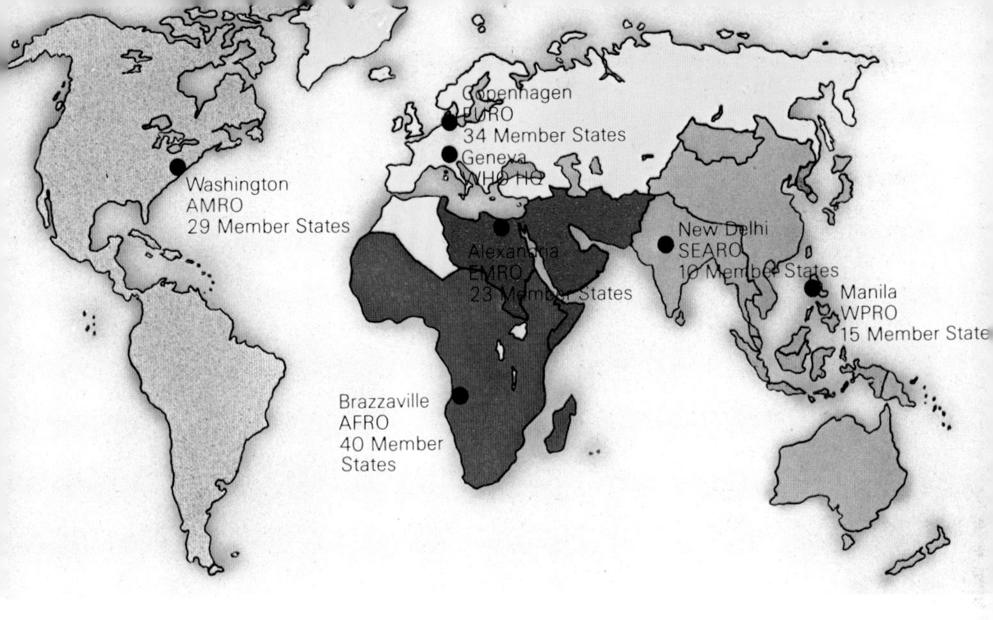

The World Health Organization's regions, covering 156 member states (1980).

France
Gabon
Gambia
Germany, Democratic Republic
Germany, Federal Republic of
Ghana
Greece
Grenada
Guatemala
Guinea
Guinea Bissau
Guyana
Haiti
Honduras
Hungary
Iceland
India
Indonesia
Iran
Iraq
Ireland
Israel
Italy
Jamaica
Japan
Jordan
Kenya
Kuwait
Laos
Lebanon
Lesotho
Liberia
Libya
Luxembourg
Madagascar
Malawi
Malaysia
Maldives
Mali
Malta
Mauritania
Mauritius
Mexico
Mongolia
Morocco
Mozambique
Nepal
Netherlands
New Zealand
Nicaragua
Niger
Nigeria
Norway
Oman
Pakistan
Panama
Papua New Guinea
Paraguay
Peru
Philippines
Poland
Portugal
Qatar
Romania
Rwanda
Sao Tomé and Principe
Saudi Arabia
Senegal
Seychelles
Sierra Leone
Singapore
Solomon Islands
Somalia
South Africa
Spain
Sri Lanka
St Christopher and Nevis
St Lucia
St Vincent
Sudan
Suriname
Swaziland
Sweden
Syria
Tanzania
Thailand
Togo
Trinidad and Tobago
Tunisia
Turkey
Uganda
Ukraine
USSR
United Arab Emirates
United Kingdom
United States of America
Uruguay
Vanuatu
Venezuela
Vietnam
Western Samoa
Yemen Arab Republic
Yemen, PDR
Yugoslavia
Zaire
Zambia
Zimbabwe

AN INTERDEPENDENT WORLD

Technology has made the world seem a much smaller place and this is particularly noticeable in the fields of trade, industry and finance. In fact, it has often been because countries have wanted to extend their trading areas that 'earth-shrinking' developments have taken place.

As the world gets 'smaller' we can see the similarities between peoples and notice how some countries are at similar stages of development. Some are advanced industrial countries, like the USA, many of the European countries, Japan and Australia. Others it is harder to classify because less is known about their development. This applies particularly to the USSR, China and countries in Eastern Europe. Then there are the developing countries, like most of those in Africa, South-east Asia and South America. The oil-rich countries of the Middle East form a class of their own.

However developed they are, all countries depend on each other to a greater or lesser extent and in different ways. Some are rich in basic *commodities* like ores for iron, copper, lead, zinc and tin, or foodstuffs like sugar, coffee or tea. But these countries may lack the technology to manufacture goods they need. So they *export*, or sell abroad, the commodities they have and *import*, or buy overseas for home use, the manufactured goods they want. Ideally a country's exports should be worth the same as, or slightly more than, their imports. If this happens, the country is said to have a favourable *balance of trade*.

Unfortunately, one country's exports are another country's imports. So not all countries can earn a trade *surplus*. But it is possible to earn money abroad in other ways. If companies make *overseas investments* by building factories abroad they can send home part of the *profits* in the form of *dividends*. Such non-trade items can

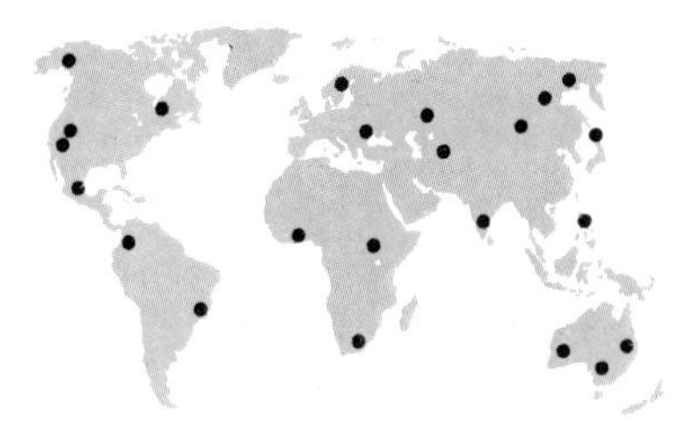
• Major gold producing areas

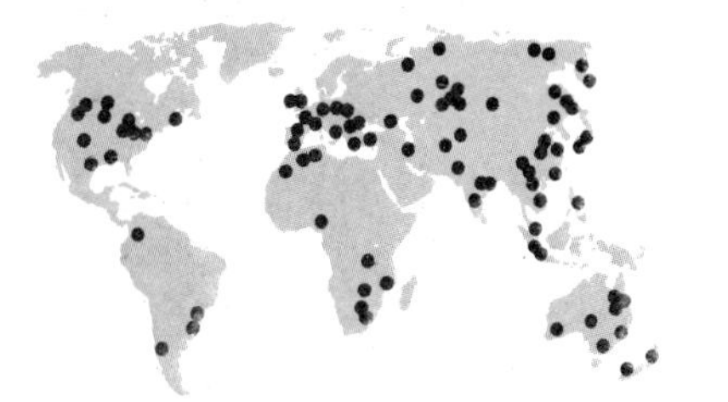
• Major coal producing areas

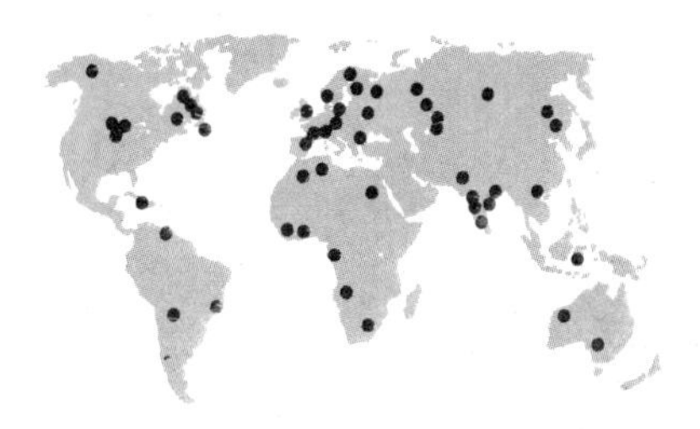
• Major iron ore producing areas

be very important. For example tourists bring in foreign money and so help to pay for imports into the country visited.

The total value of all a country's dealings with the rest of the world are summed up in figures called the country's *balance of payments*, which add the value of non-trade items to the trade balance figures.

GOVERNMENTS

As the world has become more highly industrially developed so governments have played an increasingly active and important part in daily life – and in economic matters in particular.

Today nearly half the working population in some countries work for the state – as policemen, social workers, soldiers, administrators and employees of state-owned businesses.

As a result, governments have to meet the very heavy costs of keeping a country going. In most advanced countries the major items of government expenditure are: defence and the armed forces; internal security and the police; education; health care; communications facilities and roads, railways, airports and telephone networks.

To pay for all this, governments impose a variety of *taxes* and *duties*. Direct taxes are those charged, for instance, on an individual's or a company's income and paid directly. Indirect taxes are those paid as part of the price of something else. Sales taxes and value added tax (VAT) are indirect taxes. Duties are charges raised on goods imported or charges on drinking spirits, like whisky, administered by customs officials.

Like households, governments have to balance their spending against their income. This is usually attempted by an annual *budget* which sets out what expenditure is needed and how money will be raised to meet it. If income is the same as expenditure, the country is said to have a balanced budget. But most governments tend to have a *deficit* – they spend more than they receive.

Governments are a major influence on their country's economy. For example, if a government decides to re-equip its army, it will buy weapons, vehicles, clothing and so on in huge amounts. Manufacturers, in turn, need to buy large quantities of raw materials and often hire new workers to fulfil the orders. So government spending can boost employment and prosperity.

Governments use their powers as big participants in, and regulators of, the economy to help shape prosperity by stimulating or dampening demand. If taxes on basics like food, clothing and petrol are suddenly raised sharply people have less to spend on 'luxuries' like new cars, jewellery, furniture, holidays and so on. The companies providing non-essential goods are then not so busy and reduce the number of workers they employ. Unemployed workers have less money to spend and so the impact of a tax change spreads right through the system. So raising taxes on essentials could help, for instance, to cut spending on luxury imports and restore a country's balance of trade.

MONEY

Money is essential in the modern world but it remains a confusing subject best appreciated by realizing that a coin has *no* use or value in itself but only as a *means of exchange*. The only reason for having money is to be able to acquire, conveniently, something else.

In some cases people do not bother with money. Neighbours help each other with different jobs which one may be better at than the other. And a certain amount of swapping and bartering still goes on. Swapping half a chicken for a few pints of milk is easy enough but there are problems if one wants to swap a pig for a bicycle. Who is to say they are worth the same? If they are not worth the same, how do you give change?

Having standard symbols of value, or money, solves these problems. All sorts of things have been used as money – shells, stones, iron bars, pressed tea leaves and cigarettes. As long as everyone is prepared to accept the items in exchange for other goods whose values, in terms of shells or cigarettes, is agreed, then there are no problems.

Today money comes in different *currencies* – dollars, pounds, francs, pesetas and so on – and as coins and notes. But it also exists as figures in bank accounts.

A bank may say it holds a million units of currency for its customers but it would actually hold only a small part of that as notes and coins in its vaults. The customers only need cash for a small part of their business and prefer to keep the rest as *deposits* in the bank. The point is that the word 'money' means more things than just coins and notes, and money is actually created in the banking system.

If a customer deposits 1000 units of currency, the bank knows that only about 100 units will be required by this customer for things which have to be paid for in cash. The bank also may know nine other customers each of which would like to borrow 1000 units of currency to buy, for example, some new furniture or a new car. These purchases would be made by cheque, so again each of the customers would need only a little bit of cash for day-to-day items. The bank can allow these customers to have the use of the spare 900 units deposited by the first customer and it can literally *create* new money by making loans of 1000 units each to the nine customers who want to borrow money. Each customer then has 1000 units in *money*, all recorded in the bank. And the bank has available 100 units for each customer's minor expenses.

This 'creating' of money is controlled by governments in one way or another, principally by setting rules for what proportion of customers' deposits may be used for loans.

CHESS

This is a game for two players, one taking the white pieces and the other the black. The board is of 64 squares, alternately black and white. At the beginning of the game each player has a white square in the right-hand corner nearest him or her. The lines of squares going from left to right are called *ranks*, those from top to bottom *files*, and the paths from corner to corner and those parallel to them are *diagonals*.

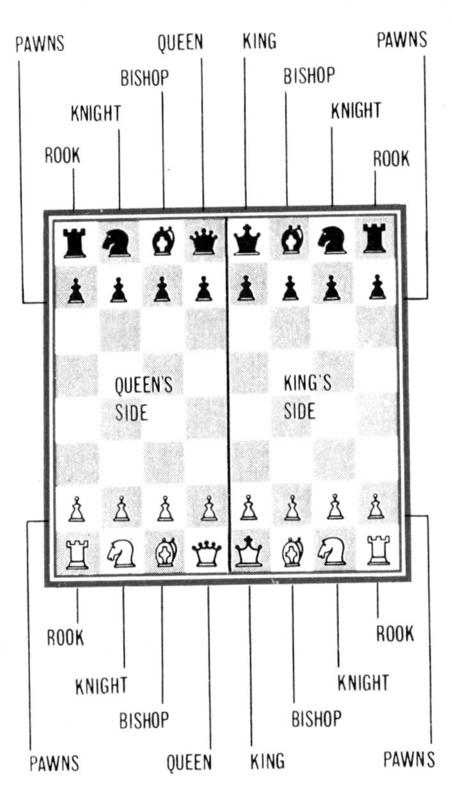

Each player has 16 pieces: a king (K), a queen (Q), two rooks (R) (sometimes called castles), two bishops (B), two knights (Kt) and eight pawns (P). At the beginning of the game the pieces are laid out as in the diagram on this page. Note that the white queen occupies a white square, and the black queen opposite occupies a black square. White moves first. When games of chess are described, each square has two numbers – one with reference to the white pieces, and one to the black. These are shown in the diagram on page 224. If in the first move of the game the pawn on the square QB2 (known as the queen's bishop pawn) is moved two squares forward the move will be written thus: 1. QBP – QB4.

The object of the game is to capture the opponent's king. Pieces capture an enemy piece by moving to the square occupied by that piece, the captured piece being removed from the board.

Pieces move as follows:

King: one square in any direction, either along a rank, a file or diagonally.

Queen: any number of squares in any direction.

Rook: any number of squares along a rank or file.

Bishop: any number of squares diagonally. It follows that a bishop on a white square can only move to another white square.

Knight: two squares along a rank or file and then one square to left or right. Looking at the diagram below, the knight on QKt1 can make its first move to QR3, QB3 or Q2. A knight in the centre of the board will have eight possible squares to move to. A knight is the only piece on the board that may jump over other pieces.

Pawn: A pawn on its first move may move either one or two squares along its file. Subsequently it may move only one square forward. Pawns, unlike other pieces, may only move forwards towards the opponent's end of the board. If a pawn reaches the end of its file, it may be exchanged for another piece, usually, of course,

Black

QR1 QR8	QKt1 QKt8	QB1 QB8	Q1 Q8	K1 K8	KB1 KB8	KKt1 KKt8	KR1 KR8
QR2 QR7	QKt2 QKt7	QB2 QB7	Q2 Q7	K2 K7	KB2 KB7	KKt2 KKt7	KR2 KR7
QR3 QR6	QKt3 QKt6	QB3 QB6	Q3 Q6	K3 K6	KB3 KB6	KKt3 KKt6	KR3 KR6
QR4 QR5	QKt4 QKt5	QB4 QB5	Q4 Q5	K4 K5	KB4 KB5	KKt4 KKt5	KR4 KR5
QR5 QR4	QKt5 QKt4	QB5 QB4	Q5 Q4	K5 K4	KB5 KB4	KKt5 KKt4	KR5 KR4
QR6 QR3	QKt6 QKt3	QB6 QB3	Q6 Q3	K6 K3	KB6 KB3	KKt6 KKt3	KR6 KR3
QR7 QR2	QKt7 QKt2	QB7 QB2	Q7 Q2	K7 K2	KB7 KB2	KKt7 KKt2	KR7 KR2
QR8 QR1	QKt8 QKt1	QB8 QB1	Q8 Q1	K8 K1	KB8 KB1	KKt8 KKt1	KR8 KR1

White

The numbering used to describe games of chess.

the most powerful, the queen. A player by this means may have two queens on the board. When capturing an opponent's piece, however, a pawn moves one square forward diagonally, either to left or right.

There are two other special moves. The first is the *en passant* move. As stated, a pawn may move on its first move two squares forward, but if by doing so it avoids capture by an opposing pawn (i.e. if by moving only one square forward an opposing pawn could have taken it), then the opposing player may capture the pawn *en passant*, and may take it as if it had moved only one square.

The second special move is known as 'castling'. If a player has not moved his or her king or the rook on their king's side, but the intervening squares are empty, he or she may castle by moving the king to KKt1 and the rook to KB1. This is known as castling on the king's side. Similarly, a player may castle on the queen's side by moving the king to QB1 and the rook to Q1. A player may not castle if his or her king is in check (which will be explained later), nor may a player castle more than once in a game.

How does a player win by capturing the opponent's king? First, the expression 'check' must be explained. If a player has one or more of his or her pieces so positioned that the opponent's king may be captured on the next move, then that king is in check, and the attacking-player must announce 'check'. The opponent must then use the next move to avert the danger, which can be done by capturing the threatening piece, by moving one of his or her own pieces to an interposing square to block the threat, or by moving the king to a safe square. If none of these alternatives is open to the player, then the king is 'checkmated', and the game is lost.

A game can be drawn at any time by agreement. A game is also drawn if stalemate occurs, which is when a player can move only his or her king, which is not in check, but can move it only to a position of check. A draw by repetition can be claimed if a position repeats itself three times, or if a player can place the opponent's king in perpetual check: that is, if a player cannot checkmate but can check the opposing king on every move, the game may be declared a draw.

At the beginning of a game, a player should attempt to get his or her more powerful pieces into play as quickly as possible. For example, if the pawn in front of the king is moved, diagonals are immediately opened up for the queen and a bishop.

There are several recognized openings to chess games, each with a name, and there are recognized counters to them, all designed to achieve good positions early in the game. There are many books published on opening gambits, as they are called, as indeed there are on all stages of a chess game, and a beginner who wishes to play well should read one of the books designed for learners.

DRAUGHTS

This is played on the black squares of a chessboard, using two sets of counters, each consisting of 12 black and twelve red or white circular pieces. These are arranged on the black squares of the first three rows at each end of the board, and they move one square forward, diagonally.

Below: layout at the start of a draughts game. Bottom: captures are effected by jumping opponent's pieces.

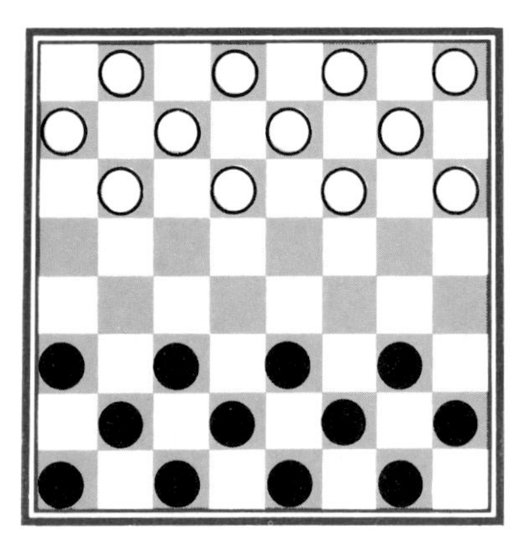

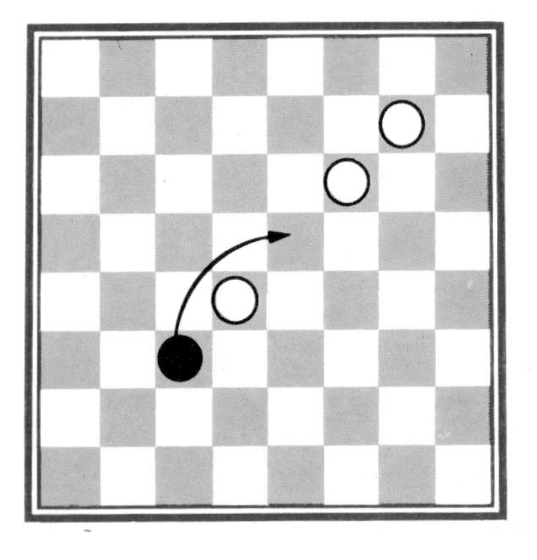

The purpose of the game is to capture all the opponent's pieces, which is done by jumping across them to a vacant square beyond. If, by so doing, the attacker then lands on a square from which it is able to capture again, it does so without waiting for the next move. On reaching the opponent's back line, a piece becomes a king by having a captured piece placed on top, and may then move forwards or back.

A player in a position to make a capture must do so.

BACKGAMMON

This game is for two players. It is played with a special board, 15 black and 15 white counters or stones and two dice. The illustration opposite shows the board at the beginning of the game. The board is divided by a bar into two halves; by arrangement one half is the inner (or home) board and one half the outer – in the illustration the right half is the inner. Projecting from each side of the board are 12 points of alternate colours (numbered in the illustration for convenience, but not numbered on the board itself). Each player rolls one die, and the higher plays first. The object is to move all 15 stones into the inner board and then off the board. The first player to remove all his or her stones is the winner. Each player moves towards his or her inner table (i.e. black moves clockwise in the illustration, white anti-clockwise).

The first player rolls both dice and may move his or her stones according to the score. The player

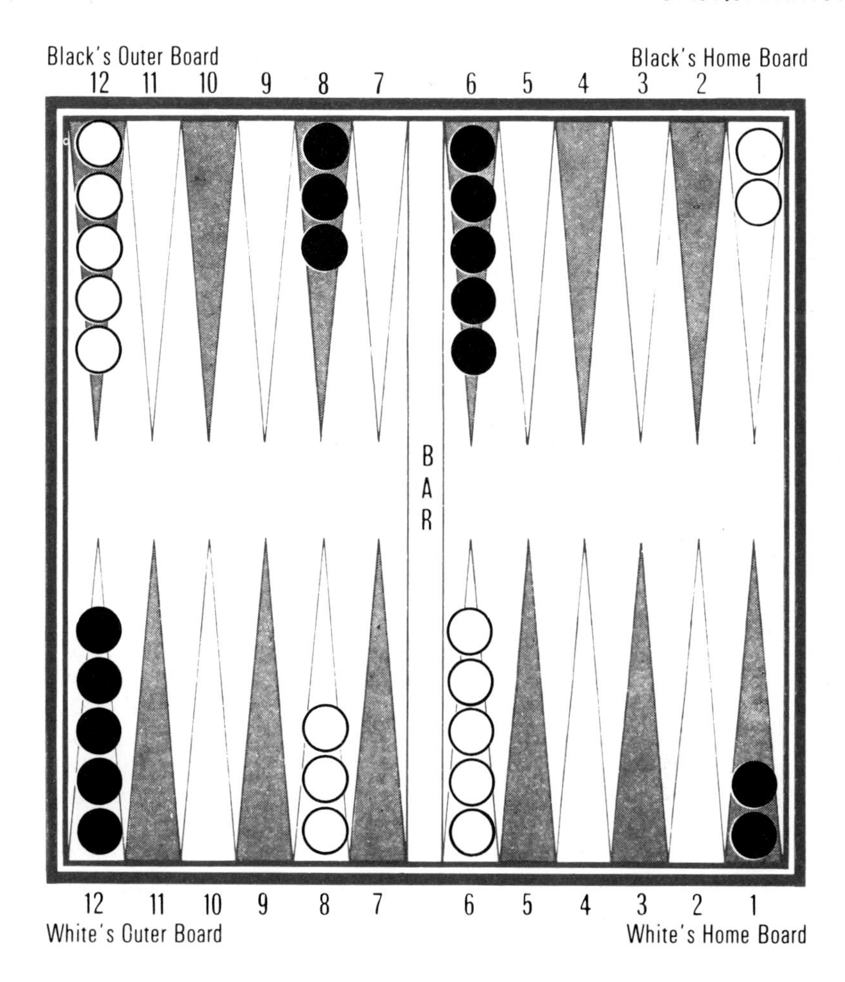

may move two stones, each according to the score of one die, or may move the same stone twice. For instance, if White rolls 6 – 3, he or she may move one stone from Black's point 1 to point 10, or may move one stone from Black 12 to White 7 and one from Black 12 to White 10. Doubles are scored twice over, for instance a double-6 would enable the player to move four stones each six points, or, if preferred, two stones 12 points. A player must always move if possible. If players cannot move, they lose the turn. If they can move only the score on one die, they must, and if they can move the score on either die, but not both, they must take the higher score.

No point may be occupied by stones of opposite colours. If a player has two or more stones on a point, he or she has made the point, and the other player must not land on it. So if White's first throw is 5-5, he or she cannot move either stone on Black's point 1, as the first 5 would take either to Black's point 6, which is already occupied by five Black stones.

A single stone on a point is called a blot. If the opponent can move a stone to that point, the blot is hit and is removed from the board and placed on the bar in the centre of the board. When a player's stone is on the bar, he or she must enter it before moving any other stone. A stone enters on the adverse inner table. Thus if Black has a stone on the bar, and White has two stones on each point of his or her own inner table, it is clear that Black cannot move, and must wait until a point is available before he or she can enter the stone.

A player's first task is to move all fifteen stones into his or her inner board. Once this has been achieved, the player may begin to take off his or her stones. A stone is taken off by throwing the number equivalent to the point occupied by the stone. Thus if White has all his or her stones in the inner board, and throws 4-2, he or she may take off stones from points 4 and 2. Or, of course, he or she may take off one stone from point 6. Or, if preferred, White may take off a stone from point 2, and move a stone from point 6 to point 2. If, at this stage of the game, a player throws a number higher than the highest occupied point, he or she may take off a stone from the highest occupied point. For example, if a player throws a 6, and his or her highest occupied

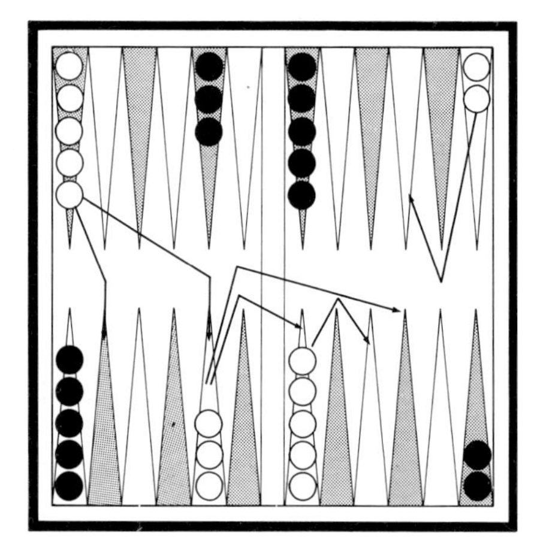

The principle of moving the stones around the board is illustrated here by showing all the possible moves for White's first throw of 5 – 2. For the two, White could move any of his or her stones, but for the five there are only two choices.

point is 5, he or she may take off the stone on point 5.

It will be seen that backgammon is in effect a race, with both players moving their stones in opposite directions round the board in an attempt to take them all off first. Players should try to make points, which render their own stones safe for the time being and also impede their opponent's stones.

Games using the principle of moving counters round a board according to the throw of dice have been known for at least 5000 years. Backgammon in most of its modern features has been played at least since the 15th century, and the name 'backgammon' dates back to 1645. The games of 'tric-trac' and 'tables' were essentially what we know as backgammon.

GENERAL INFORMATION

This section contains lots of useful information on a variety of subjects. It is arranged for quick reference, so you can easily find whatever you want to look up.

INTERNATIONAL CAR REGISTRATION PLATES

Foreign registered vehicles should display an international distinguishing sign of approved pattern, as established by international convention.

★ This signifies that the rule of the road is drive on the left; otherwise it is drive on the right.
† This signifies that the sign is unofficial and not included in the United Nations list of signs established by international convention.

A Austria
ADN People's Democratic Republic of Yemen *(formerly Aden)*
·**AFG** Afghanistan
AL Albania
AND Andorra
AUS Australia★

B Belgium
BD Bangladesh★
BDS Barbados★
BG Bulgaria
BH Belize *(formerly British Honduras)*
BR Brazil
BRN Bahrain
BRU Brunei★
BS Bahamas★
BUR Burma

C Cuba
CDN Canada
CH Switzerland
CI Ivory Coast
CL Sri Lanka★ *(formerly Ceylon)*
CO Colombia
CR Costa Rica
CS Czechoslovakia
CY Cyprus★

D German Federal Republic
DDR German Democratic Republic
DK Denmark
DOM Dominican Republic
DY Benin *(formerly Dahomey)*
DZ Algeria

E Spain *(including African Localities* and provinces)
EAK Kenya★
EAT Tanzania★ *(formerly Tanganyika & Zanzibar)*
EAU Uganda★
EC Ecuador
ES El Salvador
ET Arab Republic of Egypt
†**ETH** Ethiopia

F France *(including overseas departments and territories)*
FJI Fiji★
FL Liechtenstein
FR Faroe Islands

GB United Kingdom of Great Britain & Northern Ireland★
GBA Alderney★ *(Channel Islands)*
GBG Guernsey★ *(Channel Islands)*
GBJ Jersey★ *(Channel Islands)*

GBM	Isle of Man★
GBZ	Gibraltar
GCA	Guatemala
GH	Ghana
GR	Greece
GUY	Guyana★ (*formerly British Guiana*)
H	Hungary
HK	Hong Kong★
HKJ	Jordan
I	Italy
IL	Israel
IND	India★
IR	Iran
IRL	Ireland★
IRQ	Iraq
IS	Iceland
J	Japan★
JA	Jamaica★
K	Kampuchea (*formerly Cambodia*)
†**KWT**	Kuwait
L	Luxembourg
LAO	People's Democratic Republic of Laos
†**LAR**	Libya
†**LB**	Liberia
LS	Lesotho★ (*formerly Basutoland*)
M	Malta★
MA	Morocco
MAL	Malaysia★
MC	Monaco
MEX	Mexico
MS	Mauritius★
MW	Malawi★ (*formerly Nyasaland*)
N	Norway
NA	Curacao (Netherlands Antilles)
NIC	Nicaragua
NL	Netherlands
NZ	New Zealand★
P	Portugal
PA	Panama
PAK	Pakistan★
PE	Peru
PL	Poland
PNG	Papua New Guinea★
PY	Paraguay
RA	Argentina
RB	Botswana★ (*formerly Bechuanaland*)
RC	Taiwan (*Formosa*)
RCA	Central African Republic
RCB	Congo
RCH	Chile
RH	Haiti
RI	Indonesia★
†**RIM**	Mauritania
RL	Lebanon
RM	Madagascar (*formerly Malagasy Republic*)
RMM	Mali
RN	Niger
RO	Romania
ROK	Republic of Korea
ROU	Uruguay
RP	Philippines
RSM	San Marino
RSR or **ZW**	Zimbabwe★ (*formerly Rhodesia*)
†**RU**	Burundi
RWA	Rwanda
S	Sweden
SD	Swaziland★
SF	Finland
SGP	Singapore★
SME	Suriname★ (*formerly Dutch Guiana*)
SN	Senegal
SU	Union of Soviet Socialist Republics
SWA or **ZA**	South West Africa (*Namibia*)
SY	Seychelles★
SYR	Syria
T	Thailand★
TG	Togo
TN	Tunisia
TR	Turkey
TT	Trinidad and Tobago★
USA	United States of America
V	Holy See (*Vatican City*)
VN	Republic of Vietnam
WAG	Gambia
WAL	Sierra Leone
WAN	Nigeria
WD **WG** **WL**	Dominica★ Grenada★ St Lucia★ } *Windward Islands*
WS	Western Samoa
WV	St Vincent★ (*Windward Islands*)
YU	Yugoslavia
YV	Venezuela
Z	Zambia★
ZA	South Africa★
ZRE	Zaire (*formerly Congo Kinshasa*)

AIRLINE REGISTRATION MARKS

AA American Airlines
AC Air Canada
AF Air France
AH Air Algerie
AR Aerolineas Argentinas
AT Royal Air Maroc
AY Finnair
AZ Alitalia
BA British Airways
BN Braniff International Airways
BR British Caledonian Airways
CA General Administration of Civil Aviation of China
CP CP Air
DL Delta Air Lines
EA Eastern Air Lines
EI Aer Lingus
ET Ethiopian Airlines
FG Ariana Afghan Airlines
FI Icelandair
GA Garuda Indonesian Airways
GF Gulf Air
GH Ghana Airways
HA Hawaiian Airlines
IA Iraqi Airways
IB Iberia
IR Iran Air
JL Japan Air Lines
JU Jugoslovenski Aerotransport
KL KLM Royal Dutch Airlines
KM Air Malta
KQ Kenya Airways
KU Kuwait Airways
LH Lufthansa
LO LOT Polish Airlines
LY El Al Israel Airlines
LZ Balkan
MA Malev
ME Middle East Airlines
MH Malaysian Airline System
MS Egyptair
NW Northwest Orient Airlines
OA Olympic Airways
OK CSA
OS Austrian Airlines
PA Pan American Airways
PK Pakistan International Airlines
PR Philippine Airlines
QC Air Zaire
QF Qantas Airways
QZ Zambia Airways
RG Varig
RJ Alia The Royal Jordanian Airlines
RK Air Afrique
RO Tarom
SA South African Airways
SK Scandinavian Airlines
SN Sabena
SQ Singapore Airlines
SR Swissair
SU Aeroflot Soviet Airlines
SV Saudia
TE Air New Zealand
TG Thai Airways International
TP TAP Air Portugal
TU Tunis Air
TW Trans World Airlines
UA United Airlines
UT UTA
VA VIASA
WT Nigerian Airways

WORLD STANDARD TIMES AT NOON GREENWICH MEAN TIME

For an explanation of why different parts of the world have different times, see page 65.

Accra	noon
Adelaide	9.30 pm
Algiers	1.00 pm
Amman	2.00 pm
Amsterdam	1.00 pm
Ankara	2.00 pm
Athens	2.00 pm
Auckland	midnight
Baghdad	3.00 pm
Bahrain	3.00 pm
Bangkok	7.00 pm
Beirut	2.00 pm
Belgrade	1.00 pm
Berlin	1.00 pm
Berne	1.00 pm
Bombay	5.30 pm
Bonn	1.00 pm
Brisbane	10.00 pm
Brussels	1.00 pm
Bucharest	2.00 pm
Budapest	1.00 pm
Buenos Aires	9.00 am
Cairo	2.00 pm
Calcutta	5.30 pm
Canberra	10.00 pm
Cape Town	2.00 pm
Caracas	8.00 am
Chicago	6.00 am
Colombo	5.30 pm
Copenhagen	1.00 pm
Damascus	2.00 pm
Delhi	5.30 pm
Djakarta	8.00 pm
Dublin	noon
Frankfurt	1.00 pm
Geneva	1.00 pm
Gibraltar	1.00 pm
Hamburg	1.00 pm
Helsinki	2.00 pm
Hong Kong	8.00 pm
Islamabad	5.00 pm
Istanbul	2.00 pm
Jerusalem	2.00 pm
Karachi	5.00 pm
Kuala Lumpur	8.00 pm
Lagos	1.00 pm
Leningrad	3.00 pm
Lima	7.00 am
Lisbon	1.00 pm
London	noon
Los Angeles	4.00 am
Luxembourg	1.00 pm
Madras	5.30 pm
Madrid	1.00 pm
Melbourne	10.00 pm
Mexico City	6.00 am
Milan	1.00 pm
Montevideo	8.30 am
Moscow	3.00 pm
Nairobi	3.00 pm
New York	7.00 am
Nicosia	2.00 pm
Oslo	1.00 pm
Ottawa	7.00 am
Panama	7.00 am
Paris	1.00 pm
Peking	8.00 pm
Perth	8.00 pm
Piraeus	2.00 pm
Prague	1.00 pm
Rangoon	6.30 pm
Rawalpindi	5.00 pm
Reykjavik	noon
Rio de Janeiro	9.00 am
Rome	1.00 pm
San Francisco	4.00 am
Santiago	8.00 am
Sofia	2.00 pm
Singapore	7.30 pm
Stockholm	1.00 pm
Sydney	10.00 pm
Tehran	3.30 pm
Tokyo	9.00 pm
Toronto	7.00 am
Tunis	1.00 pm
Vancouver	4.00 am
Vienna	1.00 pm
Warsaw	1.00 pm
Washington	7.00 am
Wellington	midnight
Winnipeg	6.00 am
Zurich	1.00 pm

DISTANCES BY AIR

The distances of principal world cities from London by air, using the shortest routes.

NAME	DISTANCE km	DISTANCE miles	NAME	DISTANCE km	DISTANCE miles
Aden	6 566	4 104	Lisbon	1 565	972
Amsterdam	372	232	Madrid	1 247	775
Athens	2 416	1 501	Melbourne	19 206	11 934
Baghdad	4 929	3 063	Montreal	5 216	3 260
Berlin	954	593	Moscow	2 493	1 549
Bombay	7 887	4 901	Munich	946	588
Brussels	351	218	Nairobi	7 128	4 429
Buenos Aires	11 138	6 961	New York	5 541	3 463
Cairo	3 531	2 206	Nicosia	3 264	2 028
Calcutta	7 986	4 991	Oslo	1 162	722
Chicago	6 641	4 127	Paris	346	215
Colombo	9 421	5 854	Prague	1 078	670
Copenhagen	980	609	Rome	1 461	908
Djakarta	13 417	8 337	San Francisco	9 928	6 169
Dublin	449	280	Singapore	10 879	6 799
Geneva	753	468	Stockholm	1 447	899
Gibraltar	1 746	1 085	Sydney	17 019	10 636
Hong Kong	13 038	8 102	Teheran	5 502	3 419
Johannesburg	9 093	5 683	Tel Aviv	3 589	2 230
Karachi	6 338	3 961	Tokyo	16 200	10 066
Kingston	8 379	5 207	Venice	1 131	703
Kuala Lumpur	12 686	7 883	Vienna	1 273	791
Lagos	5 473	3 401	Warsaw	1 471	914

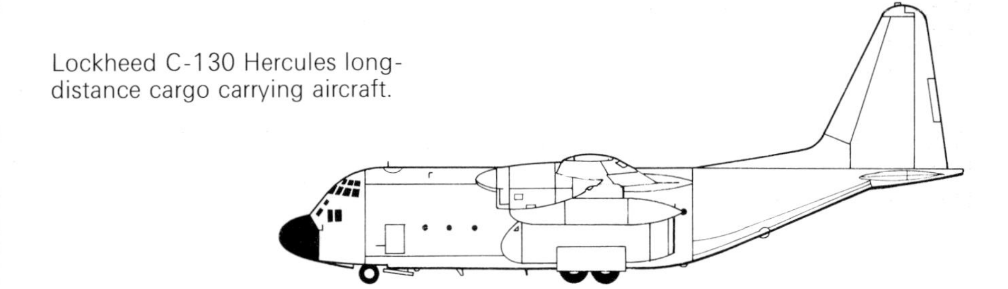

Lockheed C-130 Hercules long-distance cargo carrying aircraft.

AIRLINE INSIGNIA

Aer Lingus
(Ireland)

Aeroflot
(USSR)

Air Canada
(Canada)

Air France
(France)

Air India
(India)

Air Jamaica
(Jamaica)

Alitalia
(Italy)

American Airlines
(USA)

British Airways
(United Kingdom)

British Caledonian
(United Kingdom)

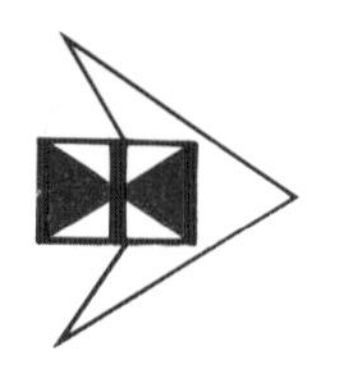

Cathay Pacific Airways
(Hong Kong)

Czechoslovak Airlines
(Czechoslovakia)

Gulf Air
(Bahrain, Oman, Qatar, UAE)

Iran Air
(Iran)

Lufthansa
(Germany)

Japan Air Lines
(Japan)

Nigeria Airways
(Nigeria)

Olympic Airways
(Greece)

Pan American
(USA)

Qantas
(Australia)

Saudia
(Saudi Arabia)

Singapore Airlines
(Singapore)

Trans World Airlines
(USA)

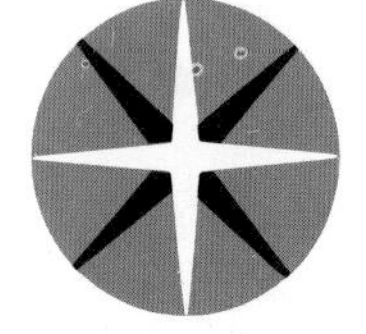

Varig
(Brazil)

FOREIGN WORDS AND PHRASES

(Abbreviations – F: French; G: German; Gk: Greek; I: Italian; L: Latin; P: Portuguese; S: Spanish).

ad hoc (L) For this special purpose
ad infinitum (L) For ever; to infinity
ad interim (L) Meanwhile
ad nauseam (L) To the point of disgust
a fortiori (L) With stronger reason
à la carte (F) From the full menu
à la mode (F) In the fashion
alter ego (L) One's other self
amour-propre (F) Self-esteem; vanity
a priori (L) From the cause to the effect
à propos (F) To the point
au contraire (F) On the contrary
au courant (F) Fully acquainted (with)
auf Wiedersehen (G) Till we meet again
au naturel (F) In a natural state
au revoir (F) Till we meet again
auto da fé (P) Act of faith
à votre santé (F) Your good health!

bête noire (F) Pet hate
billet doux (F) Love letter
bona fide (L) In good faith; genuine
bon marché (F) A bargain; cheap
bon vivant (F) Gourmet; one who enjoys life
bon voyage (F) Have a good journey

carpe diem (L) Enjoy today
carte blanche (F) Full powers
casus belli (L) Cause of war
caveat emptor (L) Let the buyer beware
chacun à son goût (F) Everyone to their own taste
chef-d'oeuvre (F) Masterpiece
ci-devant (F) Former
comme il faut (F) In good taste; correct
compos mentis (L) Of sound mind; sane
corps diplomatique (F) Group of diplomats in a capital city

de facto (L) In fact
de jure (L) By right (in law)
de rigueur (F) Necessary; compulsory
deus ex machina (L) Providential interposition; nick-of-time solution by a superhuman agency
Dieu et mon droit (F) God and my right
double entendre (F) Double meaning

embarras de richesse (F) Difficulty caused by having too much
en famille (F) At home; in the family; informal
en fête (F) Celebrating
en passant (F) In passing; by the way
entre nous (F) Between ourselves
esprit de corps (F) Group spirit

fait accompli (F) An accomplished fact
faux pas (F) False step; mistake

fin de siècle (F) Decadent

hoi poloi (Gk) The people
honi soit qui mal y pense (F) Evil be to he who evil thinks
hors de combat (F) No longer able to fight

ibidem (ibid) (L) In the same place
ich dien (G) I serve
idée fixe (F) Obsession
in extremis (L) At the point of death
in loco parentis (L) In the place of a parent
in memoriam (L) In memory (of)
in perpetuum (L) For ever
in situ (L) In its original position
inter alia (L) Among other things
in toto (L) Completely
ipso facto (L) (Obvious) from the facts
ipso jure (L) By the law itself

je ne sais quoi (F) I know not what

laissez faire (F) Leave matters alone; policy of non-interference
lèse-majesté (F) High treason; arrogant conduct of inferiors
locum tenens (L) A substitute or deputy

magnum opus (L) A great work; an author's principal book
maitre d'hôtel (F) Hotel-keeper; head-waiter
mea culpa (L) It is my fault
modus operandi (L) Method of working

nil desperandum (L) Despair of nothing
noblesse oblige (F) Noble birth imposes obligations
nom de guerre (F) Assumed name
nom de plume (F) Assumed name of an author
non compos mentis (L) Of unsound mind
non sequitur (L) It does not follow
nota bene (NB) (L) Note well

opus (L) Work of art, music or literature

passim (L) Everywhere
per annum (L) By the year
per capita (L) By the head
per centum (per cent) (L) By the hundred
per diem (L) By the day
per mensem (L) By the month
persona non grata (L) An unacceptable person
pièce de résistance (F) Chief dish of meal; main item
pied-à-terre (F) Lodging for occasional visits
poste restante (F) To await collection (from a post office)
prima facie (L) At first sight
pro forma (L) As a matter of form
pro rata (L) In proportion
prosit (G) Good health

quid pro quo (L) A thing offered for another of the same value

raison d'être (F) Reason for existence
reductio ad absurdum (L) A reducing to the absurd
requiescat in pace (RIP) (L) Rest in piece
résumé (F) Summary

sans souci (F) Without care
sauve qui peut (F) Save himself who can
savoir-faire (F) Tact
semper fidelis (L) Always faithful
sine die (L) Indefinitely
sine qua non (L) An indispensable condition
sobriquet (F) Nickname
soi-disant (F) Self-styled
sotto voce (I) In a whisper or undertone
status quo (L) The existing state of affairs
stet (L) Let it stand (ignore correction marks)
sub judice (L) Before a judge (and not yet decided)

table d'hôte (F) A set meal at a fixed price
tempus fugit (L) Time flies
terra firma (L) Solid earth
tête-a-tête (F) Private talk between two people
tour de force (F) Feat of skill or strength
tout de suite (F) Immediately

ubique (L) Everywhere

vade mecum (L) Constant companion; manual of reference
versus (L) Against
vice versa (L) Conversely
vis-à-vis (F) Opposite; face to face

wagon lit (F) Railway sleeping-car
Weltschmerz (G) World weariness

Zeitgeist (G) Spirit of the times

There are more than 3000 languages, forming less than 20 language groups. Spanish, French, Portuguese and English were spread around the world by colonizing powers and, with Arabic and Russian, have become the major international languages. The map shows the distribution of some of the world's major languages.

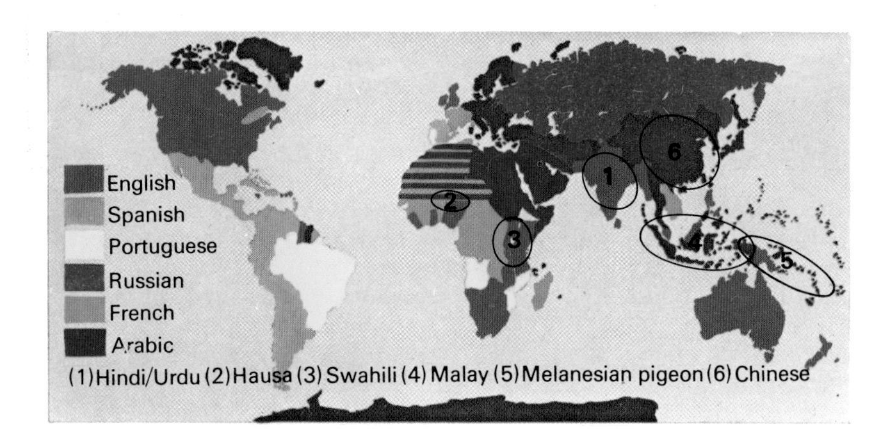

ARABIC, ROMAN AND BINARY NUMERALS

Arabic	Roman	Binary	Arabic	Roman	Binary
1	I	1	50	L	110010
2	II	10	60	LX	111100
3	III	11	64	LXIV	1000000
4	IV	100	90	XC	1011010
5	V	101	99	XCIX	1100011
6	VI	110	100	C	1100100
7	VII	111	128	CXXVIII	10000000
8	VIII	1000	200	CC	11001000
9	IX	1001	256	CCLVI	100000000
10	X	1010	300	CCC	100101100
11	XI	1011	400	CD	110010000
12	XII	1100	500	D	111110100
13	XIII	1101	512	DXII	1000000000
14	XIV	1110	600	DC	1001011000
15	XV	1111	900	CM	1110000100
16	XVI	10000	1000	M	1111101000
17	XVII	10001	1024	MXXIV	10000000000
18	XVIII	10010	1500	MD	10111011100
19	XIX	10011	1666	MDCLXVI	11010000010
20	XX	10100	2000	MM	11111010000
21	XXI	10101	4000	MV̄	111110100000
29	XXIX	11101	5000	V̄	1001110001000
30	XXX	11110	10000	X̄	10011100010000
32	XXXII	100000	20000	X̄X̄	100111000100000
40	XL	101000	100000	C̄	11000011010100000

WORLD CURRENCIES

Country	Currency
Afghanistan	afghani (100 puls)
Albania	lek (100 qindarka)
Algeria	dinar (100 centimes)
Andorra	franc (Fr) & peseta (Sp)
Angola	escudo (100 centavos)
Antigua and Barbuda	dollar (100 cents)
Argentina	peso (100 centavos)
Australia	dollar (100 cents)
Austria	schilling (100 groschen)
Bahamas	dollar (100 cents)
Bahrain	dinar (1000 fils)
Bangladesh	taka (100 paise)
Barbados	dollar (100 cents)
Belgium	franc (100 centimes)
Belize	dollar (100 cents)
Benin	franc (100 centimes)
Bermuda	dollar (100 cents)
Bhutan	rupee (100 paise) (Ind)
Bolivia	peso (100 centavos)
Botswana	rand (100 cents) (SA)
Brazil	cruzeiro (100 centavos)
Brunei	dollar (100 sen)
Bulgaria	lev (100 stotinki)
Burkina Faso	Franc (CFA)
Burma	kyat (100 pyas)
Burundi	franc
Cameroon	franc
Canada	dollar (100 cents)
Cape Verde	escudo
Cayman Islands	dollar (100 cents)
Central African Republic	franc (100 centimes)
Chad	franc (100 centimes)
Chile	escudo (100 centésimos)
China: People's Republic	yuan (10 chiao, 100 fen)
China: Taiwan	dollar (100 cents)
Colombia	peso (100 centavos)
Comoros	franc
Congo	franc
Costa Rica	colon (100 centimos)
Cuba	peso (100 centavos)
Cyprus	pound (1000 mils)
Czechoslovakia	koruna (100 haleru)
Denmark	krone (100 ore)
Djibouti	franc
Dominica	dollar (100 cents)
Dominican Republic	peso (100 centavos)
Ecuador	sucre (100 centavos)
Egypt	pound (100 piastres, 1000 milliémes)
El Salvador	colón (100 centavos)
Equatorial Guinea	ekpwele
Ethiopia	dollar (100 cents)
Falkland Islands	pound (100 pence)
Fiji	dollar (100 cents)
Finland	markka (100 pennia)
France	franc (100 centimes)
Gabon	franc (100 centimes)
Gambia	dalasi (100 bututs)
Germany, East	mark (100 pfennigs)
Germany, West	mark (100 pfennigs)
Ghana	cedi (100 pesewas)
Gibraltar	pound (100 pence)
Greece	drachma (100 lepta)
Grenada	dollar (100 cents)
Guatemala	quetzal (100 centavos)
Guinea	syli (100 cauris)
Guinea-Bissau	peso (100 centavos)
Guyana	dollar (100 cents)
Haiti	gourde (100 centimes)
Honduras	lempira (100 centavos)
Hong Kong	dollar (100 cents)
Hungary	forint (100 filler)
Iceland	kroña (100 aurar)
India	rupee (100 paise)
Indonesia	rupiah (100 sen)
Iran	rial (100 dinars)
Iraq	dinar (1000 fils)
Ireland, Rep. of	pound (100 pence)
Israel	pound (100 agorot)
Italy	lira
Ivory Coast	franc (100 centimes)
Jamaica	dollar (100 cents)
Japan	yen
Jordan	dinar (1000 fils)
Kampuchea, Democratic	riel (100 sen)
Kenya	shilling (100 cents)
Kiribati	dollar (100 cents)

Country	Currency
Korea, North	won (100 jun)
Korea, South	won
Kuwait	dinar (1000 fils)
Laos	kip (100 att)
Lebanon	pound (100 piastres)
Lesotho	rand (100 cents) (SA)
Liberia	dollar (100 cents)
Libya	dinar (1000 dirhams)
Liechtenstein	franc (Swiss)
Luxembourg	franc (100 centimes)
Macau (Port.)	pataca (100 avos)
Madagascar	franc
Malawi	kwacha (100 tambala)
Malaysia	dollar (100 cents)
Maldives, Rep. of	rupee
Mali	franc (100 centimes)
Malta	pound (100 cents, 1000 mils)
Mauritania	ouguiya (5 khoums)
Mauritius	rupee (100 cents)
Mexico	peso (100 centavos)
Monaco	franc (French)
Mongolian People's Republic	tugrik (100 mongo)
Montserrat	dollar
Morocco	dirham (100 centimes)
Mozambique	metical (100 centavos)
Namibia	rand (100 cents)
Nauru	dollar (100 cents) ($A)
Nepal	rupee (100 pice)
Netherlands	guilder (100 cents)
New Zealand	dollar (100 cents)
Nicaragua	córdoba (100 centavos)
Niger	franc (100 centimes)
Nigeria	naira (100 kobo)
Norway	krone (100 ore)
Oman	rial Omani (1000 baiza)
Pakistan	rupee (100 paisas)
Panama	balboa (100 cents)
Papua New Guinea	kina (100 toea)
Paraguay	guarani (100 céntimos)
Peru	sol (100 centavos)
Philippines	peso (100 centavos)
Poland	zloty (100 groszy)
Portugal	escudo (100 centavos)
Qatar	riyal (100 dirhams)
Romania	leu (100 bani)
Rwanda	franc (100 centimes)
St Kitts-Nevis	dollar (100 cents)
St Helena	pound (100 pence)
St Lucia	dollar (100 cents)
St Vincent	dollar (100 cents)
San Marino	lira (Italian)
Sao Tome	dobra (100 centavos)
Saudi Arabia	riyal (20 qursh)
Senegal	franc
Seychelles	rupee
Sierra Leone	leone (100 cents)
Singapore	dollar (100 cents)
Solomon Islands	dollar (Australian)
Somalia	shilling (100 cents)
Spain	peseta (100 centimos)
Sri Lanka	rupee (100 cents)
Sudan	pound (100 piastres, 1000 milliemes)
Suriname	guilder (100 cents)
Swaziland	rand (100 cents) (SA)
Sweden	krona (100 öre)
Switzerland	franc (100 centimes)
Syria	pound (100 piastres)
Tanzania	shilling (100 cents)
Thailand	baht (100 satangs)
Togo	franc (100 centimes)
Tonga	pa'anga (100 seniti)
Trinidad & Tobago	dollar (100 cents)
Tunisia	dinar (1000 millimes)
Turkey	lira (100 kurus)
Turks and Caicos Islands	dollar (USA)
Tuvalu	dollar (Australian)
Uganda	shilling (100 cents)
United Arab Emirates	dirham (100 fils)
United Kingdom	pound (100 pence)
United States	dollar (100 cents)
Uruguay	peso (100 centésimos)
USSR	rouble (100 copecks)
Vanuatu	vatu
Vatican City State	lira
Venezuela	bolivar (100 centimos)
Vietnam	dong (100 xu)
Virgin Islands	dollar (USA)
Western Samoa	tala (100 sene)
Yemen Arab Republic	riyal (40 bogaches)
Yemen PDR	dinar (1000 fils)
Yugoslavia	dinar (100 paras)
Zaire	zaire (100 makuta [sing. likuta], 10 000 sengi)
Zambia	kwacha (100 ngwee)
Zimbabwe	dollar (100 cents)

SENDING DISTRESS SIGNALS

There are several different ways of sending distress signals in an emergency. Morse code is a system of communication using dots and dashes to represent letters and numbers, which can be done by flashing a light, by sound or by using a flag. SOS in morse is known all over the world as a call of distress.

Semaphore, using two flags, can be used to send messages in daylight, and international ground-to-air signals, made with stones, clumps of weeds, clothing, equipment, in snow or sand, are easily seen by low-flying helicopters or aircraft.

Smoke signals by day and fire signals by night are sure to be seen, but great care should be taken in making fires, especially when it is

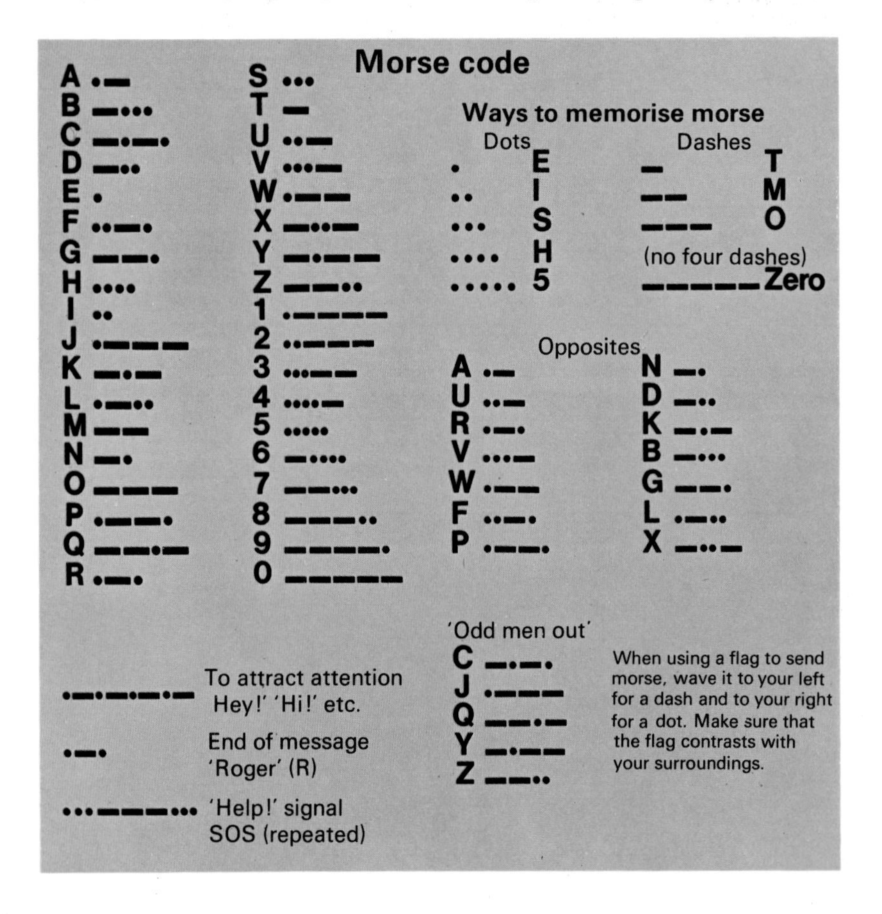

International ground-to-air signals. Use stores, clothing or equipment.

I — Doctor needed: serious injury

II — Medical supplies needed

X — Unable to proceed further

F — Food and water needed

LL — All well with us

Δ — Safe to land at this spot

K — Indicate direction and proceed

↑ — I am/we are proceeding in this direction

JL — Message not understood

N — No

Y — Yes

□ — I/we need map and compass

Semaphore, using two flags, is ideal for sending distress signals in daylight.

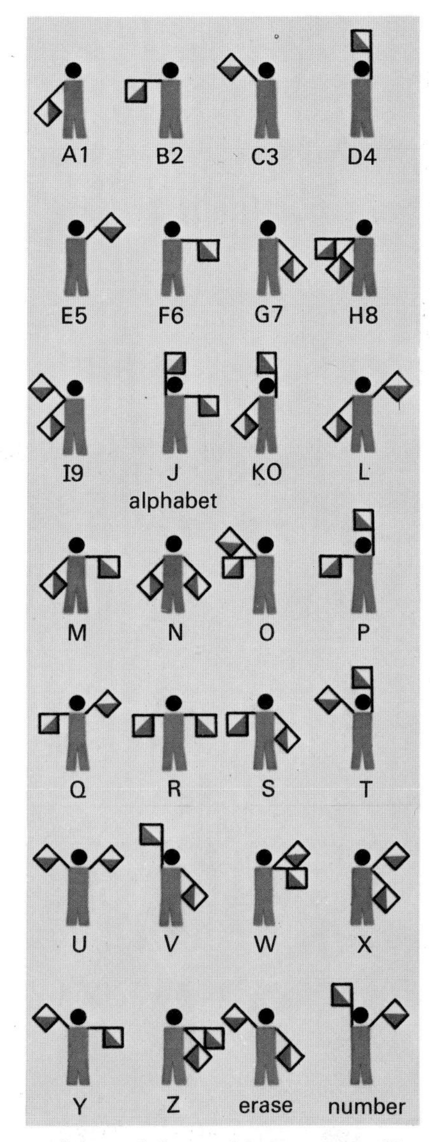

breezy. Steel mirrors can be used for signalling in the daytime – a polished tin lid is a good substitute. Or in an emergency an item of clothing can be used as a flag signal. The colour of the flag must contrast with the basic colour of the surrounding vegetation.

Another means of signalling often used in mountain search and rescue operations is flares: red indicates the position of the accident or says 'I require aid'; white acknowledges a message; green recalls a person to base.

BRAILLE

Braille is a system of writing or printing for the blind, in which combinations of raised dots are used to represent letters. The Braille alphabet is based on the six dots of a domino. A code of 63 combinations covers all the letters, punctuation marks and various abbreviation signs. The alphabet was invented in 1834 by Louis Braille, a Frenchman who was blinded in a childhood accident. He later taught at the National Blind Institute in Paris.

Today Braille typewriters enable the blind to write, and many books, newspapers and magazines are published in Braille in nearly every country in the world. There are also Braille codes for music and mathematics.

A B C D E
F G H I J
K L M N O
P Q R S T
U V W X Y
Z and for of the
with fraction numeral poetry apostrophe
hyphen dash comma semicolon colon
full stop ! ( ) ? “ ”

THE DEAF AND DUMB ALPHABET

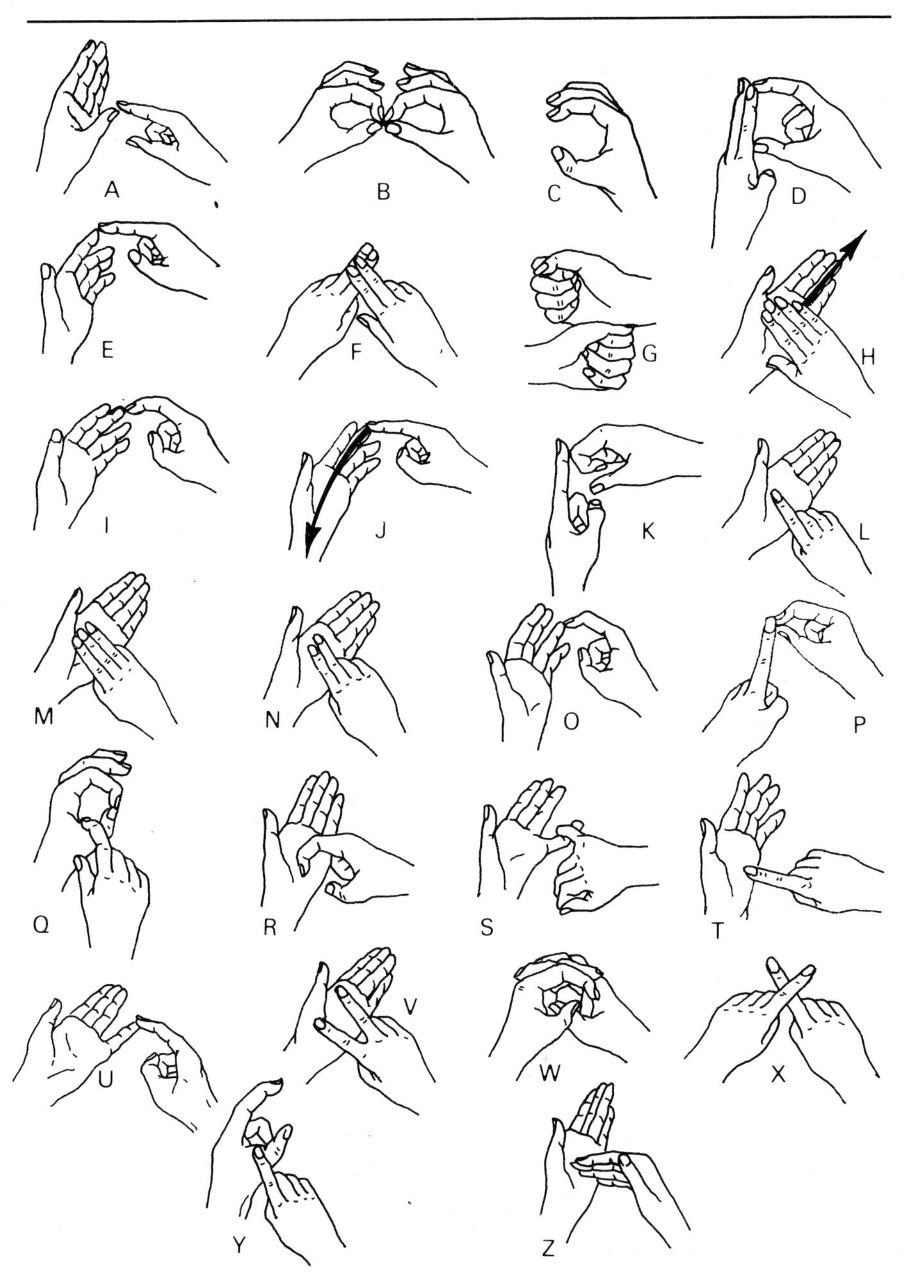

COMMON ABBREVIATIONS

AA Automobile Association
AB able-bodied seaman
AC alternating current
a/c account
AD *anno Domini* (in the year of Our Lord)
am *ante meridiem* (before noon)
ARCM Associate of Royal College of Music
AV Authorized Version (of the Bible)
BA Bachelor of Arts; British Airways
BBC British Broadcasting Corporation
BC before Christ; British Columbia
BCom Bachelor of Commerce
BD Bachelor of Divinity
BL Bachelor of Law
BMA British Medical Association
BSc Bachelor of Science
BR British Railways
Bt Baronet
c *circa* (about)
C Centigrade
CA Chartered Accountant
Cantab of Cambridge
CB Companion of the Bath
CBE Commander of the Order of the British Empire
CBI Confederation of British Industry
CE Church of England
cf *confer* (compare)
CH Companion of Honour
ChB Bachelor of Surgery
CID Criminal Investigation Department
cif cost, insurance, freight
CMG Companion of Order of St Michael and St George
CO Commanding Officer
COD cash on delivery
cp compare
DBE Dame Commander of the Order of the British Empire
DC *da capo* (from the beginning); District of Columbia; direct current
DCL Doctor of Civil Law
DCM Distinguished Conduct Medal
DD Doctor of Divinity
DLitt Doctor of Literature
DPh, DPhil Doctor of Philosophy
DSc Doctor of Science
eg *exempli gratia* (for example)
ER *Elizabetha Regina*, Queen Elizabeth
et seq *et sequentia* (and what follows)
f *forte* (loud) **ff** *fortissimo* (very loud)
F Fahrenheit
FCS Fellow of Chemical Society
FGS Fellow of Geological Society
fob free on board
for free on rail
FRAS Fellow of Royal Astronomical Society
FRCO Fellow of Royal College of Organists
FRCP Fellow of Royal College of Physicians
FRCS Fellow of Royal College of Surgeons
FRGS Fellow of Royal Geographical Society
FRS Fellow of Royal Society
FRSGS Fellow of Royal Scottish Geographical Society
FZS Fellow of Zoological Society
GB Great Britain
GBE Knight (or Dame) Grand Cross of British Empire
GC George Cross
GCB Grand Cross of the Bath
GM George Medal; Grand Master
GMT Greenwich Mean Time
GP general practitioner
HF high frequency
HM Her/His Majesty
HMI Her/His Majesty's Inspector
hp horse-power
HQ Headquarters
HRH Her/His Royal Highness
HT high tension
ib, ibid *ibidem* (in the same place)
ie *id est* (that is)
inst instant (this month)
IOU I owe you
IQ Intelligence Quotient
IRA Irish Republican Army
IWW Industrial Workers of the World
JP Justice of the Peace
KB Knight of the Bath
KBE Knight Commander of the British Empire

KC King's Counsel
KCB etc Knight Commander of the Bath, etc
KG Knight of the Garter
km/h kilometres per hour
KP Knight of St Patrick
KT Knight of the Thistle
LDS Licentiate in Dental Surgery
LLB Bachelor of Laws
LLD Doctor of Laws
LRAM Licentiate of the Royal Academy of Music
LRCM Licentiate of the Royal College of Music
LRCP Licentiate of the Royal College of Physicians
LRCS Licentiate of the Royal College of Surgeons
LRCVS Licentiate of the Royal College of Veterinary Surgeons
MA Master of Arts
MB Bachelor of Medicine
MC Military Cross; master of ceremonies
MP Member of Parliament
mpg miles per gallon
mph miles per hour
MPS Member of Pharmaceutical Society
MRCP Member of Royal College of Physicians
MRCS Member of Royal College of Surgeons
MRCVS Member of Royal College of Veterinary Surgeons
MS manuscript; *pl* **MSS**
MusBac Bachelor of Music
MusDoc Doctor of Music
NAAFI, Naafi Navy, Army and Air Force Institutes
NATO North Atlantic Treaty Organization
NB *nota bene* (note well); New Brunswick
NCO non-commissioned officer
No number; *pl* **Nos**
NSPCC National Society for Prevention of Cruelty to Children
NT New Testament
ob *obiit* (died)
OBE officer of the Order of the British Empire
OHMS On Her/His Majesty's Service
OM Order of Merit
OT Old Testament
Oxon of Oxford
p *piano* (soft) **pp** *pianissimo* (very soft)
PhD Doctor of Philosophy
pm *post meridiem* (after noon)
PO Post Office; postal order
pro tem *pro tempore* (for the time being)
prox *proximo* (next month)
PS postscript
PTO please turn over
QC Queen's Counsel
QED *quod erat demonstrandum* (which was to be shown)
qv *quod vide* (which see)
RA Royal Academician; Royal Artillery
RAC Royal Automobile Club
RAF Royal Air Force
RAMC Royal Army Medical Corps
RASC Royal Army Service Corps
RAVC Royal Army Veterinary Corps
RBA Royal Society of British Artists
RE Royal Engineers
RIP *requiescat in pace* (rest in peace)
RN Royal Navy
RNR Royal Naval Reserve
RNVR Royal Naval Volunteer Reserve
RSA Royal Scottish Academician
RSPCA Royal Society for Prevention of Cruelty to Animals
RSV Revised Standard Version (of the Bible)
RSVP *répondez, s'il vous plait* (please reply)
RV Revised Version
SOS urgent appeal for help
SRN State Registered Nurse
St Saint
TNT trinotrotoluol (an explosive)
TUC Trades Union Congress
UK United Kingdom
ult *ultimo* (last month)
UNO United Nations Organization
USA United States of America
USSR Union of Soviet Socialist Republics
VC Victoria Cross
WEA Workers' Education Association
WRAC Women's Royal Army Corps
WRAF Women's Royal Air Force
WRNS Women's Royal Naval Service
YMCA Young Men's Christian Association
YWCA Young Women's Christian Association

CONVERSION FACTORS

BRITISH AND AMERICAN TO METRIC

Linear Measure

1 inch	= 25.4 millimetres
1 foot = 12 inches	= 0.3048 metres
1 yard = 3 feet	= 0.9144 metres
1 mile = 1760 yards	= 1.609 kilometres

Square Measure

1 square inch	= 6.45 sq centimetres
1 square foot = 144 sq in	= 0.0929 sq metres
1 square yard = 9 sq ft	= 8.836 sq metres
1 acre = 4840 sq yd	= 0.4047 hectares
1 square mile = 640 acres	= 259 hectares

Cubic Measure

1 cubic inch	= 16.38 cu centimetres
1 cubic foot = 1728 cu in	= 0.0283 cu metres
1 cubic yard = 27 cu ft	= 0.7646 cu metres

Liquid Measure

British

1 pint = 20 fluid oz	= 0.568 litres
= 34.68 cu in	
1 quart = 2 pints	= 1.136 litres
1 gallon = 4 quarts	= 4.456 litres

American

1 pint = 16 fluid oz	= 0.473 litres
= 28.88 cu in	
1 quart = 2 pints	= 0.946 litres
1 gallon = 4 quarts	= 3.785 litres

Dry Measure

British

1 peck = 2 gallons	= 9.092 litres
1 bushel = 4 pecks	= 36.4 litres
1 quarter = 8 bushels	= 2.91 hectolitres

American

1 pint = 33.60 cu in	= 0.550 litres
1 quart = 2 pints	= 1.101 litres
1 peck = 8 quarts	= 8.81 litres
1 bushel = 4 pecks	= 35.3 litres

Avoirdupois Weight

1 grain	= 0.065 grams
1 dram	= 1.772 grams
1 ounce = 16 drams	= 28.35 grams
1 pound = 16 ounces = 7000 grains	= 0.4536 kilograms
1 stone = 14 pounds	= 6.35 kilograms
1 quarter = 2 stones	= 12.70 kilograms
1 hundredweight = 4 quarters	= 50.80 kilograms
1 long (UK) ton = 20 hundredweight	= 1.016 tonnes
1 short (US) ton = 2000 pounds	= 0.907 tonnes

METRIC TO BRITISH

Linear Measure

1 millimetre	= 0.039 inches
1 centimetre = 10 mm	= 0.394 inches
1 decimetre = 10 cm	= 3.937 inches
1 metre = 10 dm	= 1.094 yards
1 kilometre = 1000 m	= 0.621 miles

Square Measure

1 square centimetre	= 0.155 sq inches
1 square metre	= 10.764 sq feet
1 hectare	= 2.471 acres
1 square kilometre	= 0.386 sq miles

Cubic Measure

1 cubic centimetre	= 0.061 cu inches
1 cubic metre	= 35.315 cu feet

Liquid Measure

1 millilitre	= 0.002 pints (British)
1 centilitre = 10 ml	= 0.018 pints
1 decilitre = 10 cl	= 0.176 pints
1 litre = 10 dl	= 1.76 pints
1 decalitre = 10 l	= 2.20 gallons
1 hectolitre = 100 l	= 2.75 bushels
1 kilolitre = 1000 l	= 3.44 quarters

Weight

1 gram	= 15.43 grains
1 decagram = 10 g	= 5.64 drams
1 hectogram = 100 g	= 3.527 ounces
1 kilogram = 1000 g	= 2.205 pounds
1 tonne (metric ton) = 1000 kg	= 0.984 (UK) long ton

MISCELLANEOUS MEASURES

Surveyors' Measure

7.92 inches	=1 link
100 links	=1 chain
80 chains	=1 mile

Nautical Measure

1 span	=9 inches
8 spans	=6 feet
6 feet	=1 fathom
100 fathoms	=1 cable
10 cables = 1 nautical mile	=6080 feet (1852 metres)
1 knot	=1 nautical mile per hour
3 nautical miles	=1 league
60 nautical miles	=1 degree
1 ton (shipping, UK)	=42 cubic feet
1 ton (displacement)	=35 cubic feet
1 ton (register)	=100 cubic feet

Angular and Circular Measure

60 seconds	=1 minute
60 minutes	=1 degree
90 degrees	=1 right angle or quadrant
180 degrees	=1 straight angle
360 degrees	=1 circle or 4 quadrants

Troy Weight

24 grains	=1 pennyweight
20 pennyweights	=1 ounce
12 ounces	=1 pound

Apothecaries Weight

20 grains	=1 scruple
3 scruples	=1 drachm
8 drachms	=1 ounce
12 ounces	=1 pound

Wood Measure

1000 millisteres = 1 stere	= 1 cubic metre
1 board foot	= 144 cubic inches
16 cubic feet	= 1 cord foot
8 cord feet	= 1 cord

Cloth Measure

1 ell	= 45 inches
1 bolt = 120 feet	= 32 ells

Brewery Measure

9 gallons	= 1 firkin
4 firkins = 1 barrel	= 36 gallons
6 firkins = 1 hogshead	= 54 gallons
4 hogsheads	= 1 tun

Writing Paper

24 sheets	= 1 quire
20 quires = 1 ream	= 480 sheets

Paper Sizes

A0 = 841 × 1189 mm	
A1 = 594 × 841 mm	
A2 = 420 × 594 mm	
A3 = 297 × 420 mm	
A4 = 210 × 297 mm	
RA0 = 860 × 1220 mm	
RA1 = 610 × 860 mm	
RA2 = 430 × 610 mm	
SRA0 = 900 × 1280 mm	
SRA1 = 640 × 900 mm	
SRA2 = 450 × 640 mm	
Metric Quad Crown	= 768 × 1008 mm
Metric Quad Large Crown	= 816 × 1056 mm
Metric Quad Demy	= 888 × 1128 mm
Metric Quad Royal	= 960 × 1272 mm

THE INTERNATIONAL SYSTEM OF UNITS (SI)

BASIC SI UNITS

Unit	Physical Quantity
metre (m)	length
kilogram (kg)	mass
second (s)	time
ampere (A)	electric current
kelvin (K)	thermodynamic temperature
mole (mol)	amount of substance
candela (cd)	luminous intensity

SOME DERIVED SI UNITS

Unit	Physical Quantity
hertz (Hz)	frequency
joule (J)	energy
newton (N)	force
watt (W)	power
coulomb (C)	electric charge
volt (V)	potential difference
ohm (Ω)	resistance
farad (F)	capacitance
henry (H)	inductance
lux (lx)	illumination

PREFIXES FOR SI UNITS

Prefix	Multiplication Factor
atto (a)	10^{-18} (0.000000000000000001)
femto (f)	10^{-15} (0.000000000000001)
pico (p)	10^{-12} (0.000000000001)
nano (n)	10^{-9} (0.000000001)
micro (μ)	10^{-6} (0.000001)
milli (m)	10^{-3} (0.001)
centi (c)	10^{-2} (0.01)
deci (d)	10^{-1} (0.1)
deca (da)	10 (10)
hecto (h)	10^{2} (100)
kilo (k)	10^{3} (1000)
mega (M)	10^{6} (1 000 000)
giga (G)	10^{9} (1 000 000 000)
tera (T)	10^{12} (1 000 000 000 000)

STAR SIGNS AND THEIR ASSOCIATIONS

Sign	Date of Birth	Symbol	Element	Colour
Aries	21 March–19 April	The Ram	Fire	Red
Taurus	20 April–20 May	The Bull	Earth	Green
Gemini	21 May–20 June	The Twins	Air	Yellow
Cancer	21 June–22 July	The Crab	Water	White
Leo	23 July–22 August	The Lion	Fire	Orange
Virgo	23 August–21 Sept	The Maiden	Earth	Grey
Libra	22 Sept–21 October	The Balance	Air	Rose
Scorpio	22 October–20 Nov	The Scorpion	Water	Crimson
Sagittarius	21 Nov–20 Dec	The Archer	Fire	Mauve
Capricorn	21 Dec–19 Jan	The Goat	Earth	Black
Aquarius	20 Jan–18 Feb	The Water-bearers	Air	Black
Pisces	19 Feb–20 March	The Fishes	Water	Blue

Sign	Stone	Ruling Planet	Human Type	Affinity
Aries	Diamond	Mars	Idealistic	Leo & Sagittarius
Taurus	Sapphire	Venus	Practical	Virgo & Capricorn
Gemini	Emerald	Mercury	Sociable	Libra & Aquarius
Cancer	Agate	Moon	Emotional	Scorpio & Pisces
Leo	Ruby	Sun	Idealistic	Aries & Sagittarius
Virgo	Sardonyx	Mercury	Practical	Taurus & Capricorn
Libra	Chrysolite	Venus	Sociable	Gemini & Aquarius
Scorpio	Opal	Mars	Emotional	Cancer & Pisces
Sagittarius	Topaz	Jupiter	Idealistic	Leo & Aries
Capricorn	Turquoise	Saturn	Practical	Virgo & Taurus
Aquarius	Amethyst	Saturn & Uranus	Sociable	Gemini & Libra
Pisces	Bloodstone	Jupiter	Emotional	Cancer & Scorpio